This book provid[...] [...]-
tion of the House [...] [...]:
how it began; [...] [...]s
leaders; why it is supported by the southern Demo-
crat-conservative Republican coalition; why it needs
headlines for existence; why it travels like a
theatrical company; how it works with the FBI, the
American Legion, and other private patriotic groups.
Most of all you will be astounded at the extent
of the Committee's surveillance network. It is literally an Orwellian "Big Brother" that watches all
potentially "subversive" Americans by keeping
millions of names of individuals and thousands of
organizations in a huge cross-reference file which
is open to friends of the Committee if they want to
"get someone."

As Frank Donner says: "This Committee has broken
more records than Babe Ruth." It has spent the
most money, called the most witnesses, published
the most pages, visited more places, ruined more
lives and is responsible for the least legislation of
any Committee in Congress. This roving inquisition
drops in on a city, investigates, and leaves. Many
people have lost their jobs, and some have become
permanently unemployable: they have been
branded.

In this book Frank Donner—a constitutional lawyer
—has filed a complete brief for the American people. He has provided, in a lively, compelling style,
the factual and analytical ammunition necessary
for every American to defend himself against
THE UN-AMERICANS.

To the youth of America in quest of vanishing freedoms.

All, all of a piece throughout;
 Thy chase had a beast in view;
Thy wars brought nothing about;
 Thy lovers were all untrue.
'Tis well an old age is out,
 And time to begin anew.

John Dryden

This is an original publication—not a reprint.

The
UN-AMERICANS

Frank J. Donner

Ballantine Books   **New York**

Copyright © 1961 by Frank J. Donner

PRINTED IN THE UNITED STATES OF AMERICA
BALLANTINE BOOKS, INC.
101 Fifth Avenue, New York 3, New York

CONTENTS

1 REVOLT OF THE NONREVOLUTIONARIES

On Friday, May 13, 1960, about 100 San Francisco policemen, reinforced by a squadron of motorcycle cops in black
boots and white helmets, turned fire hoses on a group of
200 students in San Francisco City Hall. When the students sat down in the face of the hosing, they were beaten
with clubs and dragged out of City Hall, some of them by
their feet with their heads bumping down the marble stairs.

New York Post correspondent Mel Wax, describing the
bloody marble staircase in City Hall, wrote:

> It was down those 38 steps that those who protested
> the hearing were clubbed, beaten, soaked with high-
> pressure fire hoses, and dragged kicking and scream-
> ing by white-helmeted policemen.
>
> I saw it happen. Never, in 20 years as a reporter,
> have I seen such brutality. San Francisco police hurled
> women down the staircases, spines bumping on each
> marble stair. I saw one woman dragged through glass
> from a broken front-door pane.
>
> Two big cops seized a thin, gray-suited student
> from the University of California. One held him while
> the other hit him, again and again, in the stomach.

The hosing was the climax of a three-day protest against
the House Un-American Activities Committee (HUAC)
by the students of California's Bay area. Shortly after
HUAC began hearings, on Thursday, May 12, more than
1,000 students attended a protest rally. During the entire
three days, the hearings were picketed by crowds which,
at their peak on Saturday, May 14, (the day after the attack on the students) had swelled to an estimated 5,000,
including students, parents, professors, ministers and plain
citizens. They demanded HUAC's abolition, challenged its
legality and denounced its abuses.

While HUAC has never lacked for critics, this was by
far the most vigorous expression of opposition in all of its

stormy 23-year history. J. Edgar Hoover, FBI chief, promptly labeled the demonstration "Communist-instigated riots," and reported that it was "the most successful Communist coup to occur in the San Francisco area in 25 years." HUAC moved swiftly to cover itself, screaming that the demonstrators were dupes or Communist plotters. But neither Hoover nor HUAC explained how so many thousands had been persuaded to blindly surrender their independence. Nor was any identification offered of the Red Pied Pipers who had snared these victims.

Sixty-four of the protesters—most of them students—had been arrested and charged with inciting to riot, resisting arrest and disturbing the peace. When the charges against 63 were subsequently dismissed, 58 of them issued a statement: "Nobody incited us, nobody misguided us. We were led by our own convictions and we still stand firmly by them."

Why had anti-HUAC feeling crystallized so firmly in San Francisco?

This was not the first visit of HUAC to San Francisco—it was the fourth. The Committee had first come to town in 1953, again in 1956, yet again in 1957. The 1957 hearings were darkened by the suicide of William Sherwood, a subpoenaed scientist. His suicide note said he could not face the ordeal of a televised hearing.

These periodic hearings had met ever-increasing opposition and left a deposit of anger and resentment. By 1959, when HUAC subpoenaed 110 public-school teachers—40 from Northern California and 70 from Southern California —the Committee was forced to retreat in the face of outraged public protest by Democratic Party groups, churches, organized labor, educators, students and the press. The 1959 hearings were canceled. In 1960 HUAC returned to the attack.

For the students—most of them from the University of California, our nation's largest—opposition to HUAC was inevitable. They had organized a campus group, Students for Civil Liberties, for the express purpose of opposing HUAC. This movement and SLATE, a liberal political organization on the California campus, were local expressions of a nation-wide student ferment. The "beat" generation was giving way to a generation of protest. As two professors, Drs. Bernard Biggs and Albert Anderson have written, "Five years ago, the vocal minority on campuses was 'beat'—passive, cynical and pessimistic. Now they're willing to take action on issues that appeal to their moral concern."

This student movement has seen a generation alienated from the controversies of our time by fear or cynicism. Motivated primarily by ethical and moral concerns, it had gone into action on issues such as civil liberties, the Southern sit-in fight against Jim Crow, protests against the H-bomb and nuclear testing, etc. At California, this movement was widespread and lively. The City Hall demonstrations took place only seven days after the execution of Caryl Chessman, an event which had drawn a tremendous student response climaxed by a mass demonstration of protest against capital punishment.

Opposition to HUAC is not confined to students. The San Francisco violence dramatized a rapidly growing movement for HUAC's abolition which now has the support of prominent American political and religious leaders, educators, lawyers, trade unionists and writers. The church and the campus have become centers of the abolition movement.

Three of our presidents have commented critically on HUAC and its activities. President Franklin D. Roosevelt said of HUAC, "It is sordid—flagrantly unfair—and un-American." In 1959, President Truman said "The Committee on Un-American Activities is the most un-American thing in America." In the course of the presidential campaign, President Kennedy—like ex-President Truman, no stranger to the congressional investigative process—deplored abuses in legislative investigations: it can hardly be doubted that he had HUAC in mind when he said, "The legislative investigations, designed and often exercised for the achievement of high ends, has too frequently been used by the Nation and the State as a means for effecting the disgrace of private persons."

Many American newspapers which in the past had been almost solidly pro-HUAC, or at most mildly critical of its excesses, have moved to positions of sharp hostility. Some 15 large American dailies, including the *New York Times,* the *Washington Post,* the *San Francisco Chronicle,* the *New York Post* and the *St. Louis Post-Dispatch,* have editorialized for the Committee's abolition. Three Wisconsin newspapers have endorsed Wisconsin Governer Nelson's abolition plea.

As the attack mounts, HUAC rings new changes on the charge of a Communist plot; its opponents, the Committee ever more stridently claims, are either agents or dupes of Moscow. But there are more cogent reasons for the flowering of the movement to end HUAC.

For more than a decade we have been steadily losing our freedoms. The obsession with anti-Communism and security, transformed into a national psychosis during the McCarthy era, resulted in systematic attacks on free speech, press, assembly and opinion. The policing of dissent by agencies of government became a routine feature of our lives. Witness the sedition prosecutions under the Smith Act, the intimidations of the FBI, the rash of loyalty oaths, the security-screening apparatus which blankets American industry, the emergence of the informer as hero, the wave of deportation and denaturalization proceedings against the foreign-born, the restrictions on the right to travel, the manifold attacks on organizations and on the freedom of association, and the congressional witch hunts.

True, the excesses of the McCarthy era have abated somewhat: the Army, the State Department, and our libraries abroad are no longer fair game for witch hunts. But our entire society is still infected with the contagion of caution, fear and silence. At the root of the conformity which has engulfed us is a pervasive self-censorship, a loss of the sense that freedom is every American's birthright. Our people have come to live in terror of being publicly identified with the minority. The questioners, the "agin'ers," the come-outers and the dissenters simply feel themselves to be too menaced by their environment to question, to be against, to come out and to dissent. As the domestic frontiers of our freedom contract, the Government drenches the world with renewed boasts of our free democratic life—an irony which has amused even our friends and well-wishers abroad.

The mounting opposition to HUAC stems in part from the conviction that it has contributed enormously to our present plight. Because of its repressive "fall-out," its impact on our basic freedoms has been incomparably more destructive than that of any other government activity. To be sure, dissent has been stifled by restrictive legislation, but it has been wounded far more deeply by fear of public exposure and reprisal, the Committee's most potent weapon. Like salt flavoring the sea, the threat of HUAC's activities pervades the entire process of individual and group expression on the vital issues of our time. Civil liberty has been poisoned by fear of the Committee—fear of its subpoenas, fear of being "named" by its informers, fear of joining or remaining a member of a "cited" organization, fear of signing petitions, fear of supporting causes or movements which might be condemned by HUAC. In the view of many, we cannot find our way back to freedom unless HUAC is abolished.

The Committee's highly personalized use of its powers has also stirred a torrent of protest. HUAC is supposed to obtain facts in order to help Congress discharge its legislative responsibilities. Instead, it is charged, HUAC uses the investigative power to attack the witness—"to disgrace private persons," as President Kennedy put it.

A hearing is essentially a trial of the witness suspected by the Committee of subversion—but without any of the traditional safeguards of a trial. Its purpose is to alienate the witness-defendant from the protections of his society and to bring about his ruin. This use of the investigative power is called "exposure," and has been a self-proclaimed Committee objective from the very beginning.

HUAC's hearings have emerged as a modern counterpart of the ancient pillory, a form of public humiliation and punishment. The pillory was an invitation to the community to work its will on the helpless victim; so is a HUAC hearing. The use by HUAC of its hearings to expose and punish was condemned by the United States Supreme Court in 1957 as a perversion of the power to investigate. "We have no doubt," the Court ruled in the *Watkins* case, "that there is no congressional power to expose for the sake of exposure." Yet the Committee continues to point the finger of suspicion, accuse, try and punish.

Here are some facts about the anatomy of these hearings: In the first place, it is not a Federal crime to be a member of the Communist Party. In fact, the Internal Security Act of 1950 provides:

Neither the holding of office nor membership in any Communist organization by any person shall constitute per se a violation of . . . this section or of any other criminal statute.

But the Smith Act makes it a crime, among other things, to advocate knowingly the desirability of overthrow of the Government by force or violence; to organize or help to organize any society or group which teaches, advocates or encourages such overthrow of the Government; or to become a member of such a group with knowledge of its purposes. Evidence that a person is or has been a member of the Communist Party or that he attended Party meetings or associated with Party members would be links in a chain of proof that might lead to the discovery of evidence needed for a Smith Act prosecution.

Let us assume for a moment that you are, or have been, a Communist. This is a belief to which you have a constitutionally protected right. Furthermore, you have never indulged in any criminal *act* in connection with this belief. Should you plead the First Amendment (which protects your right to have a belief), you will be in contempt of Congress and liable to a jail sentence and fine, for the courts have ruled that the free speech and assembly protections of the First Amendment are not a valid reason for refusing to answer HUAC's questions. An answer might be a clue or a link in a chain of proof of a Smith Act violation. Should you plead the Fifth Amendment (which protects your right not to incriminate yourself), then, because you refuse to deny that you are a Communist, in the context of a HUAC hearing you are guilty by inference (it does not matter that guilt by inference has been specifically condemned by the Supreme Court—remember we are now in a HUAC hearing). Despite the fact that a plea of the Fifth is supposed to protect the *innocent* witness who fears *unfounded* prosecution, HUAC uses it to defame and disgrace the witness. Suppose you are ready to gamble with the risks of prosecution and to answer the $64 question right out, "Yes, I am a Communist (or have been)?" And the answer is very simple—if you answer HUAC's $64 question, in effect you waive the right to plead the Fifth to any questions that follow: thus you are forced to inform on former friends or associates, or go to jail on contempt charges.

6

But you may be completely innocent of any connection with the Communist Party whatever. You still have the right to plead the Fifth in order not to "open the door" to further enquiry. If you swear under oath that you are not, and never have been, a Communist, you may waive the right to use the Fifth Amendment to avoid answering any questions about other organizations which the Committee chooses to ask you. And even if your denial is not a waiver, it would make the plea of the privilege about other organizations so revealing as to be meaningless.

Furthermore, if you answer in the negative and HUAC refuses to credit your denial, you may be indicted for perjury.

These are the mechanics of a system which weighs and disposes of our lives. These are the rules of a game as weird as the legal proceeding described in Kafka's prophetic novel *The Trial*, in which an arm of the state, moved by dark, concealed and vengeful compulsions, plucks out and punishes men for phantom crimes.

There is a widespread feeling that the Committee's time of judgment has arrived. During the 16 years of its functioning as a standing committee, it was rarely called upon to justify itself. The pressures of the cold war disposed many to forgive its trespasses. If the relationship between what it was doing and the legislative process seemed obscure, it would be ultimately clarified. If witnesses were injured or defamed in the course of a hearing, that was an unavoidable consequence of the hunt for facts. If the facts for which the Committee claimed to be hunting never emerged, that merely pointed to the need for greater perseverance and more hearings. All the returns are now in: the Committee is ripe for a reckoning.

The reckoning, it is claimed, shows that the Committee is bankrupt; that it has enormous liabilities and no assets. In the course of its never-ending investigations, it has blasted the careers of hundreds of professionals—writers, artists, teachers and lawyers. It has made "unemployable" numberless talented men and women in the mass-communications media and has forced the discharge and blacklisting of many workers in industry. Hundreds have been branded for life as traitors and reduced to pariahs. It has ruined the personal lives and mental health of scores of its victims; its subpoena has been a trigger of unbearable anxiety and fear. A HUAC appearance, or a subpoena, contributed to the suicide or untimely death of at least 15 persons.

It has often been argued that HUAC's toll of freedom, livelihood, career, reputation and peace of mind is necessary—an unavoidable evil, a small price to pay to safeguard our security. The liabilities, it is claimed, are more than offset by the assets. But when we open the legislative account ledger and make a reckoning we discover that after all the Committee's scare headlines, its never-ending bouts with claimed threats to our existence and its sensationalized disclosures about the Red menace, it can claim credit for only one statute: the Internal Security Act of 1950, which was vetoed by President Truman and still has not been approved by the United States Supreme Court. One need not be a thrall of Moscow to conclude that on the record the Committee has not justified its existence.

HUAC is now some 23 years old. Created in 1938 as a temporary, special investigating committee, its seven-year childhood was a stormy one under the chairmanship of the redoubtable Martin Dies. In 1945, its temporary status was ended and it entered legislative adulthood as a permanent standing committee. It had been investigating Communism for 15 years when, in 1953, Senator McCarthy, a brash parvenu, broke into the act. The basic techniques of subversion-hunting were already thoroughly developed by HUAC; all that was left for the Wisconsin Senator was to intensify their application. When McCarthy's spectacular excesses brought him low, the Committee continued to do business at the old stand, the good gray dean of exposure.

This is not to say that the Committee no longer has any rivals. In 1951, the Senate, prodded by the late Senator McCarran, created a counterpart of HUAC in the form of a subcommittee of the Judiciary Committee. Under the leadership of Senators McCarran and Jenner, this Committee, from 1951 until 1955, offered stiff competition in hearings and headline-hunting to HUAC. Since 1955, the Committee, under the chairmanship of Mississippi's Senator Eastland, has grown rather dormant. More recently, Senator Dodd of Connecticut, a former member of the Federal Bureau of Investigation, has taken over the work of the Senate subcommittee and launched it on a vigorous program with targets such as the movement to ban nuclear testing and the Cuban revolution.

HUAC is not merely the undisputed leader in its field; it is adjudged by many, both in and out of Congress, "the most powerful Committee in Congress." HUAC's life and times can only be described in superlatives: it has broken more records than Babe Ruth. A 23-year-old marathon investigation into a single subject—Communism and subversion—is in itself a wonder of the legislative world. In the course of its stupendous, generation-long, nonstop probe, the Committee has published more than 50,000 pages of hearings and reports—easily outdistancing all other congressional committees combined in this respect. It has issued over 5,000 subpoenas—another record—for it is estimated that this exceeds the subpoenas issued by all other congressional committees combined for the same period. During the term of its functioning as a standing committee, it has cited for contempt five times the number of witnesses cited by all other congressional committees combined in the same period. It has heard thousands of witnesses, some two or three times. In addition to a long list of Washington hearings, it has conducted hearings in about 25 cities —in some of them several times.

Its appropriations are also startling in proportion to the costs of other committees. In addition to the huge sums which it has expended for printing, it has received and spent in salaries alone almost $5 million. Its annual appropriation for 1959, $327,000, the highest in its history, was topped only by a very few important congressional committees. Its appropriation was greater than for the Ways and Means Committee and the Judiciary Committee, more than double that for the Committees on Education and Labor, Foreign Affairs and Banking and Currency. In 1960, it received another appropriation of $327,000, a total of $654,00 for a two-year period, during which time the Committee on Armed Services received $150,000, the Ways and Means Committee $300,000, the Committee on Education and Labor $328,000, the Committee on Banking and Currency $205,000, and the Judiciary Committee $425,000.

While the appropriation for 1959-60 totaled $654,000, HUAC actually cost the taxpayers a total of $850,000— the $200,000 difference representing additional outlays, including printing. During 1960, HUAC printed about 332,000 copies of its hearings, consultations and reports at a cost of $47,270.53, a sum nearly equal to the entire appropriation of the House Committee on Agriculture ($50,000).

In 1961, HUAC asked for and received $331,000, an appropriation exceeding that of almost any other committee of the House.

Composed of nine members, HUAC has a staff of 55—12% of the total complement of House legislative-committee personnel and the largest number of staff personnel of any legislative committee.

How and why did this extraordinary committee come into being?

2 BIRTH OF A CONGRESSIONAL MONSTER

The House Committee on Un-American Activities never had—and was never intended to have—a legitimate legislative function. Its birth certificate is a blueprint of the exposure system.

The resolution of 1938 under which the Committee functioned on a temporary basis authorized it to investigate

(1) the extent, character, and objects of un-American propaganda activities in the United States, (2) the diffusion within the United States of subversive and un-American propaganda that is instigated from foreign countries or of a domestic origin and attacks the principle of the form of government as guaranteed by our Constitution. . . .

This resolution thus planted the Committee's investigative authority with both feet in the middle of the First Amendment. "Propaganda" is a method of communicating ideas. It was impossible to investigate "propaganda" without evaluating those ideas—praising some and attacking others. This was censorship by investigation.

When the Committee was created, Chairman Martin Dies

acknowledged that any attempt to prevent or punish un-American activities by legislation "might jeopardize fundamental rights far more important than the objective we seek. . . ." But he found what to him was an ideal solution. His Committee was not going to introduce legislation banning or even policing un-American activities—propaganda or otherwise. That would be unconstitutional. In unconsciously ironic deference to our fundamental laws, he promised to confine himself to exposure—independent of a legislative end. He would expose and at the same time safeguard the rights of the people against legislative trespass. What could be fairer?

HUAC was designated as a "special" investigating Committee with limited tenure. It was to submit its final report on January 1, 1939, a scant seven months after its creation. Chairman Dies told the House that he was quite agreeable to this time limitation and that he would finish the job in short order.

By the time January rolled around, however, Dies was pleading with the House to extend his mandate for a full year. This the House did on the Chairman's claim that there was more un-Americanism and more subversion in the land than he had realized—and, unsaid, more newspaper headlines than an obscure Congressman could get by any other means.

The antisubversive prober has a natural advantage in the investigative sweepstakes: the deep-seated, emotional anti-Communism of most Americans. The more farfetched his disclosures, the more welcome they are. He deals in issues which trench to the heart of the Nation's existence. Their very gravity commands that he be given the benefit of the doubt. And he knows that if he strikes the right chords of sedition and treason with sinister overtones of plotting and secrecy, a receptive press will carry his accusations and warnings to every American hearth. Above all, he must name names—he must expose—for it is always open season on Reds and nothing is more productive of headlines than an attack on individuals.

If the antisubversive demagogue knows how to go about it, he can launch a spiraling probe which it is impossible to stop. Overnight he becomes a man with a mission, a scourge of traitors, a defender of the Nation, a patriotic awakener. Millions hang on his pronouncements; his press conferences are thronged with eager reporters demanding new disclosures. He lectures Presidents, shares the spotlight with the FBI as a savior of our security, and becomes an authority on foreign policy whose warnings it is politically dangerous to ignore.

In 1939, the Committee reported that while Congress lacked the power under our Constitution to deny people the right to teach what it deemed to be subversive doctrines, "it does have the right to focus the spotlight of publicity upon their activities."

In 1940, the Committee avowed that its real purpose was not legislation but rather "to inform the American people of the activities" of subversive organizations by "turning the light of pitiless publicity" on them.

The Committee rapidly developed the notion that it had a unique, a special, function—*exposure*. "This is the only agency of government that has the power of exposure," it reported in 1941. And in 1943 it announced that "discovery and exposure" were its "special function" by mandate from the House. In that year it published the names, positions and salaries of 563 Government employees, alleged to be members of the American League for Peace and Democracy, because "the Committee felt that the Congress and the people were entitled to know who they were." This was only one of the many lists which the Committee published in the forties in the exercise of its self-assumed exposure function.

The Dies Committee never doubted for a moment that it could use the power of investigation to attack individuals, organizations and ideas on political grounds without violating the Constitution. It seemingly never occurred to the Committee that the First Amendment would be meaningless if its prohibitions were binding on the Congress as a whole but not on its investigating committees. And it actually boasted that it was engaging in a nonlegislative activity—the exposure of individuals. The Committee's "temporary" status had become a fiction: its mandate was renewed each year until 1943, when its tenure was extended to two years. Rooting out un-Americanism became a way of life.

Chairman Dies had really struck pay dirt, from his point of view, three months after the Committee was launched —in the testimony of just two witnesses. The first was

John P. Frey, President of the Metal Trades Department of the AFL, who for three days in August 1938 gave testimony attacking the CIO as a Red-dominated organization. Without any corroborating evidence at all, Frey cited scores of CIO unions as communistic and listed 283 alleged Communists in CIO unions.

Frey was succeeded on the witness stand by Walter S. Steele, Chairman of the American Coalition Committee on National Security, a confederation of 114 patriotic organizations. His testimony was significant because it marked the emergence of the vigilante network that became so important to the functioning of the Committee. Steele, who had testified before earlier antisubversive committees, charged some six and a half million Americans with subversion. He placed the names of 641 allegedly communistic organizations on the record and made Red charges against thousands of individuals. He even cast suspicion on certain Catholic organizations, the Boy Scouts, the Camp Fire Girls, and the American Society of International Law. Following what has become a persistent HUAC pattern, Steele had little or nothing to say about Fascist organizations, which, at the time he testified, were fairly prominent throughout the country.

Steele's testimony was too rambling and turgid to capture the headlines. But Frey had organized his material with the press in mind: his list of names was presented at the beginning of his testimony; each individual name was numbered and was followed by an identifying description together with data including the home city of the victim. The press blazed with headlines: "Communists Rule the CIO. CIO Communist-Dominated From Top to Bottom, Frey Testifies; He Names 283 Reds." Many of those named were discharged and blacklisted in industry. The Committee gave Frey a stunning weapon against his arch foe, the CIO, and at the same time found an opportunity to perform some antilabor bloodletting on its own account.

Thus the technique of exposure was born: the Committee would provide a libel-proof forum for charges of subversion against named individuals made without cross-examination and for no legislative purpose; the press would publish the lists of names as well as the inflammatory trumpery accompanying the names as a news story deserving the most prominent coverage because it was tes-

13

timony before a Congressional committee; the community (including the employer) would do the rest.

Kenneth G. Crawford, analyzing Dies's success, pointed out:

It was probably the very success of the Frey testimony as an experiment in publicity that awakened Dies and his associates to a full realization of the potentialities of the political gold mine that they had struck. From Frey on it was catch as catch can with no holds barred. No patrioteer was too wacky to be taken seriously.

While Frey was the prototype of a long line of friendly witnesses, J. B. Matthews, a former Methodist missionary, teacher, pacifist, socialist and reformed Marxist, was the first of a series of Committee ideologists and policy-makers. Matthews not only built up the Committee's elaborate file system, but, according to the late Howard Rushmore, was the "brain-truster back of the Committee's relentless exposures." Matthews gave the Committee its basic orientation at a time in 1938 when it was floundering, and taught the Committee the neo-Archimedean precept that with enough names in a file, one could expose the world. Matthews unburdened himself for some ten hours in executive session as a witness before the Committee, and shortly thereafter became its research director. Matthews was not only a prodigious identifier, but an indefatigable bloodhound of concealed "fronts." In his own testimony he reeled off over 100 organizations which he claimed were linked in various hidden ways to Moscow. It was Matthews who was responsible for the charge that Shirley Temple was a Communist dupe.

Matthews left the Committee in 1944 to become the behind-the-scenes high priest of the exposure operation and the custodian of what is said to be the most Gargantuan file on subversive names and activities ever assembled. In 1948 Matthews was chief investigator for an antisubversive investigation of the University of Chicago, and in 1953 he served for two weeks as executive director of Senator McCarthy's antisubversive probe, but was forced to surrender that post as a result of nation-wide protests over an article in which he linked at least 7,000 Protestant clergymen with subversion. His prior testimony remained on the record, unquestioned by the Committee.

Meanwhile, the Committee was discovering other powerful reasons to remain in existence. An antisubversive probe had found broader objectives than the exposure of individuals or the probers' political self-aggrandizement. The ultimate aim was the exploitation of anti-Communism as an instrument of political leverage, a means of handicapping the achievement of legitimate national goals. The Dies Committee unceasingly attacked the New Deal by discrediting its programs as communistic and un-American. It undermined the implementation of these programs by exposing and calling for the dismissal of "subversive" New Dealers.

A powerful stimulus to the constant renewal of the Dies Committee's powers was the drive by a coalition of Southern Democrats and Northern Republicans to influence and change the political climate in which the New Deal had been flourishing. Congressmen who were opposed to the Roosevelt program saw in the Dies operation a means of discrediting and possibly slowing it down. Besides, the flamboyant Dies, with his swashbuckling methods and headline-hunting, gave a kind of balm to a small, frustrated House group which had seen leadership and prestige slip from its hands into those of the President. Dies's barbaric yawp might be more grating than Roosevelt's cultivated accent, but it was well suited to telling the world that there was still life in the old House.

By the end of 1944, however, the six-year Committee investigation began to run out of gas and to exhibit certain signs of motor fatigue. During the entire year it had heard only one witness and published a seven-page hearing record. The peripatetic Dies ceased roaming the countryside at the head of his Committee bloodhounds and remained in Washington, his full-throated cry reduced to a whisper. In May of that election year, Dies announced, to the surprise of his House colleagues, that he would not seek re-election. To many observers at the time it seemed that the Committee had come to the end of the road. It was widely assumed, in the press and in congressional circles, that the new Congress, which was to convene in January, would decline to renew the Committee's mandate.

The major reason for this was that the Committee had become so openly anti-Administration that the Democrats, then in the majority, regarded it as a Republican political instrument. Members of the majority, with the exception of those Southerners from "safe" districts, feared that the Committee might in the future be used to try to unseat them. The fear was not groundless. The Committee had in the past done just that, not only in congressional contests, but also in state elections and in the presidential election. Democrats who supported the Roosevelt-Truman ticket in the 1944 election were angry at the Committee's release of a report on the National Citizen's Political Action Committee (NCPAC) shortly before the balloting began. It sought to create the impression that NCPAC, which had been set up to support the Roosevelt-Truman ticket by a group of labor leaders and liberals, was what the Committee was fond of calling a "Red front." The charge, made on the eve of the election, was a typical hit-and-run play, calculated to alienate support from the Democratic ticket. And although the play failed, supporters of the Administration in the House determined to kill off the Committee.

But what was past turned out to be merely prologue. The opposition to the Committee failed to reckon with the resourcefulness of Representative John Rankin, acknowledged by many to be one of the most skillful parliamentarians in the House, who made a stunning move. He proposed making the Committee a standing committee of the House, which would give it permanent status. In a blitz tactic, he submitted an amendment to the House rules which, as is customary on the opening day, were before the House. Usually, the Chairman of the Rules Committee, at that time Representative Adolph Sabath, Democrat of Illinois, brings in a resolution which, in effect, reconstitutes the Committee much along the lines of its predecessor. If members of the House desire changes in the rules, these changes are normally referred to the Rules Committee before being placed before the entire House. Rankin's amendment, however, short-circuited the procedure. The last thing he wanted was to have his proposal brought before the Rules Committee, where it would be subjected to lengthy hearings and calm deliberation. He knew it would ultimately be killed by the Rules Committee; so he used a parliamentary sneak play to force the House to act on his resolution.

The Rules Committee for the new Congress was not yet legally constituted. Therefore the Rankin amendment could not be referred to it, but had to be considered by the House as a whole. And the House could not renew the powers of the Rules Committee, vital to the functioning of the House, without at the same time voting on the Rankin amendment, either accepting or defeating it before it could vote on the main resolution.

It was a master stroke. The House, preoccupied as it was on the opening day with the details of organizing itself, was not prepared to debate any important issues, and certainly not one that was thought to be dead. Rankin, through a combination of parliamentary sleight of hand and an appeal to the patriotism and security-consciousness of a wartime Congress, was able to rekindle the Committee's dying embers.

The success of Rankin's tactical maneuver, however, only gave him his audience, not the final prize. He still had to convince a majority of the House to vote for his amendment. Time for debate was very limited, but no one could fail to see that he was proposing a congressional monstrosity: a permanent committee with the essentially transitory function of investigation. Precedent, unbroken since the founding of the Republic, had established that investigating committees are not constituted as permanent bodies. Majority leader McCormack and other Congressmen were quite aware that this was indeed a fateful decision.

"Mark what we are doing," he warned. "This is not a question of establishing an investigating committee to investigate conditions that arise from time to time; it is a question of amending the rules of the House to provide for a permanent standing committee that does not consider legislation, but has one subject, one field, the field of investigating and making a report.

"There is," he continued, "a big difference between establishing a standing committee to investigate and establishing a special investigating committee for a particular Congress. If this amendment is adopted, as far as I know, it will be the first time in this body that a committee of this kind was ever established as a permanent standing committee."

Rankin quickly assured the House that the Committee would be no different from any other standing committee; it would have a legislative assignment to conduct hearings and report out bills. This was easy to say—especially for Rankin. But what was to be the area of its assignment?

Each standing committee—such as Ways and Means, Veterans' Affairs (over which Rankin himself presided), Foreign Affairs and Armed Services—operated within a clear and well-understood jurisdiction. So would the new standing committee, Rankin feebly asserted. As an investigating committee, it would continue to probe "un-American propaganda" and "propaganda activities." As a legislative committee, it would handle bills introduced in Congress on the subject of "un-American activities." But what did that mean? It could not refer to such matters as sedition, espionage and sabotage, for these already were within the jurisdiction of the Judiciary Committee.

Was the new Committee to carve a slice of jurisdiction from each of the standing committees so as to give it authority to handle bills involving, for example, un-American activities (whatever that meant), of farmers, veterans, trade unionists and soldiers, which would otherwise be processed by the Agriculture, Veterans' Affairs, Labor and Armed Services Committees? Was the Committee to invade the Judiciary Committee's established jurisdiction over bills involving criminal penalties when such penalties were proposed for "un-American activities?" What kind of legislation did "un-American" describe?

Again McCormack protested that the new Committee's jurisdiction was vague, if indeed it had jurisdiction over any legislation whatever.

"What type of legislation?" he asked the House. "There is a question of the jurisdiction of committees, of other permanent and standing committees. Certainly the existing rules provide the type of bills or resolutions that are referred to a standing committee. This resolution establishing a standing committee, assuming it can recommend legislation, does not set forth the type of legislation." Rankin never bothered to answer McCormack's question—and it has not been answered to this day.

Rankin did not waste time trying to sell his resolution on its legislative merits. He had a much more potent selling point: the importance of the continuing role of the Committee as a political security agency. The discontinuance of the Committee, he charged, was a subversive plot to get rid of its valuable collection of political dossiers and thus leave the Nation at the mercy of its enemies. He told the House that on more than 5,000 different occasions various intelligence agencies of the Government had consulted the

Committee's records "and have found in them a wealth of information that has gone far toward protecting the Nation from sabotage of all kinds." Discontinuing the Committee, Rankin insisted, would mean "that these valuable records that probably involve the fate of the Nation, the safety of the American people, would be dissipated. . . . I want to see that these papers are kept; that is the one thing I am striving for."

This charge was false, for steps had already been taken to preserve the Committee's records. But that made no difference to Rankin. He appealed to the House to foil the plot: "some of the men who went over to look over these papers were prepared to remove them and said they would like to throw them into the Potomac River."

On a voice vote, the proposed amendment was defeated, 134 to 146. Congressman Rankin then demanded a record of the vote and on a roll call the amendment passed. The victorious majority was the same coalition of Republicans and Southern Democrats which had prolonged the Dies Committee's life. Among those who voted against the Committee were Representative Francis Walter, now the Committee's chairman, and Representative Clyde Doyle of California, now an active member of the Committee. Thus was created the strangest parliamentary body of our time—a permanent legislative investigating committee without a legislative purpose, a standing committee with no meaningful legislative assignment.

The January 1945 vote did not, however, conclude debate in the House on the merits of the Committee's activities. During May 1946 sharp differences were aired in the course of debate on a motion appropriating $75,000 for the work of the Committee in the ensuing year. The motion was vigorously opposed by a group of Northern Democrats, including the chairman of the Judiciary Committee, Representative Emanuel Celler, who complained about the Committee's tenderness toward American Fascists, and Representative Doyle, who said that the work of the Committee should be in the hands of the Federal Bureau of Investigation. He added that the Committee had ignored American principles of jurisprudence by acting as both judge and jury. Rankin counterattacked with a virulent assault on the opponents of the Committee and a threat that he would have the Committee go "after un-American elements in the House." Despite this, opponents of the

Committee mustered the highest vote against the Committee's appropriation since its inception, 81 nays. The Committee won handily, however, with 240 in favor of the appropriation.

In July, with only feeble resistance, the Committee was again made a permanent part of the House structure when the Legislative Organization Act was passed. Rankin's threat to investigate his fellow House members in a period of growing reaction undoubtedly helped to turn the tide. From that day onward the fear of the Red smear has served as HUAC's most potent weapon to hold its congressional critics in line.

Rankin's demagogic maneuvers not only rescued the Committee from oblivion, they obtained for it tremendous coercive powers. In conducting investigations the Committee (or its subcommittees) was authorized "to sit and act at such times and places within the United States, whether or not the House is sitting, has recessed, or has adjourned, to hold such hearings, to require the attendance of such witnesses and the production of such books, papers, and documents, and to take such testimony, as it deems necessary." This delegation of power was greater than that given any other committee of the House.

With all of its great power, the Committee was to have no legislative responsibilities. In theory an agent of Congress, its functions were in no way related to the duties of Congress. Its real purpose as an investigating committee was to smite the political infidel, not to report findings to Congress. The result could only be to emancipate the Committee from the supervision of the House, which exercises ultimate control over its committees through the lawmaking process. It could "investigate" whomever and whenever it wanted without concern about its legislative productivity. Congressman Dies had explained that this new power of exposure was more valuable than legislation because it avoided constitutional problems! There was no need to waste time in legislative hearings or in drafting reports on dull and technical bills; let the other standing committees, with a clearly defined jurisdiction, do this grubby work.

While other standing committees had to get authority from the House to conduct investigations with the power of subpoena, the Committee had *carte blanche,* a lifetime pass on the exposure line. All that it needed from Congress was a yearly appropriation.

Nor did the language of its resolution serve as an internal restraint. The resolution authorizing conventional investigations is an important control on investigative abuse. It marks the outer limits of the investigation; the investigating committee can probe only those matters which it is authorized to investigate. The witness can be required to answer only those questions which are pertinent to the resolution. But the Committee was authorized to operate its exposure system under a resolution with no meaningful limitations on its scope. It was to be a permanent roving inquisition into unpopular speech and ideas.

As the Supreme Court ruled in the 1957 *Watkins* case, "it would be difficult to imagine a less explicit authorizing resolution. Who can define the meaning of the 'un-American'? What is that single, solitary 'principle of the form of government as guaranteed by our constitution'?" Like "un-American," the term "subversive" is merely an epithet.

The experience of the Nation with the functioning of the Dies Committee left no room for doubt that the jurisdiction of the Committee was as broad or as narrow as the prejudices of the Chairman.

In its 1939 report, the Committee emphasized that "Americanism recognizes the existence of a God. . . ." According to Committee standards, you are un-American if you believe in the following:

(1) absolute social and racial equality;

(2) the destruction of private property and the abolition of inheritance [apparently irrespective of the means employed or advocated];

(3) the substitution of communal ownership of property for private ownership;

(4) the belief that it is the "duty of government to support the people";

(5) a system of political, economic or social regimentation based upon a planned economy;

(6) collectivistic philosophy;

(7) destruction of the American system of checks and balances with the three independent coordinate branches of government.

The *New York Times* summed it up when, in January

of 1945, it editorialized that the Dies Committee had "suffered from ambiguity of its birth. Just what is un-American activity? The law defines crimes against the state, and persons committing such crimes are admittedly un-American. But is it un-American to hold an unpopular opinion . . . or take an attitude that is also held or taken by Communists? . . . Had he [Dies] pushed his opinion to its logical end more than half the population of the United States might have been denounced . . . he used methods that old-fashioned persons regard as un-American—indictment by innuendo, refusal of defense testimony, prosecution and sometimes persecution in place of impartial investigation. . . ."

The permanent Committee has exploited the vagueness of the resolution in the same way as its predecessor, the temporary Committee. It has used its power to attack as un-American and subversive the Fund for the Republic, the National Council of Churches, the American Civil Liberties Union, and such individuals as Bishop Oxnam, Dr. Edward U. Condon, Dr. Robert Hutchins, the late Rabbis Stephen Wise and Judah Magnes, and scores of others. The present chairman has decreed that racism, anti-Semitic bombings and hate literature are not "subversive" and "un-American" within the meaning of the Committee's resolution. HUAC, he claims, has no jurisdiction in these areas. Who can say him nay?

Thus, the permanent Committee was born, fully equipped with all of the basic components of the exposure system: (1) it was functionally independent of the body which created it, because (2) it lacked legislative responsibilities; (3) its investigative power was shaped to inquisitorial ends and conferred upon it by (4) a charter to probe speech and ideas so broad and vague as to impose no meaningful restraints upon it.

3 ANATOMY OF A HATE GROUP

In the fall of 1960 a fire-bomb was thrown against the front of the office of the Citizens' Committee to Protect American Freedom, a Los Angeles group formed to oppose

HUAC. The bomb shattered the door and started a fire. The bombing came shortly after a huge swastika was smeared on the door of the Citizens' Committee offices. The mailbox was shot off. An attempt was made to set fire to the home of Frank Wilkinson, the group's secretary, a leading figure in the movement to abolish HUAC (now serving a one-year jail term for contempt of the Committee). Wilkinson's wife received anonymous telephone calls threatening his life. Wilkinson's life insurance was canceled. Los Angeles students who joined him in a TV program in opposition to HUAC barely escaped a beating by thugs after they left the studio. In the spring of 1961 the New York office of a HUAC abolition group was broken into and vandalized.

On January 2, 1961, a group of members of the American Nazi Party descended on Washington to picket the White House in support of HUAC. On the same day a screaming, threatening mob of Fascist-oriented refugees besieged a meeting in Washington's All Souls Unitarian Church held in support of a HUAC-abolition campaign. The atmosphere was electric with imminent violence; bloodshed was averted by prompt action of the police, who formed a protective cordon around the meeting. When an outbreak seemed inevitable, the police requested that the meeting be terminated as quickly as possible and supplied a motorcycle escort to protect the participants on their way out of the city. The picket signs of these fanatics were stored in Chairman Walter's office.

Two weeks later an inflamed champion of the Committee burst into the office of University of California Professor Thomas F. Parkinson, poet, Guggenheim fellow, author and teacher. The intruder carried a Bible in one hand and a double-barreled shotgun in the other. He raised the gun and fired. The shots ripped into the back of a graduate student, Stephen Mann Thomas, and brought instant death. Professor Parkinson suffered a shattered jaw which required skin grafting and plastic surgery.

The killer, John Harrison Farmer, was apprehended the next day. In his briefcase was this note: "Death to all Communists. Death to all fellow travellers. Death to every friend of Communism. Death in the name of God to all the evil hosts of Communism and its followers." Farmer had also marked for death Assistant Professor Richard T.

Drinnon. Farmer did not know these men. Both of them had opposed HUAC and were members of SLATE, a campus anti-HUAC organization. He had read about their activity and was particularly exercised by an article attacking Parkinson for his criticism of the Committee.

When a Congressman votes against an appropriation measure for internal improvement, he may get disapproving mail. But a vote in the House against HUAC results in a shower of abuse, obscenity and hate. Many of these letters are unprintable. Here are a few mild samples of congressional mail after the 1961 vote on HUAC's appropriation:

> Please, get yourself a one way ticket to Red Nazi Russia.
> Drop dead. This would be the height of responsibility to this wonderful Christian America.
> You are sharing the objectives of the insidious and diabolical Communist Conspiracy. Such flirtations with treason are gaining for you and the despicable notoriety of being at the very least an unbalanced, soft headed, bleeding heart. We, who now reverently treasure the memory of our Nathan Hales, have a venomous contempt for you Benedict Arnold types.

This is the harvest of hate, and it dramatizes the role of the Committee in the underworld of the professional hate groups.

Hate groups are established fixtures in American public life. Their pathology has been frequently described by social scientists as an expression of prejudice rooted in hate and defeat. They emerge in response to a need for a scrapegoat, an outlet for the aggression spawned by frustration. Their world is one of black and white, of sweeping, unalterable generalizations. To the bigot—organized or unorganized—the country is on the brink of disaster. He sees and invents evidences of imminent doom everywhere. He is obsessed by the conviction that there is one evil which explains all the ills of his society and of the world. Salvation can come only by destroying, by liquidating or punishing his "pet hate"—be it Catholic, Negro, Jew or foreign-born.

The world of the hate group is structured on myth,

stereotype and falsehood. It protects itself from the inroads of reason with an enormous arsenal of polemic and rhetorical weapons. The spokesman of the hate group masterfully echoes all the paranoiac fears of his followers and makes every challenge a confirmation of the power of the enemy. He slanders, lies, exaggerates, evades and forges to keep alive the particular terror on which his particular group feeds. The successful merchant of hate develops a special fear-breeding vocabulary which oozes contempt and aggression. He is a master of propaganda—the more lurid the better.

The bigot is drawn to the hate group out of an unrestrainable need for action. He is not sustained by mere belief or conviction. He has a hunger for direct action, for violence, born of a passionate resentment and anger. Means, not ends, are all-important to him. All our hate groups are unified by a hazy nostalgia for a pure America, peopled by 100% native-born, white Christian Americans and cleansed of the evils which, to them, defile it. But they have no affirmative program beyond the goal of destroying the objects of their hate. They are exclusively anti-Negro, anti-Catholic, anti-labor, anti-Semitic, anti-foreign-born.

In addition to their special obsessions, the hate groups share an enthusiasm for the political and social canons of the extreme right. Thus they believe that America is not a democracy but a republic, that the income tax should be abolished, foreign aid ended, States' rights restored and the powers of the Supreme Court restricted. Inevitably, hate groups have an affinity for one another, based on a consciousness of kind, common emotional needs and interlocking prejudices. The White Citizens Councils are anti-Negro but they are also anti-Catholic and anti-Semitic. The American Council of Christian Churches is anti-liberal Protestant, but it is also anti-Catholic and anti-Semitic. The Circuit Riders are anti-liberal Protestant but also anti-Semitic, anti-Negro and anti-labor.

Each hate group is thus naturally allied to all the others. All of them have a common dedication which unites them in a special way; they are fanatical crusaders for HUAC.

For the 23 years of its existence HUAC has had close and continuous ties with the hate underworld and the more "respectable" pressure groups which work with it. The Dies Committee's first investigator was Edward F. Sullivan, a publicity specialist for native Fascist groups and a former professional labor spy. Two years before his appointment he was the principal speaker at an Asheville, North Carolina, convention of native Fascists. (Sullivan's speech was described in the local press as "what Hitler would have said had he been speaking.") He also was a prominent speaker at Nazi Bund and Coughlinite gatherings. Another Committee collaborator was Harry Jung, Chicago propagandist of anti-Semitism. J. B. Matthews, the scholar of the patrioteer hate underworld, and Walter S. Steele, one of its principal spokesmen, were pillars of the Dies Committee.

One of Dies's strongest admirers and collaborators was Joseph P. Kamp, a professional hate merchant who was editor and publisher of a Fascist magazine, *The Awakener*. Kamp's Constitutional Educational League had a working relationship with the Committee. Kamp had access to the Committee's files, in return for which he supplied the Committee with thousands of names. The Educational League gave Dies an "Americanism" award; it was subsequently mentioned in a Federal conspiracy indictment.*

Dies enjoyed a similar relationship with Father Charles E. Coughlin, Fascist priest, leader of the Christian Front. Through his radio program and his publication, *Social Justice,* Father Coughlin disseminated quantities of Nazi propaganda. He too provided Dies with lists of names and propaganda material. In 1939 he issued these instructions to his followers:

> In your appreciation of the work accomplished by Dies employ some of your leisure moments to write him a letter of encouragement. In fact, a million letters brought to his desk would be an answer to those who are bent on destroying him and the legislative body he represents.

Paid Nazi agents were enthusiastic about HUAC and its work. A banquet for Dies was given by Fascist propa-

---

* When HUAC's continuance was threatened, Kamp wrote in *The Awakener,* "The League began a nationwide drive on its behalf, secured over 4 million signatures to petitions and deluged Congress with an avalanche of letters from aroused patriots."

gandist Merwin K. Hart in December 1939 (Mr. Hart, incidentally, was a contributor to Chairman Walter's most recent congressional campaign. His National Economic Council was charged a few years ago by the Buchanan Committee with "ill-concealed anti-Semitism.") Among those who did honor to Dies were Bundist James Wheeler Hill, and German-American Bund leader, Fritz Kuhn. When asked what he thought of the Committee, Kuhn replied, "I am in favor of it being appointed again and I want them to get more money." Convicted Nazi agent George Sylvester Viereck said, "I have the highest respect for the Committee and sympathize with its program." The Federal Communications Commission reported that "Representative Dies received as many favorable references in Axis propaganda in this country as any living American public figure." This was during the war.

Dies shared speaking platforms with Fascist James True, inventor of a special blackjack called the "kike-killer," and Reverend Edward Lodge Curran, Father Coughlin's lieutenant. Under Dies, the Committee fed material and articles by its members to Reverend Gerald B. Winrod's *Defender* and Reverend Gerald L. K. Smith's *Cross and the Flag,* both anti-Semitic hate sheets. Smith and Winrod showered Dies with praise—as did the entire hate underworld.

For example, William Dudley Pelley, the head of the pro-Nazi Silver Shirts, said, "I formed the Silver Legion in 1933 . . . to propagandize exactly the same principles." The Ku Klux Klan's Imperial Wizard, James Colescott, asserted, "[The Committee's] program so closely parallels the program of the Klan that there's no distinguishable difference between them." In 1942, Imperial Wizard Colescott arranged a private interview with Dies which resulted in his urging Klansmen everywhere "to support the work of the Dies Committee." In the Klan's publication, *The Fiery Cross,* for January 1942, he praised the Committee's "great service to our country."

It is hardly surprising that Representative Samuel Dickstein told the House in 1941: "110 Fascist organizations in the United States have had, and have now, the key to the back door of the Un-American Activities Committee."

Dies was under constant attack by liberal forces for his failure to investigate Fascist organizations. But Dies used

27

his powers to shield these groups and made token investigations only to preserve the appearance of impartiality.*

These critics failed to appreciate the underlying realities of the Dies Committee's relationship to the hate underworld. They had become partners in a joint enterprise. The hate groups gave HUAC names, propaganda and political support. HUAC used the power of the government to strike at the hatists' targets. Then this material, fed into the Committee's files and burnished with the prestige of officialdom, was used by the underworld in its press. As David Wesley has summed it up:

> What these long years did, was to create a solid establishment: an acre of files, a thoroughly indoctrinated staff, a firm tradition, a network of contacts and sources of information, a conditioned pattern of behavior, a methodology, all intricately interwoven into the whole fabric of the underworld of the peddlers of hate, with its interlocking directorship and its broad, cross-pollinating system of propaganda organs.

After HUAC was reconstituted in 1945, it continued its collaboration with the hate groups. The Committee was dominated by Congressman John Rankin† of Mississippi, one of the most virulent anti-Semites ever to sit in Congress. Rankin had been honored by the Nazis and did not hesitate to attack Jews and Negroes as inferior peoples whenever he found an opportunity. On November 18, 1943, he announced that I. F. Stone, a Washington liberal journalist who had attacked him for his anti-Semitism, was

---

* In June 1947, HUAC, in response to liberal pressure, set up a subcommittee on Fascism, headed by Representative John McDowell, himself an anti-Semite, of Pennsylvania. The subcommittee was promptly challenged by Representative Sabath to take action by investigating a group of prominent Fascist organizations. The subcommittee met for ten minutes and decided there was nothing to investigate.

Chairman Velde, in 1945, in a move to win support for HUAC, then under severe criticism for its attack on the clergy, carefully selected for investigation the two smallest hate outfits he could find: The National Renaissance Party and the magazine *Common Sense*, both of whose supporters could be housed in the same telephone booth. No witnesses were called, but a report was issued.

† The nominal Chairman was Representative Edward J. Hart of New Jersey, who resigned in July 1945 and was succeeded by Representative John J. Wood of Georgia.

really named Isidore Feinstein.* When a group of women called on him to protest his bill denying the right of franchise to all American soldiers, Mr. Rankin said of these ladies: "If I am any judge, they are Communists, pure and simple, probably more simple than pure. They looked like foreigners to me. I never saw such a wilderness of noses in my life." Speaking on the floor of the House on February 21, 1944, he referred to Walter Winchell as "the communistic little kike."

In the first major debate on the new HUAC in the House, members of Congress complained that HUAC was doing business at the same old stand. Representative Hook of Michigan described the Committee as a "sounding board for the un-American Fascist groups," and he informed the House that "Gerald L. K. Smith [the notorious anti-Semite] is not only the Committee's adviser on un-Americanism, he is also the confidante of the Committee's plans." Representative Savage of Washington complained: "It seems to me all Gerald L. K. Smith has to do is yell 'sic 'em' and the Committee's counsel takes after whatever party Mr. Smith is peeved at." Representative O'Toole of New York said: "The Committee has permitted itself to become a forum for the dissemination of racial and religious theories that are not part of our democracy."

The Wood-Rankin Committee's hate-group connections sparked a number of investigations in the forties. One of the first was the attempt to purge the radio of a group of liberal commentators who were critical of the hate groups. In October 1945 the Committee obtained 78 scripts of radio commentators. In December the Committee introduced a bill which would "by proper and frequent announcements clearly separate and distinguish programs consisting of news items from those programs based upon, or consisting of, personal opinion or propaganda." On February 2, 1946, Rankin said, "I want to tell you now, some of this stuff that is going over the air should be stopped. Of all the dirt and filth I ever heard, those filthy attacks on me and the Committee on Un-American Activities by Walter Winchell are the worst."

The Committee then turned its investigative talents to proving that the United States is not a democracy—the favorite thesis of the lunatic fringe. Early in 1946 liberal

* Interestingly enough, Chairman Walter told the House the same thing when Stone criticized the Committee.

organizations which had concerned themselves with "democracy" were reminded in letters from Committee Counsel Adamson that "this country was not organized as a democracy." Adamson wrote as follows to columnist Drew Pearson: "Several people have called to my attention the closing line of your Sunday night broadcast, 'Make democracy work.' I should like very much to have your definition of the word 'democracy' as you are using it over the radio. If you will be good enough to supply this information, I will give the matter further consideration to determine whether it should be called to the attention of the members of the committee for such action as they deem proper."

The Hollywood probe of 1947 also had strong hatist links. The files on Hollywood had been developed by Fascist publicist Edward F. Sullivan, and the pressure for the investigation had come from an assortment of native Fascists. Gerald L. K. Smith finally turned the trick. In 1948 he wrote in *The Cross and the Flag,* "We do take credit, we Christian Nationalists, for the recent investigation into Hollywood."

In 1949 HUAC made a sally into the field of education. It asked more than 100 schools and colleges to submit textbooks for a check on subversive content. This probe, too, was inspired by a lunatic-fringe outfit, the National Council for American Education, which was run by the notorious anti-Semite Allen A. Zoll. It boasted on its Board of Governors the Coughlinite priest Edward Lodge Curran and a Committee member, Representative (late Senator) Karl Mundt.

With the emergence of McCarthyism, HUAC was no longer limited to old-fashioned hatist and crackpot sects for investigative suggestions and support.* Hate became everybody's business. The function of the private organization in HUAC's operation continued to be important. It's principal role was to act as HUAC's agent and collaborator in the hearings held to expose HUAC's targets. The old-line professional hate groups together with patriotic societies, reactionary fraternal orders, individual bigots and patrioteers (the Network),† undertook the

---

* The most striking of HUAC's present relationships to the classic hate groups are in the field of religion. These are discussed in a later chapter.

† Throughout this book I use the term "the Network" as a shorthand description of a large group of organizations and

punishment of HUAC's victims, a perfect outlet for the aggressive action the hate group craves. The primary weapons used against HUAC's victims are denunciation and discharge pressures. The hatist adds to these his own special weapons: the anonymous telephone call, the "crank" letter, boycott, vandalism and physical violence. During the fifties, too, HUAC's dossiers and files—the house that hate groups built—multiplied fantastically. The two-way flow—of names into the Committee and of "official" smears back to their hatist source—became a vast standardized operation.* In addition, these files were being stocked with names and propaganda from new sources: the FBI files and ex-Communists. Every hate group was able to become a little do-it-yourself HUAC. These groups, too, emerged as the major consumers and distributors of HUAC propaganda, which they disseminated in millions of copies. It costs them nothing and gives the cachet of official support to their own programs. HUAC, on its part, is a national clearinghouse for the merchandise of hate.

The Committee is not merely functionally linked to hate groups. Its own operations reflect the hate-group syndrome. It is itself a hate group. HUAC's extremism, its exaggerations, deceptions, and distortions, its willful oversimplification of the complex, its division of the world into black and white, its response to all forms of criticism with the Red smear, its overheated, fear-mongering rhetoric, and its rivers of antidemocratic propaganda, are the techniques and practices which have been made familiar to us by the operations of the hate groups.

HUAC hates the "subversive" in much the same way that the anti-Semite hates the Jew, the racist hates the Negro, the fundamentalist hates the Catholic, the patrioteer hates the alien. But unlike its frequently frustrated non-

movements which cooperate with HUAC in a variety of ways.
HUAC's network covers the ultra-rightist ("the radical right") segments of the political spectrum, the patriotic and nationalist organizations and their "Americanism" commissions, the crackpot hate sects, the irredentist refugee formations, certain religious movements and groupings, and specialized blacklisting services and organizations.
These organizations are HUAC's "public" in the theatrical sense—its wildly approving audience. They are also HUAC's political base and its collaborators in the exposure process.
* See Chapter 14, "Big Brother Is Watching You."

governmental counterparts, HUAC can do something about its hate. It can give direct expression to its hostility by punishing its object. What tells us most clearly that HUAC is a hate group is the exposure system. Exposure speaks the language of the hate group; it is hate in action.

The personalities of many of HUAC's leaders and staff members are figures in a gallery of hate.* Let us begin with J. Parnell Thomas.

Thomas, born John Parnell Feeney, became a member of the Dies Committee when it was formed, and its Chairman in 1947. An insurance broker and a conservative Republican, he brought to his task a savagery and arrogance rarely equaled in the annals of the Committee. A man of vast prejudices, with a truculence to match, and not overly bright, he had apparently convinced himself that stern measures—even though legally and morally questionable—were necessary to save the country from immediate overthrow by subversive forces.

As Professor Carr has written, "Not the least of Thomas' faults was his complete lack of dignity as the Committee's presiding officer. Seldom has an important congressional agency been so handicapped by the vulgarity of its leader . . . . Again and again Thomas conducted Committee hearings as though he were a cheap comedian or a participant in a street-corner political harangue."

He knew little or nothing about the technical content of the hearings he staged. All this was the work of the Committee's chief investigator, Robert Stripling, who, together with a junta of informers and favorite newsmen, ran the Committee. Stripling was a major HUAC policy-maker. He left HUAC and today is an agent of "Freedom in Action," a group dedicated to "vigilant constitutional patriotism."

But Thomas knew how to bully a witness, ridicule his arguments and impugn his motives. He knew the witness was guilty before he ever reached the stand. He was impatient to shower him with abuse.

He dismissed the constitutional arguments of the Hollywood unfriendly witnesses as "a concerted effort on the part of the Communists, their fellow-travellers, their dupes,

---

* In an over-all evaluation of HUAC's staff, Professor Robert K. Carr wrote in 1950, "The Un-American Activities Committee has not been famed among congressional committees for the high quality of its membership . . . in the main, respected and intelligent representatives have not sought service on this committee."

and paid apologists to create a lot of fog about constitutional rights, the First Amendment and so forth." Thomas's attack on lawyers for witnesses are legendary. During the course of the Hollywood hearings he called Robert W. Kenny, a lawyer, to the stand, and asked him what he was advising his clients. He proceeded to read to Kenny the Federal Conspiracy Statute, and charged that Kenny, in advising his clients, had conspired with them to commit a criminal offense—deliberate refusal to answer questions.

Thomas conceived of HUAC as a means of smearing the Roosevelt Administration and gloated over how many New Dealers the Committee had exposed. In a speech in June 1940 he said, "The Fifth Column in the United States has flourished under the New Deal rule. In some respects it is synonymous to the New Deal so the surest way to remove the Fifth Column from our shores is to remove the New Deal from the seat of government."

All of HUAC's activities under his leadership were poisoned by a blatant partisanship. The Hollywood hearings in 1947 were launched with noisy fanfare that the evidence would show that the New Deal had reduced the film industry to turning out pro-Soviet propaganda. No evidence at all was introduced in support of this thesis. Yet Thomas falsely stated in a subcommittee report that "some of the most flagrant Communist propaganda films were produced as a result of White House pressure."

One of Thomas's most shameful performances was the Condon case. A HUAC subcommittee headed by Thomas issued a report in March 1948 charging that Dr. Edward U. Condon, director of the National Bureau of Standards, "is one of the weakest links in our atomic security." The report was a mass of misstatements, distortions and omissions. The most shocking of the latter involved a letter which J. Edgar Hoover had written in May 1947 to Secretary of Commerce W. Averell Harriman. Thomas simply excised from the letter a key exculpatory sentence. He later said that this was "inadvertent." There was also evidence for the view that Thomas "improved" on the original letter through language insertions. Dr. Condon had demanded a hearing before the issuance of the report, and pressed for one after it appeared. But he repeated his requests in vain. The attack on Dr. Condon was a clumsy attempt by Thomas to attack the Roosevelt Administration by impugning the loyalty of an important employee—a practice in which Dies had specialized. This report was timed to win support for the largest appropriation the Committee had ever requested.

In November 1948, Thomas was indicted on charges of conspiracy to defraud the Government and filing false claims against it. He had put two women on his payroll, although they were not bona fide employees, and then required them to turn over their paychecks to him. He also pocketed the salary of a phantom clerk-typist who was assigned to HUAC's staff but did no work for it. Ironically enough, he refused on self-incriminating grounds to appear before the grand jury. He was convicted in December 1949 and served nine months at Danbury, a Federal penitentiary where Ring Lardner, Jr., one of the "Hollywood Ten" who had been convicted for contempt of his Committee, was also incarcerated.

Thomas was succeeded as Chairman of HUAC by John S. Wood of Georgia, who served for four years. He had also put in a two-year stint in 1945-46, but he was actually Rankin's puppet. A Georgia White Supremicist, he made himself famous by the observation that the activities of the Ku Klux Klan were "an old American custom." Wood was violently anti-labor, and under his aegis HUAC conducted repeated forays against the labor movement.

In 1952, Wood's Committee returned to the Condon case, and, to the surprise of hardly anyone, concluded that "because of [Dr. Condon's] propensity for associating with persons disloyal or of questionable loyalty and his contempt for necessary security regulations, that he is not qualified for acceptability to any security position." Thus was the departed Thomas vindicated.

Under Wood's leadership, HUAC began the practice of organizing hearings for the specific purpose of publicizing information in FBI files. It extended the hospitality of its witness stand to the perjurious informer Harvey Matusow and solemnly reported that "Matusow told of the use by some members of the Communist Party of narcotics, but that he possessed no knowledge as to whether their use was encouraged by the Communist Party."

Under Wood, the Committee also converted its annual report into a showcase for the names which it had unearthed during the year's investigations—a great convenience for the blacklisting fraternity.

After the Republicans took over the 83rd Congress in 1953, Representative Harold Velde of Illinois assumed HUAC's helm. His prior FBI service had attracted him to HUAC, and he became one of its members when he was elected in 1948.

Unlike Wood, Velde conducted the Committee in the wide-open, free-wheeling style, reminiscent of Dies. He was an indefatigable headline-hunter and made windy speeches on the Red menace at the drop of a hat.

In March 1950, he astonished most Americans when, in a speech to the House, he opposed a measure for a mobile library service in rural areas because "Educating Americans through the means of the library service could bring about a change of their political attitude quicker than any other method. The basis of Communism and socialistic influence is education of the people. If we are opposed to socialism in America as we all say we are, we must all conscientiously oppose this bill." Presumably acting on these views, Velde, in 1952, launched a probe of the Nation's most respected universities.

One of Velde's characteristic "security" brainstorms was a proposal that the Library of Congress compile a list of subversive material in the Library's millions of volumes. In another speech in 1950 on Communists in Government, he derided Attorney General McGrath's advice that "all of you may rest secure—you don't have to look under your beds every night." Velde replied, "I, too, will continue to look under my bed every night." He harangued the House endlessly about the Red menace. On one occasion he advised his colleagues, "The influence of Eleanor Roosevelt in the promotion of Communism, of immorality and indecency among so-called minority groups in Washington, should be explored."

He attacked Henry Wallace and Adlai Stevenson as Red-tainted. He agreed that the U.N. film "Of Human Rights" was subversive propaganda and that, while "we all hate to be squealers and stool pigeons," informing was necessary to HUAC's functioning.

Velde shocked the country when, in connection with the Harry Dexter White affair, he subpoenaed ex-President

Truman, Supreme Court Justice Tom Clark and ex-Secretary of State Byrnes. None complied. President Truman wrote, "In spite of a personal willingness to cooperate with your Committee, I feel constrained by my duty to the people of the United States to decline to comply with the subpoena." He explained that such Committee action threatened the principle of separation of powers.

In justification of the Truman attack Velde wrote: "Harry S. Truman has a long history of disrespect for congressional investigating committees' exposures of subversives in Government . . . on September 22, 1948, President Truman made the vicious statement 'the Committee is more un-American than the activities it is investigating.' Had President Truman shown more regard for the truth developed by the Committee, the issues of today would not exist."

Velde's probe of the clergy in 1953, climaxed by a gavel-wielding grilling of Bishop Oxnam, resulted in a torrent of criticism. Velde concealed his own ties with reactionary Methodist groups such as the Circuit Riders—the hate group primarily responsible for the probe.

Velde-conducted investigations had a peculiarly oppressive quality. He didn't bluster, shout or bully, as did Thomas and Rankin. He simply told the witness what a deep-dyed subversive he was. Sometimes he amplified—that he had met types like the witness as an FBI agent. Velde was the House's answer to Senator McCarthy.

It must not be assumed that only HUAC's Chairman can tell us about how it works and thinks. One of the most vocal of HUAC's spokesmen is Republican Gordon Scherer of Cincinnati. A former assistant prosecuting attorney and municipal official, he was assigned to HUAC when he came to Congress in 1953, and is now its ranking Republican member.

With Scherer, it was a case of love at first sight. His very first speech as a Congressman was to an American Legion post in which he attacked leading members of the clergy and quoted from their comments on HUAC witch hunts. Scherer said that one could understand these criticisms if they came from the pen of the editor of the *Daily Worker*, but that they were not "in keeping with the basic precepts of Christian brotherhood as I was taught in the church." He continued, "I would not want you to believe that these violent attacks come only from members of the cloth.

Prominent educators and intellectuals have made similar abusive and unwarranted attacks."

Scherer has the Committee assignment of defending HUAC from attack. He is the keeper of its flame. Since the Committee is under constant attack, his talents are in great demand. His role has made him an indefatigable practitioner of the Red smear. Any attack on HUAC is automatically denounced as a Red plot.

All hate groups fantastically exaggerate the power of their enemies and find everywhere frightening new proofs of their evil influence. This formula is basic in HUAC's operations. HUAC has a great advantage over other hate groups in its application of this formula, for HUAC's enemy is undefined—a "subversive" is whoever HUAC says is a subversive. The web of subversion—the "conspiracy"—constantly expands to meet HUAC's needs. When HUAC itself comes under attack, this technique is exploited to heroic proportions. Since Communists oppose HUAC, all criticism of HUAC becomes proof that (a) the critic is a Communist or a supporter, a dupe, an ally, etc., and (b) the "conspiracy" is more powerful than ever for it includes not only the "hardcore" Communists but the supporters, dupes, allies, etc. Thus criticism of HUAC confirms the desperate need to continue HUAC, for it alone can save us from this gigantic conspiratorial octopus. HUAC naturally tries to bring its targets as close as possible to the core of evil—actual Party membership. To achieve this it has developed a special logic of its own based on crudely strained inferences, falsified proofs, and emotionally defined terms. The problem of assimilating the non-Communist to the Communist is solved in a way which has become HUAC's trademark: The use of guilt by parallelism, mutual object and association. (An amusing current example is Chairman Walter's charge that a newspaper story criticizing HUAC members' extravagance and abuse of expense accounts "directly played into Communist hands.") As HUAC applies and expands this formula it becomes clear that it regards *all* of its opponents as subversive.

This "Red Magic"—the latter-day counterpart of the black magic used in a primitive society for inflicting injury on an enemy—is Scherer's special province. The hallmark of the art of Red magic is a ritualistic use of the phrase, "It is significant that . . ." or a variant thereof. Without it

Scherer would be speechless. No matter what his opponent says, Scherer inevitably finds, "It is significant that" Reds say the very same thing.

Since Scherer is no mental giant, he uses the formula to the point of ludicrousness. In December 1959, he attacked Senator Young of Ohio for accepting an invitation to speak at an Emergency Civil Liberties Committee (ECLC) dinner. Young tartly replied, "When I was on the Anzio beachheads, he was safety director of Cincinnati." Scherer triumphantly claimed in a press release that it was "significant" that Young had "used almost the identical language that has been used by the Emergency Civil Liberties Committee, the Communist *Daily Worker* and the Communists who have appeared before the Committee." Scherer, of course, cited no such "almost identical language."

When a statement of Congressman Roosevelt, in a speech on the House floor, charged that "The Committee is closer to being dangerous to America in its conception than most of what it investigates," Scherer made this response—only a slight variant of the standard formula:

> This is a paraphrase of a remark I have heard time and time again since serving on the Committee. It has come repeatedly from sullen, defiant and contemptuous members of the Communist Party who have been subpoenaed to testify before our Committee as witnesses. I have read the remark many times before in Communist and pro-Communist publications but I never dreamed I would see the day when a member of this House would repeat it on the floor. [He forgets Harry S. Truman—although it is possible that in Mr. Scherer's lexicon, Harry Truman is a Communist.] It is the use of the phrase and some other phrases and appellations in the speech of the gentleman from California that makes me wonder if he actually wrote the particular remarks.

Scherer continued in this vein for about 30 columns in the *Congressional Record,* full of ominously "significant," "even more significant," and "most significant," parallels.

Congressman Walter, too, made a statement that "It is significant that. . . ." Roosevelt's speech came after he had introduced a bill directed at subversive maritime workers.

But he did not explain why it was significant. Lenin's writings are often found to contain statements which significantly parallel or explain something said or done by HUAC's critics. Walter used this gambit to attack, on the House floor, hundreds of signers of an advertisement urging HUAC's abolition.

Scherer's zeal as HUAC's ideological sergeant-at-arms is so great that he frequently interrupts the hearings to assail the critics of the Committee. At the beginning of the Committee's 1959 hearings in Puerto Rico, Scherer vilified Clark Foreman, ECLC director, an opponent of HUAC, who was in the audience. He threatened to subpoena Foreman, charging that Foreman had organized the opposition to the Committee and coached local lawyers on ways to resist it. This outraged the lawyers (appointed to represent the witnesses by the Puerto Rico Bar Association). Judge Abraham Diaz, a distinguished Puerto Rican advocate, retorted, "That's a lie." Scherer subsequently discounted his protest as coming from a "lawyer for an identified Communist."

Scherer is thoroughly at home with the distortion and deception required by the practice of Red magic. In 1957 he charged that Red lawyers had helped to organize a demonstration of hostility to the Committee in Newark. The proof? Pickets carried signs which had been prepared by "experts." He assured his audience that some of these experts were members of the bar. The proof? "Ninety percent of the people in the picket line . . . could not understand the impact of the signs they were carrying." Scherer did not say how he reached this statistically precise conclusion. Indeed, said Scherer, crowning the recital of the Committee's sufferings, "One of the Communist lawyers who had almost driven Judge Medina to distraction" actually represented a witness at the Newark hearings.

Scherer tirelessly screams that the end is near; we have managed to survive only because he and a few other long-suffering super-patriots on HUAC have kept their fingers in the dike. But how much longer can they hold out against "the conspiracy" which hourly gains new adherents? There are some who assert that Scherer does not consciously exaggerate or distort. His quivering self-righteousness simply carries him away.

Scherer has turned up as a member of the Committee of Sponsors of the John Birch Society, a secret pressure group with hatist overtones fully equipped with the regular complement of ultrarightist objectives, plus some special ones of its own. Scherer should be happy as a lark in this group, whose founder, Robert Welch, is convinced that ex-President Eisenhower and Milton Eisenhower, John Foster Dulles and Allen Dulles, are all Reds. Welch has also accused 7,000 of the Nation's Protestant ministers of Communism or of Communist sympathy. Here, indeed, is God's plenty for such as Scherer, who can find no rest from his nightmares of "the conspiracy."

The John Birch Society Committee has also opened its welcoming arms to another HUAC alumnus, ex-Congressman Kit Clardy. He, too, should find its objectives and methods congenial. Clardy was a perennial rabble-rouser who idolized Senator McCarthy. He was of the no-nonsense, "let-me-at-'em" school of Red hunters.

When a lawyer once complained to Clardy that HUAC had been rough on his clients, Clardy replied:

> Pretty rough on those Communists? If we had been really rough on them we would have taken them apart. As it was, we were treated in a way that I think exhibited on their part the utmost contempt for the Congress and their government, and they left the stand and lied like horsethieves and we called them back and they took the fifth amendment again. If I had my way and we had any power, they would really have been punished by putting them in the dungeon the first time. . . . A few years ago this committee had, and may have at the moment the right to put witnesses down in the dungeon underneath the Capitol if they refused to cooperate with the committee. Some day perhaps I will test that out.

As far as the record shows, Clardy never did realize his dream of putting witnesses in "the dungeon." But he did conduct hearings in May 1954 in his home district, Flint, Michigan, in which he not only abused the witnesses but incited violence against them. He recalled that during his college days in 1937, his college mates had thrown UAW-CIO organizers into the Red Cedar River. He said: "I was proud of those kids. They should also have tossed into the river the then Governor, the late Frank Murphy." Clardy's conduct of the hearing contributed to the lynch spirit which swept the city. A number of workers were dragged

40

from their jobs in automobile plants by lynch gangs and beaten; hostile witnesses were evicted from their homes; their families had to go into hiding to escape the fury of mob hoodlums; the office of the lawyer for the witnesses was smeared with red paint.

The following letter was written in August 1954, by a victim of the hearings and addressed to civic leaders of Flint, Michigan:

Dear Sir:

I am earnestly seeking your help to stop the violence against me that was instigated by Representative Clardy's hearings.

I have been a responsible citizen for forty-three years. I have lived in this community since coming here in 1927. I have an unchallenged record as an employee at Chevrolet Manufacturing Company for twenty years. I served conscientiously as a soldier in World War II, and was decorated with the Bronze Star Medal. During three and one-half years of military service I fought in North Africa, Italy, Corsica, France and Germany. I am married and the father of two daughters.

Since the hearings I have worked only two weeks. I was severely beaten on returning to work and was placed under a doctor's care for thirty days with broken ribs and contusions. Again last Wednesday I was viciously beaten by a small but well organized gang of hoodlums at the factory gates.

I have had police protection for two nights on leaving work but expect there to be more violence both entering and leaving the plant, unless a real effort is made to obtain adequate police protection and to establish order on the streets of Flint.

I would appreciate anything you can do in my behalf,

Sincerely yours,

When Clardy heard that workers had been physically dragged from their jobs by a goon squad, he crowed, "This is the best kind of reaction there could have been to our hearings."

Francis Eugene Walter, Chairman of HUAC since 1955, is, with the exception of Martin Dies, the most important single figure in HUAC's history. A Democrat and a banker, he has served in the House since 1932 and on the Committee since 1949. Walter is proud of the fact that he opposed making HUAC a permanent committee in 1945. He suggested in 1954 that HUAC be made part of the House Judiciary Committee. He explained to Douglass Cater of the *Reporter Magazine* in the spring of 1955 that the reason for this suggestion was HUAC's lack of legislative purpose, "since the Judiciary Committee, not the Un-American Activities Committee, bears primary responsibility for drafting legislation dealing with subversives."

Walter is a political conservative (he was once almost a New Dealer and Fair Dealer), but unlike his predecessors on the Committee, he is no reactionary. His position on most issues is close to that of Speaker Rayburn, who is Walter's political mentor. Walter is Rayburn's favorite Northern Democrat, and the first Northern Democrat to guide HUAC's activities.

He is unlike his predecessors in two other ways. He is enormously competent and he wields unusual power. He is the second ranking Democrat on the Judiciary Committee, where he is head of its Immigration Subcommittee. He also chairs the Democratic Patronage Committee and the House Democratic caucus.

Walter is no tub-thumping bully boy of the stripe of Thomas or Clardy, no fumbling gumshoe like Velde, no calliope of inanities like Scherer. Acute and dignified, he is said to have been urged by Speaker Rayburn to take the HUAC chair to reform the Committee. But, under his leadership, HUAC has continued the basic pattern of witch-hunting which has marked it from the beginning. Thus Walter has denounced the National Council of Christian Churches, the largest and most respected church body in the United States, as Red-infiltrated; tried to use hearings to physically extract passports from witnesses to whom they had been validly issued; smeared the Fund for the Republic because he opposed its study of blacklisting; harassed a Quaker group for hiring a woman as a librarian who had pleaded the Fifth Amendment before a congressional committee; recruited ultrarightists and extremists as HUAC consultants and witnesses; openly used the Committee to force the discharge of unfriendly witnesses; and conducted a vendetta with the Supreme Court because he differed with its decisions in security cases.

Walter's zeal has produced widespread and powerful hostility to HUAC. He has increasingly used the powers of the Committee for its self-perpetuation by exposing its critics, cultivating a grass-roots Network political support, and by increased output of propaganda.

Walter's power in Congress has driven Congressional opposition into the cloakrooms. As Chairman of the Democratic Patronage Committee, he controls the disposition of jobs on the House side of Capitol Hill. As head of the Immigration Subcommittee, he can block a private immigration bill offered by his Congressional critics. This means that Congressmen who cross him must give up hope of bringing a constituent's relative into the country (or having him remain here) through a private immigration bill. As Murray Kempton has acutely written of Walter: "He thus stands as policeman over two of the fundamental interests of constituents of almost every Congressman, the jobs of their backward children, the entrance visas of their displaced uncles. Without his consent, a Congressman is almost debarred from performing service for his constituents; and a Congressman is a personal servant or he is no Congressman."

Walter has two pet hates—the Reds and the foreign-born. He is a highly articulate representative of a familiar "know-nothing" strain in American life which equates the alien with the subversive. But Walter is more than that: he is an unabashed, all-out xenophobe, an attitude which his political caution forces him to conceal, but which his rage brings to the surface often enough.

This special prejudice of Walter's is the central clue to an understanding of his role in the gallery of hatists. Walter is Chairman of the House Immigration Subcommittee—as gruesomely ironic a bit of legislative casting as one could conceive. And he is the author and champion of the Walter-McCarran Act of 1952. Of this legislation, which embarrasses our foreign relations, breeds resentment against us everywhere abroad, and mocks our protestations of equal opportunity, Cardinal Cushing has written, "It cannot be defended without recourse to the discredited and un-Christian tenet of racism."

It is hard to think of another statute which has stirred such enormous protest and demand for amendment. It was passed over President Truman's veto and its revision was repeatedly urged by President Eisenhower. But it is

43

Walter's proudest achievement, and his defense of it is a revealing measure of his prejudices. To Walter, criticism of the law is itself a proof of subversion. He has decreed that immigration is a "security" matter which is not to be treated in a "fraudulently humane" manner. When the law is under attack, Walter's emotions get out of control. He has called Jewish critics of the law "professional Jews" who shed "crocodile tears" over it. He has characterized as "throat-slitters" the crew of a French vessel, referred to certain aliens as "scum," and uses the term "hyphenated-Americans" to describe foreign-born groups. His considered judgment is, as he told the House, "I don't think these people [today's immigrants] are the kind of people our ancestors were."

When a critic of the Act, Edward Corsi, was appointed to head the State Department's Refugee Service, Walter really showed his fangs. On March 27, 1955, Mary McGrory, reporter for the Washington (D. C.) *Evening Star,* wrote:

> Mr. Walter, at an open hearing several weeks ago, charged Mr. [Edward J.] Corsi with membership in several left-wing organizations. Mr. Corsi denied the charges.
>
> In defense of Mr. Corsi, the State Department said that his presence on its roster indicated he had met the Department's high standards. Mr. Walter, however, contends that Mr. Corsi has not been cleared. . . .
>
> Aside from the alleged left-wing association, Mr. Walter indicts Mr. Corsi on a second count—his outspoken opposition to the Walter-McCarran Act. . . .
>
> "I'm not afraid of dagoes," said Mr. Walter. "And were 14 members of Congress [sponsors of the Walter-McCarran Act] psychopathic. . . . ?"

Walter never produced evidence of the organization to which Corsi was supposed to have belonged (some 20 years earlier). Corsi had not charged that the sponsors of the Walter-McCarran Act were psychopathic. He had said that those who "believed in racist theories" were "Nazis" or "candidates for an insane asylum."

On April 4, Congressman Walter inserted in the *Congressional Record* the text of a letter he wrote to Congressman Rodino of New Jersey denying statements attributed to him in the McGrory story. He complained he was misquoted, his statement was falsified, and "all my life I have been an admirer of Italy and a true friend of the Italian people." He said he opposed Corsi's appointment as advisor on immigration matters to the Secretary of State because "I believe that Mr. Corsi's association for a long period of time with highly objectionable groups and organizations continued long after it became obvious that these organizations were dominated by Communists, and they, in fact, became Communist dominated organizations." He added that he opposed Corsi because Corsi did not believe the Walter-McCarran Act was a good law. Walter insisted that Corsi had to go, and Secretary of State Dulles yielded.

The vendetta against Corsi is merely illustrative of a characteristic method of operation—for spite and anger rule this man. In 1956, Walter made an appearance before a House Appropriation subcommittee and urged it to investigate the political backgrounds of two appellate judges who had handed down decisions hostile to HUAC. He was attacked for this attempt to bully the judiciary by the national director of the Americans for Democratic Action. Walter proclaimed to the House that this critic had been a member of the Washington Book Shop, a defunct organization which had been cited ten years earlier by the Attorney General as a Communist front. Walter is an old hand at this kind of smear, in which Senator McCarthy thoroughly indoctrinated the Nation. In 1948, Walter charged a political opponent, Roy E. James, with subversion because of his membership in the American Veterans Committee, the Federal Bar Association, and the Institute of Pacific Relations, which he claimed were Communist fronts. Even though James lost the election, Walter pursued him when he returned to Government service and forced him out of his job.

Like Senator McCarthy, Walter is adept at suggesting the existence of derogatory files about an opponent but never producing them. This technique, which he used in the Corsi case, he found most useful in the course of a 1953 television debate on the Walter-McCarran Act. When a participant asked critical questions about the statute, Walter flourished a piece of paper before the cameras and said that he knew all about this man's record. After the debate he refused to divulge the ominous evidence he claimed he had compiled.

On a similar occasion he vetoed the appointment of J. Donald Kingsley as director of the Intergovernmental Migration Committee because he claimed that Kingsley had two Communists on his staff. His proof, he said, could be supplied by Senator McCarran. Senator McCarran, when asked about the matter, said he had never heard of the two men.

Walter does not hesitate to use the Committee's power directly against his critics. After Marquis Childs, the newspaper columnist, wrote that a legal officer in the Defense Department had blasted HUAC's film "Operation Abolition," Committee investigators appeared at the Defense Department and demanded its files.

In the same way he lashed out, in 1955, at a West Coast jurist who handed down a decision in a case which offended Walter because, in his view, it had wrongfully barred the deportation of a Chinese. A fellow jurist, Chief Judge William Denman of the Ninth Circuit Court of Appeals, then 83 years old, charged that Walter was "guilty of cowardly conduct which warrants the widest possible public denunciation." Walter, determined to have the last word, introduced a bill requiring the chief judges of circuit courts to retire from that post at the age of 70. The *Washington Post* said that Walter was "unfit" to hold public office: "A man with so little capacity for governing himself seems scarcely fit for the governing of his countrymen."

Inevitably, the truth is sometimes crushed and frequently bruised when it conflicts with Chairman Walter's powerful drives. He conceded to the *Washington Post* that the HUAC film "Operation Abolition" had erroneously placed Harry Bridges at the scene of the 1960 San Francisco student hosing and arrests when in fact he was at lunch at the time. Yet, in a telecast some months later, in January 1961, he told the audience that Bridges was a leader in the affair. He then compounded the deception by stating that the original error about Bridges was not that the film's narration had placed Bridges at the scene of the demonstration when he had arrived after it was over, but in placing him there on another day.

"They [the narration] stated that Harry Bridges was there on Friday when he was there on Thursday, or vice-versa. That is the terrible error that was made, but nobody has mentioned the fact that Mr. Bridges was there, Mr. Bridges, the well-known notorious Communist."

When Robert Weaver, Federal Housing Administrator, was nominated to his post by the President, he was widely attacked as a Red by racist members of Congress. They insisted that HUAC files supported the charge. Walter told newsmen there were no HUAC files to support this charge. But he did not tell them that on February 13, 1956, HUAC had released files on Weaver to Congressman Gathings of Arkansas, who used them to smear Weaver and other board members of the National Association for the Advancement of Colored People.

Walter suffers from strange memory lapses. In the 1961 trial of folksinger Pete Seeger for contempt of the Committee, the defense sought to prove that the hearings at which Seeger had testified had been improperly motivated and called Walter as a witness. He was asked whether he knew one Vincent Hartnett, author of the blacklisting manual *Red Channels* and a director of AWARE, a Network organization in the television field. Walter replied, "I have never heard his name." Yet Hartnett himself testified that he had interviewed Walter late in January or early in February 1955. Such a lapse in memory might be understandable, but Hartnett testified further that he sent Walter and the Committee's investigators materials which were used in the hearings. This, too, might have slipped Walter's mind, but the record shows that in a hearing the following year Hartnett testified as a friendly witness before Walter for an hour and 25 minutes.

Walter was asked whether he was familiar with Godfrey P. Schmidt, head of AWARE. He replied, "No, sir; I am not . . . I don't remember the name at all." This was strange. Just prior to the hearing, Schmidt had presided over a meeting of a Network organization at which Walter appeared as the guest of honor. At that time Walter had also appeared as Schmidt's partner in a television debate. Schmidt, like Hartnett, had testified before Walter in 1956. As Murray Kempton, columnist for the New York *Post* wrote, "Walter is . . . highly fortunate that he is not a Communist in a perjury case."

Equally dubious is Walter's explanation of the reason for HUAC's failure to probe the wave of racist violence and bombings of schools and synagogues, in the South. To all demands for HUAC investigations of these matters,

Walter has replied that the Committee's jurisdiction is not broad enough to authorize such investigations. In a telecast ("Youth Wants to Know") on January 28, 1961, Walter gave a youthful interrogator the following novel account of the limitations on HUAC's jurisdiction:

"Question: Sir, for our own information, could you tell us just what is considered un-American, by your Committee?"

"Representative Walter: Well, any activity that strikes at the basic concept of our Republic."

"Question: Sir, don't you agree that such subversive organizations as the American Nazi Party and Ku Klux Klan constitute a threat to the liberties of Americans?"

"Representative Walter: I don't think so. Actually, they haven't engaged in any activity on behalf of a foreign power and that, of course, is the big difference."

"Question: But sir, don't you believe that the suppression of minorities is against the Constitution of the United States?"

"Representative Walter: Of course, it is, but it is not within the jurisdiction of the Committee on Un-American Activities to make inquiries into that field. Our inquiries are limited by the statute creating the Committee, and this, of course is Communism and Communist activity."

Even Dies did not dare make this contention. He knew better. For the Dies resolution was merely a continuation of the Dickstein-McCormack resolution, which was expressly intended to cover racist and Fascist "propaganda activities" of both domestic and foreign origin. And this was the primary reason why the Dies resolution, of which the present Committee's is an exact copy, was passed in the first place.

Walter's decision that HUAC has no jurisdiction over subversive activities other than Communist activities is particularly strange since Walter was a Committee member when HUAC probed two native Fascist and anti-Semitic groups in 1954. But Walter knows that a probe of racist hate groups would bite the hands that feed him. HUAC's support comes from racist Congressmen. Racist groups are among HUAC's noisiest supporters. They write the letters and pass the resolutions demanding the continuation of HUAC. They distribute its literature, show its film, "Operation Abolition," and are paid-up members of the Network in good standing.

So, too, the cry for investigation of the John Birch

Society ignores the inner dynamics of HUAC's functioning. The society's program prominently includes support for HUAC; it is a most active distributor of its film. But it would be fascinating to learn whether HUAC, in such a probe, would summon its ranking Republican member, Gordon Scherer of the Society's Committee of Sponsors.*

Walter is one of the few Congressmen with high seniority who has not emerged with the chairmanship of an old-line committee. He was once a candidate for majority leader, if not for Speaker. Many believe that the appointment to his present post was ashes in the mouth and that he yearned for the chairmanship of an old-line committee; in particular, the Judiciary Committee. But he had to make do with this tarnished substitute in the hope of converting it into the real thing. He assumed the chairmanship at a time when the ebb of McCarthyism was expected to run it aground. Behind his tactics of intimidation, political blackmail and smear is an ultimate strategy of transforming a disreputable posse into a security bureaucracy of a new kind. Under his leadership, the Committee is being shaped into an adjunct of the FBI, a permanent political police force masquerading as a legislative committee.

Chairman Walter has sought to give HUAC a firm institutional underpinning in another way: by politicalizing the work of the Committee. HUAC's ever-increasing political propaganda activities are needed to keep the fear glands properly stimulated, to justify its own existence, to maintain its ties with the Network and, in recent years, to give expression to a preventive-war line in our relations with the Soviet Union and a tough policy on Red China.

As our chief political propaganda agency, the Committee operates an enormous publishing business. It has published hundreds of publications and distributed them in millions of copies—hearings, reports, indices, handbooks, pamphlets, biographical sketches, etc. It issues more publications and circulates more copies of them than all other House committees combined. The Committee's publications include tracts (*100 Things You Should Know About Communism*), "consultations" with experts (*Language as a Communist Weapon, The Crimes of Khrushchev, Com-*

---

* I should emphasize that I do not urge such an investigation, for it would be subject to the same objections as the Committee's investigations under scrutiny in this book.

munist Persecution of Churches);* popular political biographies of Communist figures (the *Who Are They?* series), and long-range propaganda works. The most ambitious of the latter is a multivolume encyclopedia *Facts on Communism*, which, Committee Chairman Walter says, will be one of the most comprehensive studies ever undertaken.

HUAC's most urgent theme is that the Communist Party is getting ready to take over. The evidence to the contrary is dismissed as the result of a crafty plan by the Reds "to mislead many non-Communists into believing that the Party is shattered and ineffective." HUAC warns that those who refuse to believe that the Communist Party has deliberately contracted in order to make itself stronger are to be viewed with suspicion, for they may well have a "deadly axe to grind."

HUAC's propaganda publications are as violently tendentious† as they are repetitious, but they afford the Network philosophers and theoreticians a forum and an economic watering place in dry seasons. They give the faithful the latest word from Washington on the dangers of the conspiracy. A recent campaign has sought to extend the circulation of HUAC's publications to industrial workers.

HUAC's latest experiment with self-justifying propaganda is the film "Operation Abolition,"‡ the successor to an earlier bit of cinematographic press-agentry which HUAC released in 1958.

HUAC's propaganda activities are sinister, unauthorized by its mandate, and, indeed, not a legislative function at all. But HUAC may thus have found a function for itself as a political hate-mill which gives it the political leverage, continuity and expanding power for which Walter hungers. In all but name, HUAC functions as our first ministry of propaganda.

In 1956, Walter found a kindred soul in Richard Arens and made him HUAC's staff director. Arens is a passionate

---

* One of HUAC's "consultations," Dr. Fred C. Schwarz's *The Communist Mind*, is claimed to be the most widely distributed document printed by the Government Printing Office.

† The *Crimes of Khrushchev, Part II* informs us that Khrushchev "played a very significant role" in the 1930-33 famine in the Ukraine. Khrushchev was a student at a Moscow technical school at that time.

‡ The film is discussed in detail in Ch. 11„ "San Francisco Revisited."

alien-hater and Red-baiter. He is a prophet of the Network organizations and patrioteer defenders of America's security. They have awarded him the following honors, according to a listing in a Congressional staff "Who's Who" presumably furnished by Arens himself:

Certificate of Merit "for great and inspiring public service" by the Natl. Camp. Patriotic Order, Sons of America; Citation of Merit and Commendation by the Natl. Convention of the Amer. Leg.-54 (one of six persons to receive this honor); Citation for "outstanding public service," Amer. Coalition of Patriotic Societies; Medal of Honor, Order of the Founders and Patriots of America; Citation of Merit and Distinction, Natl. Women's Patriotic Conference on Natl. Defense; Certificate of Merit, Daughters of American Revolution.

Arens won his spurs in 1947 and 1948, when, as an aide of Senator Revercomb, he was instrumental in barring from asylum in the United States thousands of displaced persons, many of them Jewish victims of World War II. When Revercomb was defeated, Arens, a Republican, soon found his affinities, Senators McCarran and Eastland. In 1949, Arens helped Senator McCarran defeat Congressman Celler's proposal to permit at least 25,000 displaced Jews to come to this country from Germany.

Prior to 1955, Arens had worked for both the Internal Security Subcommittee and the Subcommittee on Immigration and Naturalization of the Senate Judiciary Committee. In 1955, he came into sharp conflict with Senator Watkins, who was the Administration's spokesman for amendments to the Walter-McCarran Act. Despite pressure from the FBI, he was forced out of the Senate Immigration and Naturalization Subcommittee and became a Red-hunter. He sat at Senator Eastland's side when, as a one-man Internal Security Subcommittee, Eastland held a hearing in New Orleans and used the perjurious Paul Crouch to weave a web of subversion around Supreme Court Justice Black.

Arens boasted that, while serving the Internal Security and Immigration Subcommittees of the Senate Judiciary Committee, he drafted, or helped to draft, the Internal Security Act of 1950, the Walter-McCarran Act, and the Communist Control Act of 1954. In August of 1956, after he had been appointed Walter's staff director, continuing in his capacity as Senate Internal Security Subcommittee Staff director, he fed Senators Eastland and Jenner material for bitter speeches against a mild bipartisan amendment to the Walter-McCarran Act. When the Senate passed the measure, he helped Walter's parliamentary maneuvering to prevent a vote in the House. Congressman Celler has said of Arens that he "has created more havoc than dozens of men in Washington in reference to immigration and naturalization."

Arens' tenure came to a rather sticky end as a result of a series of disclosures by the late Ronald H. May, Washington correspondent for the York (Pa.) *Gazette* and *Daily,* and the *Capital Times* of Madison, Wisconsin. May revealed that Arens had served as a paid $3,000-a-year consultant to Wycliffe Draper, a multimillionaire amateur geneticist who had dedicated himself to prove that Negroes are an inferior people and should be repatriated to Africa.

When respectable geneticists refused to support his theories, Draper formed two research committees—one on immigration and one on genetics. Congressman Walter was named by Draper's lawyers as head of the former committee and Senator Eastland of the latter.

Arens refused to tell May what work he did for the Draper project, except that it consisted of finding beneficiaries for research grants in the fields of "immigration and genetics." May also discovered that Draper made grants to "patriotic" anti-Communist organizations and that Arens had given advice to other wealthy men (such as H. L. Hunt, the Texas oil man, and Smith Richardson, North Carolina pharmaceutical magnate) on grants of funds to patriotic organizations.

It was revealed that one Arens-approved grant was made to Dr. Anthony Bouscaren, a McCarthy admirer. Bouscaren had toured the patrioteer circuit with Arens, lecturing before such organizations as the Christian Anti-Communist Crusade, had been ousted from Marquette University over the Draper grant, and had served as a HUAC consultant.

Walter himself at first admitted that he had spent some time in Africa looking for universities which might profit from Draper grants and had had conferences with officials of the University of Dakar for this purpose. By the time the interview ended, he denied knowing Draper or anything about his grants. In a later statement to the *Washington Post* about the Draper project, Walter said, "I'm in a broad general way aware of its activities, but not to any extent." He left unexplained why, under these circumstances, he made his trip to Africa. Mr. Draper was not so forgetful; he made the largest contribution to Walter's congressional campaign fund—$5,000.

In August 1960, Arens appeared with Bouscaren and others at a superpatriotic school at Gleenview, Illinois, where Arens spoke on "Youth and Communism and the Web of Subversion." Arens' address on the latter subject is nationally distributed in recorded tape form by the Christian anti-Communist Crusade.

In one of his doom-laden speeches (in Des Moines, Iowa), Arens questioned President Eisenhower's patriotism for introducing his grandchildren to Khrushchev, whose invitation to come here, Arens said, was "morally wrong."

The DAR distributes a speech by Arens which charges that 180 Communist-controlled organizations in this country are dedicated exclusively to the purpose of destroying the Walter-McCarran Act.

Speaker Rayburn said that he considered it improper for Arens to receive pay from a private source while working for HUAC. Arens resigned and became a Commissioner of the United States Court of Claims in September 1960. But it can hardly be doubted that the mounting protests against HUAC, its abuses and hatist practices, contributed to Arens' departure.

It is generally recognized that the Walter-McCarran Act has brought Walter to the end of the line politically. But Walter cannot admit a mistake, especially one of such magnitude as the Walter-McCarran Act. His defense of the statute and his chairmanship of HUAC have carried him out of the main stream of American political life, where he was once firmly launched, and into the embrace of the fanatics of the Network, a mandarin among the hatists. He stands on a crag from which there is no descent, shrieking defiance at his critics. In the spring of 1961 he announced that reasons of health had forced him to end his congressional career at the end of the current congressional session.

4 EXPOSURE: THE CONGRESSIONAL PILLORY

In 1951, Congressman Walter, presiding as a Committee member at Honolulu hearings, made no secret of his hope that the "power of public opinion" would implement the Committee's exposure of witnesses.

The exposure system is a concealed, and, indeed, an unconstitutional form of law enforcement; it has no place in a tripartite system of government such as ours, which requires that each of the three coordinate branches of government—legislative, executive and judicial—respect the integrity of the others.

Legislative power is concerned with the enactment of laws setting general standards of conduct which apply to everyone. Investigations in aid of the legislative power are directed at patterns of conduct, at behavior which reflects a general condition, illuminating the need for a new law or measuring the effectiveness of an existing law. An investigation—a *legislative* investigation—cannot be conducted for the purpose of passing judgment on and determining the guilt of an individual. The prosecution of individuals under duly enacted law is the exclusive responsibility of the law-enforcement branch, which is part of the *executive* department. The determination of guilt or innocence falls exclusively within the province of the courts, which is the *judicial* department. Or, to put it simply, one body makes the law, the second carries out the law, the third judges guilt or innocence under that law.

Our governmental structure was erected on this tripartite underpinning, not for reasons of symmetry or convenience, but *because no better way could be found to reconcile the use of governmental power with the claims of individual freedom.*

As John Adams noted in 1775:

A legislature, an executive, and a judicial power comprehend the whole of what is meant and understood by government. It is by balancing each of these powers against the other two, that the efforts in human nature toward tyranny can alone be checked and restrained, and any freedom preserved in the Constitution.

About 150 years later, one of our greatest Supreme Court Justices, Brandeis, pointed out:

The doctrine of the separation of powers was adopted by the convention of 1787 not to promote efficiency but to preclude the exercise of arbitrary power. The purpose was not to avoid friction, but, by means of the inevitable friction incident to the distribution of the governmental powers among three departments, to save the people from autocracy.

The doctrine of separate and coordinate powers is a fundamental precondition to the functioning of democratic government itself, the means of preserving a system of checks and balances. Its purpose is not merely to correct abuses of power in a particular instance, but to discipline its exercise, to institutionalize arrangements which will prevent abuse from arising in the first place. Its integrity is the profound concern of all of us.

There are aspects of our Government which cannot be squared with the separation-of-powers principle. For example, there is no question that the executive veto power is a legislative function and that the senatorial power to confirm appointments is an executive one. The development of our administrative agencies has imposed a considerable strain on this principle, for those bodies exercise both executive and judicial functions. But their activities are subject to judicial review to ensure that they do not exceed their charters or violate individual rights.

Whatever modifications the principle of separation of powers has suffered since the Constitution was framed, its basic substance remains intact.

Throughout U. S. history, Congressional committees have occasionally abused their power: they have investigated for nonlegislative ends, to expose individuals for public condemnation or to act as a court to try individuals. The hunt for headlines, political ambition, the zealousness to benefit or injure a particular economic group, or to influence the outcome of a labor dispute, the temptation to have a fling as a prosecutor (many lawyer-Congressmen suffer from a "Mr. District Attorney" complex)—all of these, singly or in combination, have led Congressional committees on occasion to depart from legislative ends.

What must be emphasized here, however, is that, in contrast to the occasional lapses of other committees, the Un-American Activities Committee systematically and deliberately uses its powers for nonlegislative ends. Moreover, these nonlegislative ends are achieved not in the context of a legitimate inquiry, but through an investigative apparatus which is specially tailored to do one thing and one thing alone—injure the witness. Exposure is not the by-product of the Committee's hearings; it is the primary product—the way in which the Committee exercises its jurisdiction. It is not that the Committee fails to comply with the rules of the game. It plays a different game in a different ball park.

HUAC has dedicated itself to the special and unique function of exposure. Thus the Committee and its members have openly and proudly dedicated themselves to the abuse of the power vested in them by Congress. In 1947 the Committee explained that its function was to "expose activities by un-American individuals and organizations which, while sometimes being legal, are nonetheless inimical to our American concepts and our American future."

In the same year, J. Parnell Thomas, then Chairman of the Committee, proclaimed in a radio address:

> The chief function of the Committee . . . has always been the exposure of un-American individuals and their un-American activities. This is based upon the conviction that the American public will not tolerate efforts to subvert or destroy the American system of government, once such efforts have been pointed out. The Congress' right to investigate *and expose* [itals ed.] undemocratic forces is as established and untrammeled as our Constitution.

This fine-sounding phrase merits examination. The citizen might reasonably ask: Established by whom? And when? And obligingly, in 1951, the Committee provided their answers in a publication distributed in more than a million copies (*100 Things You Should Know About Communism*): "Exposure in a systematic way began with the formation of the House Committee on Un-American

Activities. May 26, 1938 . . . with instruction from the United States House of Representatives to *expose* people and organizations attempting to destroy this country. That is still its job, and to that job it sticks." There's that word "expose" again. Yet the Congressional instruction to the Committee says nothing about "exposure"—this was merely Martin Dies' interpretation of the function of the Committee.

Again in 1952, before Representative Velde assumed the Chairmanship of the Committee, he confirmed that exposure was the Committee's objective: "If the Committee on Un-American Activities is to execute its duty and obligations to the American people, I feel that we must do all in our power to obtain the confessions of former Communists and subversives, not only as to their own membership in subversive organizations, but also as to the membership of their associates." During his tenure, Velde, a former FBI agent, repeatedly announced that "ferreting out" Communists was the Committee's basic job.

During the past decade the Committee has continued to dedicate itself to exposure objectives. However, the Supreme Court's decision in the *Watkins* case has forced it in recent years to soft-pedal its public statements and to deceive the witness, the press and the courts about its purpose and its being. It has not in any way departed from its exposure practices. Indeed, since the eclipse of McCarthyism and the decline of mass hysteria about the Red menace, HUAC has had to sharpen the exposure system in order to maintain its effectiveness.

Whatever may be the ultimate purpose of a bona fide legislative investigation—recommendations for new legislation, the appraisal of a law already on the books, a check on the conduct of executive personnel—it centers on some problem, some issue, some evil: e.g., "payola," the prizefight racket, the operation of the Port of New York Authority, the high price of drugs. The need to throw factual light on "the matter under inquiry," is all-important. It determines the nature of the evidence to be sought, the kind of witnesses, the number, time, and place of hearings. When the subject is exhausted, the investigation is over.

But HUAC has created for itself an inexhaustible subject. It can always find "subversives" who must be exposed.

The "issue" with which the Committee is grappling is supposedly Communism. But the hearings held are designed to shed light not on the issue, but on the witnesses. HUAC's basic purpose is dual: first, publicly to identify the political affiliations of the witness and his associates and, second, to punish the witness because of those affiliations.

The identification itself is a serious interference with the rights of free speech and association. To a far greater extent than is generally acknowledged, our political and social freedoms are dependent on privacy and anonymity. The secrecy of the ballot, the confidential character of trade-union membership, the assurance that subscribers will receive publications in "plain brown wrappers"—in these and in scores of other ways we recognize that free association, thought and speech require privacy and anonymity.

Indeed, free speech became possible only when the conditions of life made anonymity possible. The right remained an abstraction in a pre-industrialized society when each man was at the mercy of his neighbor's prejudices and was bound to the mores, the religion and the politics of his community. As Professor John P. Roche has written, "In a very real sense the very impersonalization of urban life is a condition of freedom; it is quite possible to live differently from one's neighbors without their knowing, much less caring, about deviation." The right to dissent on fundamental questions, proclaimed by the founders and enshrined in the Constitution, is meaningless without anonymity.

The conformist pressures under which we live have made individual speech so perilous that organizations are indispensable to give dissent strength and anonymity. But now it has become dangerous even to join organizations. The Committee relentlessly seeks the identification through "pitiless publicity" of members of organizations in order to undermine our most meaningful freedom—freedom of association. Thousands might be willing to join the Committee for a Sane Nuclear Policy (SANE) because they are convinced that nuclear testing is the road to final incineration. But how many are ready to act in the face of the fear that their names may be published by the Committee as subversives and reprinted in the newspapers of their community?

The Committee's major achievement has been the transformation of the hearing into a public identification device which destroys the privacy essential to freedom. Because it strikes at the preconditions of freedom, the ever-present threat of being dropped into the Committee's goldfish bowl has been more stifling than all the repressive legislation on the books.

The effectiveness of the Committee's use of the identification device has shaped the basic strategy of modern repression. Compulsory disclosure has emerged in our time as the most widely used and most effective form of restraint on our basic freedoms. Senator Dodd insists that Dr. Linus Pauling turn over to him the names of American scientists who assisted him in circulating petitions in opposition to nuclear testing. New Hampshire Attorney General Wyman sends Dr. Willard Uphaus to jail for refusing to divulge the names of guests at the World Fellowship Camp. A Florida legislative committee jails the Reverend Theodore R. Gibson for his contempt of the committee in refusing to produce membership lists of the NAACP.

Arkansas, Texas, Tennessee, Virginia, Georgia and Louisiana have all tried to destroy the effectiveness of the NAACP by requiring the disclosure of its membership lists. The Southern attempt to "disclosure" the NAACP to death has been rebuffed in five Supreme Court decisions ruling that compelled disclosure violates the constitutional guarantee of freedom of association. In *NAACP* v. *Alabama,* 357 U.S. 449, the Supreme Court noted that:

> Effective advocacy of both public and private points of view, particularly controversial ones, is undeniably enhanced by group association. . . . It is hardly a novel perception that compelled disclosure of affiliation with groups engaged in advocacy may constitute an effective restraint on freedom of association. . . . [The] vital relationship between freedom to associate and privacy in group association may in many circumstances be indispensable to preservation of freedom of association, particularly where a group espouses dissident beliefs.

The theories which justify identification and compelled disclosure lured many liberals in the forties. "Stand up and be counted!" became the battle cry when the cold war touched off a drive for a means of policing dissent which might not collide with constitutional guarantees. Disclosure was widely touted as a needed counterpart to the labeling requirements of the Pure Food and Drug Act. The provisions of the Securities and Exchange Act for public registration of stock issues gave rise to proposals for an "SEC of ideas." These theories have been murdered by the realities. The supporters of these theories exaggerated the need to protect the "consumer" of ideas from deception and ignored the key relationship of privacy to freedom. In addition, they failed to recognize that disclosure of dissenting opinions would inevitably lead to reprisal and punishment by hostile forces in the community.

Nor did they foresee that the requirement that a person disclose his own present or past political affiliations can easily lead to a requirement that he identify others—and become an informer.

The invasion of the privacy of the witness and the restraint upon his freedom of association are just the downpayment on the full damage which the Committee does to him. The hearing is intended to destroy him as a person, to violate his dignity by forcing him to confess his political "sins," and to deprive him of his livelihood. This is the Committee's punishment for his offense of being, not even a *proven,* but a suspected "subversive"—not by any means only a Communist, or an ex-Communist, but anyone whom HUAC expediently chooses to consider "subversive," whether it be because of affiliation with the NAACP, or the National Council of Churches, or SANE, or any other organization which falls under its disapproval. The witness has violated no law; he has merely declined to answer the "Sixty-four dollar question," ("Are you now or have you ever been a member of the Communist Party?") on the basis of a constitutional amendment—usually the Fifth Amendment—privilege against self-incrimination. This plea, as the Supreme Court has repeatedly ruled, cannot give rise to an inference of guilt. Moreover, even if the witness had been a Communist Party member, such membership is itself an exercise of constitutionally protected rights of free speech and association. The exposure process seeks to brand its victim as subversive for the rest of his life on the public record, a visible continuing target for hostility and reprisal. The goal is to make the unfriendly witness permanently unemployable by attaching to him an indelible stigma—democracy's counterpart of the yellow armbands which Hitler forced on the Jews.

The exposure punishment is actually closer to us than Hitler's Germany. We are dealing here with a latter-day version of the pillory and stocks, the devices used in the 17th and 18th centuries to hold offenders on exhibition in a public place, in an uncomfortable and degrading posture. These archaic instruments physically punished and humiliated the offender, and at the same time exhibited him as a warning to others. Most importantly, the pillory held a man helpless in its grasp as fair game for the community; it was intended that he be spat upon, cursed, taunted and stoned. The pillory was used—especially in the 17th century—to punish dissenters.

It is no mean achievement to engineer the punishment of an American for nothing more than resorting to rights protected by his Constitution. To ensure the destruction of the witness, the hearing is carefully staged to reach and inflame, through the press, radio and television, a wide audience beyond the hearing room: the community at large, employers, bar associations, local police authorities, boards of education. The exposure hearing is a highly efficient weapon. Professor Daniel Pollitt, studying the results of two years of hearings, showed that of 64 unfriendly witnesses appearing before the Committee on whom information was available, 50 lost their jobs.

The knife of exposure sometimes cuts too deeply and wounds even the cooperative witness. Justice Black, in the *Barenblatt* case, pointed out that: "Even those the committee does not wish to injure are often hurt by its tactics, so all-pervasive is the effect of its investigations."

When the individual's privacy is invaded on the witness stand, the shield of urbanization and large-scale industry is transformed into a sword. A powerful press rubs the community's and the employer's noses in the disclosure. The likelihood is strong that the victim is a stranger to his neighbors, without protection against their suspicions. The giant size of our employing units, their interrelatedness and close ties to the defense establishment, make it easy for the Committee to hound the unfriendly witness out of employment in an industry. In a highly integrated society, the victim has no place to hide, no economic or geographic haven of tolerance. By the early fifties, many powerful employers (General Electric, Westinghouse, R.C.A., Bethlehem Steel, U.S. Steel, to name only a very few), and indeed, whole industries, proclaimed a new ground for automatic discharge or suspension—being an uncooperative witness, or a variant thereof.

In the professions, the Committee struck a gusher. Long-established tenure protections were uprooted overnight as boards of education made noncooperation with congressional committees a ground for termination. Many American universities, the United Nations, newspapers, symphony orchestras, private schools, social agencies and research organizations adopted the same policy.

Only a corporal's guard out of the large number of public-school and university teachers who were unfriendly witnesses have survived exposure. It is charged that there are still 200 writers and performers who are blacklisted in Hollywood as a result of the operation of the exposure system. With the exception of a few *New York Times* reporters, almost all other journalists who were exposed by the Committee or its Senate counterpart were fired.

There are even a number of states which during the fifties denied unemployment benefits to those discharged for being uncooperative witnesses (Maryland, Pennsylvania and Massachusetts). In some states an unfriendly witness cannot obtain a license to sell liquor, tend bar or perform as a wrestler. The District of Columbia will not permit an unfriendly witness to tune pianos. And the Network once forced the cancellation of a chess tournament in Baltimore because a leading contender was an unfriendly witness.

The victims of the old-time pillory sank or swam on the tide of community judgment; thus the pillory of popular dissenters such as Daniel Defoe and John Lilburne was made the occasion for public triumphs in their honor; but Titus Oates, the notorious informer, emerged half-dead from the pillory. The Committee cannot afford to leave the fate of its victims to chance.

For all of the fear-mongering stagecraft of the hearing, there remains the possibility that the exposure will not "take." The Committee needs some representatives in the community who will make sure that all goes well in its absence. To this end, it has perfected a system of collaboration with the Network of rightist organizations which I have already referred to. Among the most prominent of these are: the American Legion, the Veterans of Foreign Wars, AWARE, Inc., the Christian Anti-Communist

Crusade, the Daughters of the American Revolution, and the American Council of Christian Churches. In addition, the Network includes scores of individuals and *ad hoc* organizations which spring up in connection with particular hearings.

The Committee's organization Network serves a variety of functions. Its members get access to the Committee's files and dossiers for the low-down on local suspects. Network members are instrumental in bringing the Committee to their communities. They are the beaters and the advance men for the hearing and drum up favorable publicity. At the hearing, special seats are reserved for them.

But the Network members are more than supporters and well-wishers. They act as the Committee's agents and do for it what it cannot do for itself. The Committee cannot officially require public or private employers to discharge the unfriendly witness—although it frequently comes pretty close to doing so anyway. For such open pressures would fatally discredit its claim that the hearing is merely a legislative investigation. The Network enables the Committee to ensure the injury of the witness and at the same time to avoid legal responsibility for it. To make it easier to force the witness out of employment, the Committee publishes his name over and over again, first in a special index to its public hearings, then in its annual report, and again in a huge cumulative index.

Members of the Network visit the local newspapers to develop pressure on employers. They personally write, call and visit private and public employers. They organize the forced removal of unfriendly witnesses from shops—"run outs," as they are called. They circulate copies of the hearings, write letters to the newspapers demanding the discharge of the unfriendly witnesses, pack board of education meetings called to discuss the fate of the teachers who were unfriendly witnesses, and organize telephone campaigns to force sponsors to fire performers and writers. The dynamics of this partnership between a public agency and private power groups was put forth with striking candor by Representative Walter before he became Chairman of HUAC:

Rep. Francis Walter (D. Pa.) who will take charge in the new Congress of House activities against Communists and their sympathizers, has a new plan for driving Reds out of important industries. He said today he plans to hold large public hearings in industrial communities where subversives are known to be operating, and to give known or suspected commies a chance in a full glare of publicity to deny or affirm their connection with a revolutionary conspiracy—or to take shelter behind constitutional amendments.

"By this means," he said, "active Communists will be exposed before their neighbors and fellow workers, and I have every confidence that the loyal Americans who work with them will do the rest of the job."*

5 HOW EXPOSURE WORKS

Exposure is not simply a process of identifying a witness as a subversive at a public hearing. It might be difficult to engineer the punishment of the witness merely for exercising his constitutional rights. Careful preparation is needed so that the identification is made in an atmosphere of pervasive hostility; fear must rule people's thoughts and drive out reason so that Network groups can call the turn the Committee wants called .

The Committee strives to inflame the community to destroy the subversive and, in the process, to discredit and attack all kinds of liberal causes and activities. The exposure system produces a planned political overkill.

The community movement which HUAC shapes to destroy the exposed witness spreads like a brush fire. A Committee hearing, if properly planned, can influence the decision in a local tax issue, kill a housing referendum, defeat slates in trade unions, PTA's and cooperative elections, blast the hopes of a candidate for Congress or a local council, reduce participation in a community forum, force a change in the school superintendent, remove books from library shelves, and plunge the community into a miasma of suspicion, hate and fear.

* *Washington Daily News,* November 19, 1954.

Early in March 1956, HUAC subpoenaed 35 members of the Hollywood Musicians Union, Local 47, American Federation of Musicians, for appearance at a hearing in April 1956. It became necessary to leak the names in order to smear a group within the local which was then engaged in a dispute with the international. On March 9, the *Los Angeles Examiner* listed the names and employers of 22 of those subpoenaed. As a result of these disclosures, a foreign cultural tour was canceled by the Symphony of the Air and three of the subpoenaed musicians were barred from a tour by the Los Angeles Philharmonic. The release of the names effectively accomplished its exposure purposes long before the hearing even opened.

In February 1953, HUAC announced, even before a subpoena was issued, that it planned to call John T. Gojack, a trade-union leader, to testify at a hearing in Fort Wayne, Indiana. This announcement was made on the eve of a hotly contested collective-bargaining election and for the purpose of influencing its outcome.

The hearing was subsequently canceled and a new hearing scheduled—also just prior to a collective bargaining election. Before the issuance of the second subpoena for Gojack's appearance at the adjourned hearing, Chairman Walter told reporters that the purpose of the hearing was to put Gojack's union out of business. While the subpoena was still unissued, a local newspaper, the *St. Joseph* (Michigan) *Herald-Press,* where Gojack's union functioned as a collective-bargaining agent for the employees of the Whirlpool Company, printed an interview with Chairman Walter stating that the hearing would expose Gojack and that "the rest is up to the Community." The newspaper commented that "the hearing will precede by three days the NLRB representation election at Whirlpool."

The advance release of the information that the subpoenas would be issued had its intended effect in each instance. The union lost the election.

These are examples of some of the preliminary effects of a hearing. Meanwhile, the buildup to the hearing is steadily proceeding.

The news of the hearing slowly seeps into the community. A HUAC investigator visits a potential witness at home and asks him to cooperate. He is warned that a refusal might lead to loss of job, or (in the case of a naturalized citizen) to denaturalization. If the potential witness remains hostile, he is visited at his job. The employer is requested to make the employee see the light.

When the roster of witnesses is complete, an alert goes out to security officers of corporations, boards of education, local politicos and other interested individuals. Included among the insiders are the Network leaders, who are jubilant over the arrival of *der Tag*. The Committee frequently works with a local journalistic tout who gives its investigators tips on suspects. In exchange, he is permitted to break the story, "Red Probe Due in February"; "Committee Investigators Gather Evidence"; "Commie Probe to Call 40, Express Learn!" The story quotes a "reliable Committee source" that HUAC has uncovered a serious threat to the community's security.

By now gossip and rumor fill the air with the names of the victims. Some of them are called in by their employers for "quiet talks." The special hum that fear makes—of loss of job, of injury to family and career—becomes louder. There are anxious telephone calls—has a stranger appeared with a piece of paper, a subpoena? HUAC's supporters are mobilizing. The community is still passive, but curious—waiting for the next development.

While stoutly insisting that it is a firm policy not to release the names of those subpoenaed, HUAC ("a source close to the Committee") frequently leaks the names to the press. The announcement of the subpoena in advance of the hearing makes it easy to develop discharge pressures. The local vigilantes ride harder. Resolutions are passed; trials are held; halls are closed; shrill-voiced patriots call employers, school boards and professional societies to put them on the spot about subpoenaed employees and members.

At last the subpoenas are actually served—usually about a month before the hearing. Now the Committee issues a press release. It frequently promises sensational disclosures of some particularly grave peril which will be aired at the hearing ("Probers Fear Port Menaced"; "Defense Area Declared Infiltrated"; "Sabotage Threat to Be Probed by House Committee"). As the hearing day approaches, the press goes into action with "background" stories ("Red-Led Unions Here Overdue for Probe"; "Teachers Cell Ten Years Old"). When the tempo lags, "dope" stories (inside advance information) appear about the unfriendly witnesses ("Area Salesman to Be Called by Probe"; "Six Defense Workers Subpoenaed").

By the time the hearing opens, the normally passive anti-Communist members of the community have been gulled into believing they are genuinely threatened, while the community Network is riding high on a tide of vociferous hostility. The press waits to cash in on the scare headlines it has been running; expectant citizens await with alarm the disclosure of information that menaces their community; unfriendly witnesses, anticipating the rack for weeks, reach a crescendo of anxiety. The cry of "Communist!" has been made to echo the panic of an insidious disease once proclaimed by another cry, "Unclean!" The climate of fear is prepared, the stage set.

In the typical case, the person who is served with a subpoena knows he has been singled out for public exposure. Sometimes he is summoned to a private, executive session. He hopes that the private session will shield him from further harassment. But if he refuses to answer in executive session, he is called for a public appearance.

Here is the statement of a witness who appeared at an open hearing, in November 1959, purportedly dealing with subversion among Puerto Ricans in the continental United States and their homeland:

1. A representative of this committee first approached me in December of 1957 and I was interviewed by him in my office. On November 3, 1958, almost a year later, two representatives of the committee, Mr. Williams and Mr. Gerhard, visited me at my home in New York City. At this time these representatives noted that my graduate studies as a candidate for Doctor of Philosophy were nearing completion. They suggested that I had a promising career ahead as a scientist and that it would be a pity to ruin my career before it was even started. They stated that if I did not provide them with the information they requested, I would be served with a subpoena by the committee. They stated that if I refused to testify and invoked the protection of the Fifth Amendment the consequent publicity would result in reprisal by persons outside the committee

who disapproved of witnesses invoking the Fifth Amendment. They reminded me that other careers had been ruined by such exposure. They stated they had delayed service of the subpoena in the hopes of eliciting cooperation. At the end of the interview, when they decided they had been wasting their time, they announced that a subpoena would be forthcoming and commented, "Let the chips fall where they may."

2. I appeared before the committee in executive session on August 6, 1959. At that time I declined to answer questions concerning my past or present political associations and personal affairs. I was continued under subpoena until today. I can only conclude that my summons to this open hearing is an attempt to make good the threats to carry out this punitive action. It would seem that the broken careers that have been left behind by the committee are not an unfortunate by-product of information-gathering for legislative purposes, but rather a primary purpose of the hearings.

Torn between his fears and his principles, the unfriendly witness is plunged into an agonizing crisis. He knows that the Committee demands his physical presence in the hearing room for no reason other than to make him a target of its hostility, to have him photographed, exhibited and branded.

Life in a democracy has not taught him how to cope with these attacks. He knows that the vandalism, ostracism, insults, crank calls, and hate letters that he and his family have already suffered are but the opening stages of a continuing ordeal to which he is to be relentlessly subjected. He knows that he may lose his job—if he hasn't already lost it—and that his family faces a kind of community outlawry. Most of all, he is tormented by the awareness that he is being punished without valid cause, and deprived, by manipulated prejudice, of his fundamental rights as an American and of the moral and ethical protections which a civilized society extends to every man. He is sickened by the realization that an agency of Government has pandered to the bigotry of the community and now proposes to make his personal life a prey of that bigotry.

He must choose a lawyer (and pay him a fee). If he is

still employed, he must explain to his employer that he will be away from work—and why. If the hearing is out of town, he may lose several days' work (and incur extra legal fees and expenses). Will the witness' wife share his feelings? (A blacklisted witness, Alvah Bessie, has written, "Personally, I know of at least fifteen broken marriages broken because husband or wife became an informer or refused to. . . .") Shall he tell his coworkers about the subpoena? Will they understand? Or should he pray that the story of his appearance will be buried on the back pages? His youngsters have been taunted, shoved off the sidewalks and spat upon. What about the children's school? Should the teacher or principal be spoken to? Should he consult the minister?

As he approaches the hearing, the fear, the sense of shock, intensifies. A subpoenaed person, interviewed in the course of The Fund for the Republic's investigation of blacklisting, describes it this way:

> Even though you know what takes place in that committee, you are so accustomed to respecting government in all its forms, that your fear is enormous. Intellectually, you understand what's happening, but you can't control the fear. An insidious form of self-guilt sets in. You accept the views of the committee in spite of yourself. It's quite bewildering. Afterwards, you find yourself guarded and evasive whatever you do, wherever you go.

While the Committee likes to see the unfriendly witness exposed and destroyed by publicity even before the hearing, it is careful to shield the identity of the friendly witness, especially if his name and role have never before been disclosed. These witnesses are frequently issued subpoenas as though they were unfriendly. The Committee will not identify them before the hearing because, it says, they might be assassinated or their families injured by the bloodthirsty Reds. Besides, this heightens the discomfiture of surprise, the drama of confrontation, and minimizes the possibility of cold feet, second thoughts, or the development of discrediting material (always a danger with an informer) which might dampen community enthusiasm.

Moreover, it is important for the friendly witness to share the confidence of the unfriendly witnesses until the opening of the hearing so that he can testify about the hostility with which the unfriendly witnesses responded to the Committee, the steps they planned to resist it, and the advice that they received from their lawyers—something that might be difficult if the friendly witness were not subpoenaed and impossible if his "friendly" status were disclosed. In the 1959 Pittsburgh hearings, the Committee, with great relish, elicited testimony from a friendly informer about the reaction of the unfriendly witnesses to the hearing, and how, armed with his own subpoena, he penetrated their meetings with counsel and, masquerading as an unfriendly witness, shared in the legal advice that they received—a tactic which outraged even the Pittsburgh press.

The public hearings throb with hostility. When the hearing is held on the road, the Committee arranges in advance to pack the room with its Network supporters. The 1954 Seattle hearing was so jammed with members of the American Legion Auxiliary and Pro-America that many of the witnesses and their lawyers had difficulty getting into the hearing room. The friendly witnesses are separated from the unfriendly ones and are usually seated in an enclosure reserved for the Committee itself, members of the United States Attorney's office, the FBI, employers and members of the local antisubversive squad. When the hearing is held in Washington, similar efforts are made to ensure a hostile audience. At the 1953 Washington hearing of Reverend Jack E. McMichael, the best seats in the hearing room were reserved for members of the Circuit Riders, a reactionary religious group which shares the Committee's views. Each seat was lined in advance with copies of its literature.

When the hearing begins, the Chairman of the subcommittee conducting the hearings makes a statement in which he freshens up the fears of the audience and inspires them to finish off the unfriendly witnesses. The Reds are more menacing than ever; their machinations are more diabolical; do not be deceived by the number of individuals who have left the Communist Party; these are sinister tactics to screen a revolutionary plot, etc.

After this ritualistic denunciation, there follows a special local appeal. Chairman Velde's opening gambit in the

1954 Seattle-Portland hearing is a classic example of the genre:

> There is probably no section in the United States that possesses a more strategic importance than this area. We members of Congress recognize this fact and, unfortunately, so have enemies of this country.

In the Committee's world it is always high noon—there are no unstrategic areas, every industry is the most vital to our defense and every example of subversion the most devilish it has ever encountered.

Sometimes the need to make a good first headline for the afternoon press will drive the Committee into particularly silly charges. In July 1959, the Committee opened hearings on "Communist Training Operations" with an announcement by Chairman Walter that one of the witnesses had "received orders from the Kremlin, which have now been transmitted to the comrades in the United States. . . . to intensify the training of key revolutionaries in sabotage, subversion and penetration." There was not a word of evidence adduced in the hearing to support this charge, but it was good for a headline: REDS STEP UP SABOTAGE WALTER SAYS.

In the late forties and fifties, it was easy for the Committee to bring about an employee's discharge simply upon the basis of his failure to answer "No" to the question, "Are you now or have you ever been a member of the Communist Party?" It is more difficult today. Our traditions of tolerance and fair-mindedness are beginning, albeit sporadically, to reassert themselves. By 1956, the Supreme Court in the *Slochower* case had said that "We must condemn the practice of imputing a sinister meaning to the exercise of a person's constitutional rights under the Fifth Amendment."

Ambushed by these unforeseen developments, the Committee, with a new Chairman, Francis E. Walter, fought back. It set about to recreate a Red hysteria and to translate that hysteria into a readiness to hate and injure the unfriendly witness. As a first step, Chairman Walter engaged as staff director in 1956 Richard E. Arens, the greatest living expert in the art of exposure, and a disciple of such masters as Senators Eastland, McCarran and Jenner.

When the informer takes the stand, even Arens can do very little to recreate the mingled sense of fear, awe and excitement which his revelations produced in an earlier day. But Arens does his best to invest the performance with melodrama and menace. After the preliminaries are disposed of, the Committee gets to the heart of the matter—the listing of names. The Committee already has the names, but it wants them on the public record. For example (Communications, 1957):

Mr. Arens: Now during the course of your membership in the Communist Party did you know a number of people as Communists who were engaged in the communications field?

Mrs. Greenberg: I did.

Mr. Arens: Do you have before you now a list of names of persons that you have given to the staff here, persons known by you to a certainty to have been members of the Communist Party?

Mrs. Greenberg: I have.

Mr. Arens: As to each of these persons, have you observed him or her in a closed Communist Party meeting?

Mrs. Greenberg: I have.

Mr. Arens: Would you kindly tell us the names of each of these persons, and give us just a word of description concerning each one of them?

The witness then proceeded to list the names previously given to the Committee.

If the witness forgets a name, he is prompted (New England, 1958):

Mr. Arens. May I make the record clear here? The names which I have, from time to time, been prompting your memory with and suggestions are, in each and every instance, names which you have heretofore given us?

Mr. Penha: That is absolutely correct.

Mr. Arens: In private sessions, is that correct? Now may I suggest the name of——

The witness then characterizes the political position and importance of each person named. In most instances, the

72

victims turn out to be of the leadership elite. There are few unimportant Communists in the informer's world. Hearings rarely fail to turn up a headline: WITNESS NAMES NO. 1 RED IN AREA PROBE.

When the informer leaves the stand, he is held in reserve for confrontations and for spot appearances.

It must be remembered that the subpoena and the Committee appearance is only one path to the Committee's goal of exposing and ruining its victims.

As the friendly witness recites the list of names, each one described and the spelling verified, when necessary, to pinpoint the victim, newspaper reporters relay their stories of the disclosures. At once the machinery that worked on subpoenaed witnesses now goes to work on people who have merely been *named*. The named victim's phone rings; the press is calling for a statement. Discharge and trouble strike; the entire community becomes an exposure mill. The next edition carries as front-page news the list of those named—with photographs when they are available. Stores and homes are picketed, calls to boards of education are made, boycotts are threatened, blacklists are imposed, emergency meetings are called. The named victims can be exposed and ruined on a wholesale scale without a subpoena or an appearance—simply on the testimony of an informer.

The following recital by a named, and subsequently subpoenaed, doctor tells it own tale.

On September 21, while you were questioning a doctor, you asked him whether there was a certain type of meeting in my home, and you mentioned my name twice, and you spelled out my name to make sure that everybody got it, and the following day at 10 o'clock in the morning the superintendent of the hospital asked me to resign because of the associated publicity. This, mind you, after seven and one-half years of excellent service, admitted by the superintendent of the hospital.

The meeting referred to was a "meeting of the medical division of the Arts, Sciences and Professions."

Finally, the dreaded moment arrives. The subpoenaed

unfriendly witness, named by the friendly witness who has just left the stand, is called to testify. The Committee moves in to complete the exposure; members of the FBI staff and local Red squad look him over as he moves toward the witness stand to fix his face in their minds. He is overborne and bewildered by the naked hostility of the governmental forces confronting him.

The picture which the Committee presents is as harsh as it is false. The Government of the United States, in the persons of members of the Committee, panoplied by its staff, United States marshals and friendly witnesses, has trapped an enemy of the Nation, lurking and plotting in his community and place of employment, and is bringing him to book. The Committee members sit high on the judges' seats of the local courthouse (where field hearings are usually conducted), or on the dais of the august caucus room in the old House Office Building in Washington. The witness proceeds to a table below with a gagged counsel at his side, to be judged and punished at the same time. And this highly direct use of power is as arbitrary as it is harsh, for it is unredeemed by any of the procedural decencies of the Anglo-American legal system.

The witness makes his way to the stand, amidst the popping of flash bulbs, the grinding of television, the clicking of still cameras, and the bustle at the press table. His lawyer complains of the unnecessary bedlam and requests that the cameras be halted and the televising cease. The Committee solemnly explains that it has no jurisdiction— and this frequently in a Federal courthouse—over the photographers or television cameramen until after the witness is sworn. This reason for evading Speaker Rayburn's ban on the televising of all committee hearings is akin to a claim that the Committee would be powerless before a witness is sworn to prevent a spectator from smoking or brawling at the place where it is conducting a hearing.

Moreover, the cameramen know very well that the Committee really does not intend that they cease photographing or televising the witness during his testimony. They usually continue while the witness or counsel protests in vain. For example, in the 1958 New England hearings the Chairman ruled at the request of a witness that "no pictures will be taken during the course of the testimony. . . ." The photographers persisted after she took the stand. She protested, "The photographers are getting me very nervous,

Mr. Chairman." Her counsel added, "I thought the pictures were not to be taken, according to your own ruling." For this simple reminder, counsel was rebuked for "taking this opportunity to make speeches."

When the cameras continued, the witness pleaded, "Please I am very nervous when the pictures are taken. Please, I ask that no pictures be taken." The Committee, still declining to enforce its own ban on photographers, told the witness, "If you would answer the question you would not be so nervous." There followed an attempt to terrorize the witness into answering with the help of the grinding cameras. Another request to halt the televising ("I want to call your attention that you are still permitting the cameras to go after you already said they would not"), was ignored as the Committee pressed harder and threatened contempt. The witness again protested, "Mr. Chairman, the photographers are still taking pictures here"— and they continued to do so until the witness left the stand.

While objections to photographers are frequently futile, a failure to object sometimes brings the taunt that the witness is avid for publicity. In a recent hearing in Chicago, a 70-year-old witness who had been hospitalized with a heart attack asked the Committee to consider his age and health in its interrogation. When his counsel said that there was no objection to the photographers, Congressman Scherer sneered, "You don't think that would hurt his heart condition?"

As in a slaughterhouse, nothing in an exposure hearing is wasted. The very first questions asked (residence, occupation, place of work) are all designed to contribute to the witness' ruin. The Committee knows where the witness works, but how can the Committee be sure that a witness will lose his job if the nature and place of his employment are not put on the record? Similarly, the public identification of the witness' home address, which the Committee also knows, is indispensable if his neighbors are to be reached. Matters such as these could hardly be left to chance.

The Committee invariably threatens contempt against witnesses who refuse to answer such questions. Even when the witness pleads with the Committee that previous disclosures have resulted in molestation, it does not relent.

The Committee has refused to permit a witness to withhold his address when he pleaded that, as a result of a previous appearance, "we had many anti-Semitic letters." Another witness pleaded in vain: "We have been molested every time there was such a hearing. I have small children and we have been molested by some hoodlums."

The witness' office address is an equally vital piece of information (Los Angeles, 1952):

Mr. Moulder: Where is your office located from which you engage in the practice of law?

Witness: In the City of Los Angeles.

Mr. Moulder: In what building and office number?

Witness: Does that have any pertinency?

Mr. Moulder: To properly identify you as to who you are. We are trying to designate as to just exactly who you are.

Witness: I believe it is in the telegram as correctly stated here, Mr. Moulder. That is the telegram which I received summoning me to this postponed hearing.

Mr. Moulder: Then do you refuse to answer that question?

Witness: Well, my address, as I say, is correctly stated in the telegram. I believe you have a copy.

The witness answered the question.

In the 1959 Los Angeles hearings, the Committee tried to force a witness to state whether he was a doctor or a dentist and to give his street address. He gave his address as "Los Angeles County." But this did not satisfy the Committee. First Committee Counsel Tavenner tried to justify extracting his address from him on the ground that it was necessary "to locate him geographically so as to be able to know what his opportunities are for knowledge of Communist activities" in the particular area under investigation. Congressman Jackson suddenly sprouted a concern that the Committee might be confused. There was, he claimed, another individual with the same name; the residence was important to eliminate the possibility "of confusion with another doctor with the same name."

The doctor's lawyer unsuccessfully tried to offer this information off the record. The Committee wanted it on the record. To satisfy both Tavenner and Jackson, the witness specified the area of the county where he lived.

Throwing pretense to the winds, the Committee demanded, "Where, what address, that is a very general area." The witness then gave his street number. Surely there could not be two doctors with the same name, living in the same area, and at the same street number. But the Committee closed in on him: "What city?"

"Well," continued Mr. Tavenner, "it has been a long time finding that out. Where do you maintain your office?" The witness' lawyer, again to spare his client harassment, offered to supply this data off the record. When the Committee refused, the witness pleaded the Fifth Amendment.

In the Newark hearing held in September 1958, a witness resisted giving his residence and occupation because he had appeared in executive session where he had already given the Committee answers to these questions. He lost his job.

A witness (Youngstown, 1956) is asked to state her occupation. She answers, "If I state my occupation, I will be fired. I prefer to withold that."

Mr. Arens: You are required to state your occupation. . . . I respectfully request that the witness be ordered and directed to answer the question. . . .

Witness: I am a social worker.
Mr. Arens: And you work where?
Witness: I expect if I made public where I work, that I will be fired. I hope that I do not have to make public that information.
Mr. Arens: Maybe it would be in the public interest if we would divulge where you work. . . .

Mr. Willis and Mr. Velde assure the witness that she will not lose her job, if she answers the questions.

Mr. Arens: What do you do at the place where you are employed?
Witness: I am a social worker.
Mr. Arens: And what do you do where you are employed?
Witness: I do the usual duties of a social worker.
Mr. Arens: And among whom do you work?

The witness again begs the Committee not to force her out of her job. Let's start on another question, Mr. Arens suggests, and then we will return to your job. "Are you a Communist?" When the witness declines to answer on constitutional grounds, Arens again insists, "Now tell the Committee where you work."

Again the witness appeals to the Committee not to take away her job. Arens offers her another bargain: If the Committee doesn't require an answer to the employment question, will she talk about other organizations. She is asked about those and again about the Communist Party. The witness declines to answer on constitutional grounds.

> Mr. Arens: Now we are back where we started from. Tell us where you work.
>
> Witness: Your Honor, I am a social worker for a private social agency.
>
> Mr. Arens: And what is the name of that private social agency?
>
> Witness: As I said, if I give the name, I will certainly be fired.
>
> Mr. Arens: Did you have a discussion with your employers respecting your membership in the Communist Party when you accepted this position with this private social agency?

This last question is the standard question used to cue the employer to fire a witness and at the same time to supply a reason for the discharge. Arens was beginning to weary of the cat-and-mouse game he was playing with the witness, for in his next question he indicated that he knew all along where she was employed, and worked in the "brainwashing" theme.

> Do you think your losing your job might be because the parents of the children that you influence in Communism, try to influence in Communism, protest a little bit if they knew they had a Communist on the grounds? Do you think that is what might be in the back of your mind?

After taunting the witness a little more and permitting her to thrash about as the net was being drawn tighter, Arens asked, "Are you presently employed at the Jenny E. Clarkson Home for Girls at Valhalla, N.Y.?"

But it was not enough for Arens to torment the witness,

first, by seeking to use economic pressure to force her to surrender her constitutional rights; second, pretending that the Committee did not know where she worked and needed to know for a legitimate reason; third, by suggesting without any factual warrant at all that she deserved to lose her job because she had abused her relationship to her charges; and fourth, by naming her employer after the witness had made it clear that such a disclosure would result in discharge. When she repeated that the disclosure of her employment was "unfair" and "unfortunate" and would injure her, Arens baited her in a new way: "You didn't lose your employment with the Western Pennsylvania Committee for Protection of Foreign Born because somebody said something bad about you, did you? . . . You didn't lose your job as executive secretary of the Civil Rights Congress in Pennsylvania because someone said something bad about you, did you? . . . Did the Communist Party ever deprive you of a job?"

After another try at the "brainwashing" theme ("how old are these girls? . . . how many are there in the home?"). Arens tried a new gambit and asked the witness to identify her name on a *Daily Worker* wrapper: "We are going to give you an opportunity now to make your employer proud of you, and these little girls proud, that you are here serving your country, telling us all about the conspiratorial apparatus that would destroy this country. Just tell us if you are she. Perhaps you receive the *Daily Worker* to use it in uncovering other Communists or something. We receive it in our work all the time."

The Committee's tactics succeeded—the witness lost her job.

What conceivable relationship does this inquisitorial savagery bear to the process of gathering facts to help Congress discharge its legislative responsibilities? The hate, the drive of almost pathological intensity to wound and hurt which breaks through the records of this (and so many other) hearings, echoes with chilling fidelity the grillings of Jews by the Nazis—before worse came. To bring the matter closer to home: where could one find a more vivid counterpart to the 17th century arraignment and trial of a witch?

When the prehearing publicity does not get the witness fired, the Committee tries to have the subpoena served at the place of employment (See Chapter 9). If this gambit does not succeed, the Committee uses the hearing to exert pressure on the employer. In the 1956 Youngstown hearing, a witness had already stated her employment. Mr. Arens then asked, "Tell us a little more about your present job. . . . How many members of the faculty or of the organization are there, paid employees, in a comparable status to yourself? What are your functions or duties? To whom are you a secretary? Have you discussed with your employers your appearance here today?"

To the last question, the witness replied, "I was served a subpoena at work, and my employer was right there, and I explained it to him." Arens asked, "Did you have a discussion with your employer on the issue of Communism?" This frequently posed question is intended to suggest to the employer that the witness concealed his or her political views in applying for employment. Anticipating a possible attempt to discharge her after the hearing, he warns her not to return to her employer and deny that she is a Communist. She was subsequently forced to resign and her husband also lost his job.

Another question which is sometimes used to cue an employer and give him a ground for discharge is: Did you recruit anyone into the Communist Party while at your work. Or, Did you engage in Communist activity at your job?

On many occasions it becomes unnecessary for the Committee to pursue the subject of the witness' employment. He has already been fired as a result of the subpoena:

My name is ———, and I live in Newark, N. J. As to my occupation, I am now unemployed as a direct result of this Committee. I was called before an executive session. I appeared there and I was subpoenaed to an open hearing and when I so informed my employers, I lost my job. [Newark, 1958]

Mr. Tavenner: What is your profession or business or trade.

Witness: At the present time, for the last 2 days I am unemployed, having lost my job 2 days after I was served a subpoena by the Committee. [Los Angeles, 1955]

I am ———— from Roanoke, Virginia, and I am unemployed, thanks to the Committee; after I got your subpoena, I was fired.

The last witness went on to explain that she worked for two doctors. "They said that they . . . couldn't keep me on with the kind of newspaper publicity that was coming out about me [Atlanta, 1958]."

The Committee's obsession with the witness' occupation has other significance besides the need to tell its supporters where to go to have him fired. The Committee shapes the hearing so as to create the inference that the witness' entire life is the product of a subversive design. Occupational questions are intended to suggest that the witness is a dangerous person—uncovered by the Committee in the very act of assaulting our ramparts.

HUAC thinks nothing of tracking down a witness' job history through his entire lifetime in the hope of turning up exposable material. In the course of a brief examination of a witness in 1958, Arens asked him some 65 questions about how he had earned his living for 24 years prior to his interrogation!

The worker-witness is invariably painted as a potential saboteur, no matter how remote his work from the area of defense. In the 1956 New Haven hearings, the Committee sought to sensationalize the fact that a number of unfriendly witnesses had been employed at the Bridgeport General Electric plant and hence had their hands on the Nation's throat. The fact that washing machines were manufactured at the plant apparently made no difference to the Committee. A textile worker is asked, "Do you know whether Wamsutta Mills had any army contracts?" The Committee even regards insurance agents as "defense workers" in a "basic industry."

A war veteran is treated by the Committee not as a fine citizen, deserving of praise, but as a disguised revolutionary with access to guns, a betrayer of secrets, a collaborator with insurrectionists. A wounded and decorated officer is asked (Youngstown, 1956), "During the course of your period of service in the Army, were you under the discipline of any organization controlled by a foreign power?"

A worker in a plant who came from another city, or

who has more than a high-school education is a "colonizer"; sent by the Communist Party to penetrate a new stronghold.

A teacher of teen-agers or tots—it does not matter—is merely a "brainwasher" in pedagogical disguise. Whether the witness is a social worker, a lawyer, a bookseller, a doctor, or a longshoreman—the Committee strives to facilitate his exposure by portraying him as uniquely sinister. Nor must it be supposed that the unfriendly witnesses came to their strategic posts by accident. The Communist Party works unceasingly, the Committee reminds us, to penetrate, infiltrate, colonize, etc., so as the prepare itself for the revolution. And even ties with the PTA, YWCA, or a church are depicted as the product of a sinister effort of the never-resting octopus to acquire new prizes for the Kremlin.

A favorite "identifying question" seeks to establish alienage or noncitizenship. A foreign-born witness automatically suffers the Committee's hostility and suspicion—particularly if he is not naturalized.

In the 1953 Philadelphia hearings, Congressman Walter, an unabashed xenophobe, commented acidly on the large number of foreign-born unfriendly witnesses.

It should be more than clear by now that the hearing is not a legislative investigation at all, but an inquisition. The initial question about the witness' residence and occupation are not mere formalities to identify him in a preliminary way, but dodges in a game of exposure.

These tactics are used solely because the witness is unfriendly. The witness can escape this grilling simply by becoming friendly. For example, if the witness does not want to give his address or his occupation, he can indicate his readiness to cooperate. ("You do not want to give your street address? There is no necessity for giving your street address.") In one instance, after being asked if he were a member of the Communist Party, and before answering, a witness requested the removal of the camera. Chairman Velde replied:

Well, now, may I ask the witness this: If I do order —or if the committee does order—the cameras turned off and the lights turned off, would the witness then answer the questions put to him by the counsel?

Witness: Well, I would feel more at ease.

Mr. Velde: Well, would you answer the question as to your membership in the Communist Party if the lights were turned off and the television and newsreel cameras ordered to desist? Would you then be willing to cooperate with the committee in that regard?

The heart of the hearing—the $64 question, "Are you now or have you ever been a member of the Communist Party?" and its variations—have no investigative meaning or purpose. The Committee's claim that this question is not a destination, but a journey to the facts, a "preliminary question," is a deception. The absurdity of the claim that the $64 question is asked as a matter of unavoidable necessity to establish the witness' qualification to report the facts which alone interest HUAC is best demonstrated by the savagely accusatory character of the "questioning" of the witness about his politics.

It is not Arens' style just to ask the witness the $64 question and let it go at that. He has perfected a ripe anti-subversive baroque, so freighted with prejudicial rhetoric that a failure to respond will yield a maximum of exposure value. Arens asks a witness if "he is now or has ever been a member of a Godless conspiracy based on perversion and deceit," if he is a member of the "army of the Kremlin steeled to overthrow our institutions and operating behind a façade of humanitarianism," if he is part of a Kremlin-controlled world Communist operation aimed at the nerve centers of our Nation." Here is a full-blown example (Ohio, 1956):

Are you a member of an organization that is dedicated to the destruction of religion, dedicated to the destruction of the entire Judo[sic]-Christian concept upon which his Nation is founded?

Picking up steam, he continues, "Are you a member of any organization which is an atheistic organization, dedicated to the destruction of religion, the sterility of the individual, of all concepts of God. . . . ?"

The witness, who of course has been sworn, is called upon not merely to answer the question, but to answer it, "Now that you are under oath. . . ." When Arens asked a leading West Coast minister a question so prefaced, his lawyer in vain protested. "Is there any suggestion the witness is not under oath? . . . There is no point in asking this man, this witness, if he is under oath while he is under oath. This is unnecessarily offensive to the witness."

When the witness challenges the pertinence of a question, it is a cue for a renewed exposure attack. Listen to Arens explain to a witness why he is being interrogated: "We understand, and we have received testimony from live witnesses identifying you . . . as part and parcel of that movement, as a dedicated zealot of the Communist conspiracy in the United States who masquerades behind the Constitution of the United States, and would desecrate the flag of this great Nation. . . . And I propose, if you will tell us whether or not, while you are under oath, you are in the conspiracy of the Communist Party, to interrogate you at length with reference to plans and proposals and designs of this conspiracy which were taken from premises under your custody and control."

When the witness takes refuge in the plea of the privilege against self-incrimination, or of the First Amendment, Arens has another go at him (New England, 1958): "Maybe you do not know what you are declining here. I just ask you if you think that is a pretty serious charge to level against a man. He is in the underground apparatus of a foreign-controlled conspiracy to overthrow the Nation, under whose flag he obtained protection. Don't you think that is a kind of serious charge to make against a man? Would you like to express yourself on that, or am I probing into your thoughts?"

A witness who declined on constitutional grounds to discuss his participation in a group known as "Coalition for Freedom and Democracy" was asked, "You certainly wouldn't be ashamed of being in a coalition for freedom and democracy would you—unless it was a false freedom and false democracy under the auspices of a conspirational apparatus?"

When the witness objects to the loaded character of the questioning, he finds himself attacked from a new direction. A witness in the Los Angeles 1956 hearings was asked about his relationship to an organization known as the Southern California Peace Crusade: "Kindly tell us while you are under oath now and in the aura of patriotism which you have surrounded yourself in the opening statement, whether or not you betrayed your country by being executive secretary of this organization designed to subvert the security of this great Nation?" The witness protested that "there is a condemnation attached to the question." Arens tauntingly rephrased it, "For the moment may we change to say were you executive secretary of this innocent little organization, this patriotic organization, this organization for the uplift of humanity, the Southern California Peace Crusade?" Note the sarcastic diminutive in the preceding quotation. Arens is very fond of this device: "In 1949 did you go to New York City for a little session of the American Committee for the Protection of the Foreign Born?" (Youngstown, 1956).

A minister complains that the question, "Are you now, or have you ever been, a member of a godless conspiracy controlled by a foreign power" is improper because its characterization contains a value judgment based on opinion. Arens insists that the protesting witness has waived the privilege against self-incrimination and should be required to answer because he has "voluntarily" dealt with the subject matter of the question.

Many witnesses fear that to answer any "political" question (even about espionage) might be considered a waiver of the privilege for all purposes and ultimately lead to an informing demand. Arens asks the questions of the witness which he knows could be truthfully answered in a completely exculpatory way, but which the witness feels obliged to decline to answer in order to preserve his constitutional privilege—a trick perfected by the late Senator McCarthy. When it becomes clear that the witness intends to plead the privilege broadly out of fear of waiver, Arens throws all restraint to the winds and wallows in what amounts to a parody of a movie-style courtroom scene. In a loud staccato, he asks (perfectly sure that the question will be unanswered): "Now, sir, I put it to you as a fact and ask you to affirm or deny the fact that you are part of an enterprise to destroy the very constitution of the United States under which we all have protection, that you are the agent of the Communist Party as an arm of the international Communist conspiracy sent into Atlanta for the purpose of engaging in conspiratorial activities on behalf of the Communist Party. If that is not so, deny it under oath."

Arens is not always sure how far he can use the question

as a means of testifying against the witness. Thus, in the 1956 Seattle hearings, he first tested out a witness: "I . . . ask you while you are under oath to affirm or deny the fact that you are an expert in the Communist underground conspiratorial apparatus and in garroting?" When the witness pleaded the self-incrimination privilege to this question, Arens tells him: "I put it to you as a fact, sir, that you were trained in the underground school to garrote for the International Communist conspiracy. Now deny that, you are under oath."

Not a scrap of evidence was introduced in the record to supply a factual foundation for these questions. A staff writer of the Seattle *Times* commented the next day:

> But while the Communist witnesses used traditional American liberties as their shield, across the table, Richard Arens, committee counsel, at times stooped to tactics that were unbecoming to an employee of Congress.
>
> Arens appeared to be more intent upon assailing some of the witnesses than he was in extracting information.
>
> Arens used his position to testify against the witnesses to the point of accusing one of being a murderer and trained saboteur. Arens offered no substantiating evidence.
>
> The Constitution provides that no person—not even tough, unyielding Communists—shall be held to answer for a capital crime except on an information or indictment. His questions at times clearly were out of bounds.

The Committee rarely gets an answer from a witness which it does not know will be helpfully lurid. Still, there are a few witnesses about whom it is hard to be sure. They are willing to talk about themselves and appear to be thoroughly disillusioned with Communism. Will they give the Committee the kind of answers that will contribute to the exposure process? This is a problem familiar to the cross-examiner in a courtroom. He tries to protect himself by phrasing the question with care and preparing another question deflecting the impact of a possibly unwelcome answer. Here is how Arens maneuvers this dilemma in quizzing a recently resigned member of a Communist Party state committee:

Mr. Arens: Did the Party emphasize heavy industry?

Witness: I would say Yes. Rather, actually the emphasis was not heavy. It was industry that had a large number of workers.

Mr. Arens: Was there any espionage operation conducted to your knowledge by the colonizers, or was that separate and distinct?

The witness refused to be cued into a helpful answer.

I have absolutely and unequivocably [sic] no knowledge of anyone in the Communist Party mentioning the subject. . . .

And now Arens' repair work—for he coudl hardly permit denial of Communist espionage by a disillusioned Communist official to stand untampered with on the record: "Our information is that it is a separate channel." What "separate channel" and what "information" are, of course, never elucidated.

Now a try for a more helpful answer about sabotage. "Did the Party in your experience have its sabotage operations operating through the conduits or channels of the colonizers?" The question, of course, assumes that this or some other witness had testified that the Party had a "sabotage operation." The witness answers, "I could not even begin to answer such a question. I don't know what existed besides those things I am familiar with."

Here is how Arens neutralizes this answer by a Communist official denying knowledge of sabotage: "That confirms our information of elsewhere, that that is a separate operation." The "information of elsewhere" is, of course, never disclosed.

The witness, although fully cooperative in other aspects, was subsequently indicted for refusing to name his former associates. A doubt persists: Would he have suffered this fate if he had been more helpful on the subject of heavy industry, sabotage and espionage and had not forced Arens to treat his denials as confirming the existence of a "separate channel" for Communist espionage and sabotage operations?

On occasion, early in the hearing, the Committee stages a confrontation, which is a device for dramatizing the un-friendly witness' identification by the informer. The in-former physically points to (the argot is "fingers") the vic-time and states that he knew him as a Communist. The feat is usually performed by an undercover agent; few ex-Communist friendly witnesses are called upon to do it.

Mr. Arens: While you are under oath, would you kindly look at the gentleman who has just testified? Look him in the face and tell this committee while you are under oath and while he is under oath, did he or did he not tell the truth when he said he knew you as a Communist?

Mr. Scherer: I ask that you direct the witness to look at the witness Wereb.

Mr. Doyle: So that the record will show, I instruct you to face the witness, Mr. Wereb, who has, under oath, sworn that he knew you as a member of the Communist Party, and ask if you recognize him.

A more conventional form of confrontation runs like this: "The previous witness laid his liberty on the line, and said that he knew you as a member of the Communist conspiratorial apparatus. While you are under oath, stand up like a red-blooded American and tell the Committee was he lying or telling the truth."

The witness, of course, would never be permitted to cross-examine his accuser—that is not the practice of legis-lative investigating committees, explains Mr. Arens. As for the informer laying his liberty on the line, it would be the height of fantasy to suppose that the Committee would bite the hand that feeds it by challenging in any way the veracity of the undercover agent.

It may be recalled that Bishop Oxnam revealed in June of 1954 that Harvey Matusow had twice confessed perjury. A month after this announcement by Bishop Oxnam, the Committee summoned its former star witness. When asked by Congressman Clardy whether he had ever admitted lying, he referred to a recanting affidavit he had given to the *New York Times*. Congressman Clardy first tried to take Matusow off the spot by suggesting that the affidavit was not "under oath" (as though that somehow made the recantation false). But when it appeared that it was, Clardy triumphantly brushed it aside on the ground that "it was not a statement before the Committee."

Dealing with the Oxnam charges, Matusow explained that his statements to Bishop Oxnam were simply the product "of the instability of a young veteran." This response the Committee translated to mean that, "You were telling the truth when you were before this and other committees?" When Matusow indicated that Bishop Oxnam should be given "the benefit of the doubt" in construing the press statements about his interview with Matusow, Clardy put in, "You haven't heard the Bishop very often?" Thus cued, Matusow responded nobly, if he was accurately reported by the newspapers, "The Bishop is a dishonest man."

After Matusow was thus encouraged by the Committee to call Bishop Oxnam a dishonest man, the former Attorney General of the United States, J. Howard McGrath, wrote to Oxnam's lawyer that Matusow had in June come to him and confessed falsely identifying many people. When the letter was released on July 10, 1954, not only did the House Committee take no action, but Velde brushed aside the Oxnam-McGrath charges as "curbstone gossip."

If neither a former Attorney General, nor a respected bishop of one of our largest denominations could induce the Committee to question the word of a self-confessed liar, how can Mr. Arens seriously claim that an informer "lays his liberty on the line" when he charges a witness with subversion? When it subsequently became clear that the bishop and the former Attorney General were correct and that the informer had lied even about whether he had recanted, the Committee then changed its tune—but in a characteristic way: Congressman Walter announced that Matusow was a sort of E. Phillips Oppenheim double agent who had been directed by the Party to lie to Congressional Committees and then to confess in order to discredit congressional investigations!

Confrontations are good for headlines; they make the hearings coruscate with sinister emanations of hidden guilt. Another device which accomplishes a similar purpose is the offer of immunity from prosecution. Most lawyers are convinced that the Committee lacks the power to give immunity to a witness. But that makes no difference—it creates the impression that he is concealing secrets of such vast import to the Nation's security—espionage, sabotage—that every legal resource must be exploited to overcome his silence. Other favorite tactics are votes to recommend contempt, denaturalization, deportation, withdrawal of defense contracts. Department of Justice investigation into the bona fides of a Taft-Hartley non-Communist affidavit, etc.

As the hearing moves along, the Committee never loses sight of the main problem—to steep the witness in an atmosphere of crime, treason and sedition. One way of building a record against the witness is deliberately to force him to plead the Fifth Amendment over and over again by asking a flurry of questions all falling within the same area. The Committee knows from the initial response that the witness will refuse to answer, but a high score is good for headlines (Local Man Pleads Fifth Forty Times) and helps sharpen the exposure consequences. Sometimes the Committee pointedly comments in the record on the frequency of the plea. (Congressman Clardy: "I hope the gentleman isn't a drinking man . . . thirty-four fifths taken in less than half an hour is quite a lot.")

The questions are frequently used in this multiplication game to give the Committee the air of a prosecutor who is on to something big but is frustrated by the silence and evasiveness of the witness. (Did the witness have a mimeograph machine in his basement ten years ago? Was he present at a party at which the guests consumed a cake frosted with a hammer and sickle? Did he ever live at a given address 15 years earlier?) The impression which the Committee wants to leave with its audience and the press is that it has access to damning intelligence data implicating the witness in serious crimes.

A special contribution of Mr. Arens to the "cops and robbers" sweepstakes is to request the witness to sign the voucher for his witness fee on the record. He explains to the witness (and to the press) that he wants the signature to compare with the signature on a document in the Committee's possession (a letter, election petition, or a certificate of incorporation) which it regards as proof of subversion. A witness, fearful that he might lose the fee, may sign. Usually he pleads the Fifth Amendment. Arens then informs him that when he signs for his fee after the hearing, the signatures will be compared—a marvelous ploy for the gooseflesh trade.

A special form of the numbers game is the practice of ordering the unfriendly witness to identify others. HUAC knows that the witness will refuse—many witnesses plead the Fifth Amendment primarily to avoid becoming informers. The Committee likes to do this in order to smear particular individuals whom it dislikes, such as critics of the Committee. It thinks that the refusal of an unfriendly witness to identify others on Fifth Amendment grounds helps to expose him. The Committee will do this even where it is obvious that the individuals asked about have nothing to do with the matter under inquiry. It asks a recalcitrant witness to testify about persons attending a social gathering at which he was present. A witness who ran a summer camp for children was grilled in this way by Congressman Doyle:

Mr. Doyle: Counselors?

Witness: These are high school kids who help the kids have a good time.

. . . .

Mr. Doyle: Tell me definitely the name of one counselor that you had last summer. . . . Tell me the name of one person. . . . You would not have any hesitation about giving the names of your counselors in executive session, would you? . . . Do you have a list of the counselors who were at your camp last summer? . . . And the addresses of the counselors are on that list . . . are they not?

The grand strategy of the Committee is, of course, to discredit the Fifth Amendment and to equate its use with guilt. The witness is frequently told that this plea is a direct clue to his guilt. A favorite ploy is to "test the good faith" of the pleader by asking a question which has no revelance to any legitimate inquiry but which invites the surmise that the witness is a knave—especially when he refuses to answer on the Fifth Amendment grounds. ("Are there any organizations [addresses] that you could tell us about which would not supply information which might be used against you in a criminal proceeding?")

Witnesses, with increasing frequency, try to foil the Committee's exposure game by denying present membership, but pleading the Fifth Amendment as to the past (the diminished Fifth). The Committee tries hard to make it appear that this is a trick, a Communist tactic. It asks a series of questions which push back by small increments of time the period of denial. Were you a Communist before you entered this room? A month ago? Six months ago? A year ago? In 1958?

This creates an unpleasant dilemma. The witness can answer "no" at a given point and plead the privilege beyond that point. But this answer in effect surrenders the plea by pinpointing the failure to deny earlier than a particular date. If he pleads as to each question in the time sequence (after having denied generally as to the past), the Committee makes it appear that he is a concealed Communist of one sort or another: "under discipline," "a member not of the formal entity but of the Communist operation," "a part of the Communist underground," etc.

The logic of the exposure process compels the Committee constantly to move to ever more direct forms of condemnation, naked of even a fig leaf of legislative pretense. This sometimes takes the form of rhetorical questions:

Have you formed any Committee for the Protection of the Hungarians?

Now tell us what you have done to protect the flag of this country by your activities in connection with congressional committees?

You are certainly not ashamed as one who has sworn to defend this great Republic to state what you have done to protect the helpless foreign-born, would you? Unless they happened to be Communist conspirators?

Have you betrayed the flag that you were sworn to uphold?

Are you familiar with the very first Psalm, "Blessed is the man that walketh not in the counsel of the ungodly"? [asked of a minister].

Mr. Velde asks a witness (Youngstown, 1956): "Whose side are you on in the revolt, Soviet Union's or the rebels?" The witness replies, "I am on the rebels' side."

But Velde is not satisfied with the witness' answers to other questions, so he concludes, "From the witness' appearance and demeanor before this Committee, I am satisfied that he bears watching by the duly constituted authorities. I do not think he is on the side of the rebels. I think he is on the side of Moscow, the Soviets."

The late Tom O'Connor, a liberal newspaper man, was interrogated in 1952 about a charge that he had been a Communist in 1938. Congressman Velde asked him:

"Are you a member of the Communist Party now?"

"No, sir," O'Connor replied.

"Were you a year ago?"

"No, sir."

"Were you five years ago?"

"No, sir."

"Were you ten years ago?"

"No, sir."

Velde had no further questions, but made the following comment:

> I personally can draw only one inference, that you are not only a past member of the Communist Party, but that you continue to be a member of the Communist Party and that you are an extreme danger to the country as the managing editor of a large New York newspaper.

The Committee uses the record to injure the witness in other ways. It recently held hearings in Pittsburgh to which it called a number of foreign-born witnesses who cannot be deported because the proof of their deportability is defective or because there is no country to which they can be deported. It filled the entire record with the Immigration and Naturalization Service dossiers on each of them. If a witness has been in trouble with the law—a tax case, contempt of court, a labor offense—HUAC brings it out "for purposes of identification."

As the frenetic Arens slows down, the Committee members take over. A few of them take an active role in the assault on the witness. The fire-eating Scherer glares at the witness, sneeringly comments on his responses, throws out a running fire of disparagement and insult. He specializes in perfecting the record for a contempt case. He stands guard to make sure the witness does not "dance away from," or "weasel out of" a question.

Congressman Kearney—a former general and a leader of the Veterans of Foreign Wars—grunts his disapproval of the witness and joins in the attack in a rough-hewn style ("I am astounded at this character").

Congressman Doyle—a lawyer—likes to take over the questioning when the witness is about to be excused, seeking to wear him down into making disclosures he has already refused to make. He specializes in an evangelical approach: "Why don't you get yourself and keep yourself in shape as a young American citizen, when you don't have to plead your constitutional privileges. . . . This country has honored you by giving you birth. Why the dickens do you get into an atmosphere . . . where you have to refuse to help your own Congress . . . to work out what is just and fair in the field of legislation involving the cold war we are in with Soviet Communism. I suggest if you do it, you will feel a whole lot better inside."

As with many a frustrated evangelist, Doyle rains curses on the unconverted, virtually inciting a lynching of his hapless victim: "I think the great majority of people who are in this room, as well as the American public, whenever they think of you, will look at you with shame when you have called this sort of thing an inquisition. . . . The trouble is, we do not have enough help to expose the real intended purpose of people who write filth such as you have written in these papers."

An important part of the exposure hearing is the glorification of the informer witness. Some of them have been previously "named" by other informers—an incestuous form of betrayal which the Committee's name-hungry thoroughness makes almost unavoidable. The Committee voices its compassion for the economic and social hardships which they have endured, seemingly unconscious of the irony, in view of its attempt to force the same hardships on the unfriendly witness.

In a few instances, we encounter a case of double exposure—the informer who is twice named by other informers. In the Chicago (1959) hearings, the informer Joseph A. Poskonka, an FBI operative, complained to the HUAC that "there are a couple of errors that had taken place previous where I had been pinpointed as a Communist. The hearings in 1952, at the time when I was pinpointed out by Roy Thompson, a guy which testified for the Bureau." Board member Willis consoled him with the thought that his accuser "was testifying truthfully." Mr. Poskonka replied:

"But at the same time my family and myself have been discriminated very badly and hurt, cut up to pieces because people pointed and thrown bricks and slapped me in the face and done everything imaginable because the neighborhood I lived, there are no Communists and they can't stand a Communist."

It came as no surprise to Mr. Willis that an exposed person and his family are the targets of thrown bricks, slaps and "everything imaginable." "That is always the case," he noted. The witness then complained that he got another dose four years later: "Just a minute. Also in 1956, the same thing, the kid was going to school, was pointed out; and I was coming home from church. People out of the church would come out and say, 'Here goes a Communist.'"

HUAC praises the contributions of the informer, "Your contribution may be as great as that of a division in the Army," Congressman Walter tersely puts it (Gary, 1958). A characteristic tribute is General Kearney's (New England, 1958),

> Let me tell you something if I may. You are going to be called names by these people, but pay no attention to these Fifth Amendment Americans. They are no good. They will call you an informer, they will call you a two-timer, they will call you every name in the book, and we know all those names. But let me tell you now that you can walk out of this hearing room with your head held high. You are a credit and thank you.

As the hearing draws to a conclusion, the Committee congratulates itself on the valuable information it has acquired. At some point in these windup ceremonies there is a lecture about the Menace—its chameleon-like forms, its unceasing perfidies and constant growth. A quotation from J. Edgar Hoover frequently crowns this recital.

So ends the revels—as true a flowering of our anti-Communist frenzy as the Inquisition was of the Middle Ages' dark superstitions. This institutionalized latter-day inquisition makes a conventional criminal trial look like a tea party. It has something of the crushing quality of a 17th-century state trial in which a lone, unprotected individual, foredoomed and prejudged, confronts his all-powerful adversaries sitting in judgment upon him. As in the case of many state trials, guilt is assumed: the prerogatives of power overwhelm the requirements of proof. A committee of Congress insists that the witness is subversive—shouldn't that be enough for anyone? Those who reserve judgment are regarded as accomplices—fit subjects for future exposure.

One observer has characterized the Committee's hearings as a "Roman Coliseum spectacle with Arens and the committee members playing the parts of the hungry lions." An English jurist, after observing a number of hearings, commented that for all the world they resemble some sort of military inquisition in which Arens and the Committee —temporarily in mufti—examine enemy prisoners, crow over their capture, and abuse them, but don't quite know how to proceed further. "If those chaps had a more literate script and the right costumes," he added, "they might film the hearings as a sequence in a war movie."

The ordeal of the unfriendly witness by no means ends with the hearing. He must now fight for his job—if he hasn't already lost it. If he is a public employee (a teacher or a civil servant), he is almost certain to be fired. If he works in a private welfare agency, a foundation, a university, his prospects are also dim—although they are improving. If the witness works for a large corporation, he can be discharged on the ground that he is a "security risk" or that his testimony has imperiled his employer's qualification for defense work, has diminished public confidence in the corporation's loyalty, disturbed the stockholders and demoralized his fellow workers. If the employer is a small businessman, a ground for discharge is that the establishment cannot stand the publicity. An unfriendly witness who is an actor, a screen writer or director becomes fatally "controversial." If he is a doctor, dentist or lawyer, his practice suffers.

The unfriendly witness may be forced to dig a cold-war foxhole for himself—become a day laborer (if the union will give him a card), buy a launderette or an antique shop, sell storm windows, printing or encyclopedias, rent a stall in a farmers' market. He may be a gifted mathematician like Chandler Davis, or Lee Lorch; a promising psychologist like Lloyd Barenblatt; or an established radio figure like Louis Hartman—his exposure endangers his career. He may be forced to sell a prosperous business like Rose Anderson's Washington Investment Pharmacy, or Max Shlafrock's Florida contracting business. (Shlafrock had built the addition to the structure in which HUAC's Miami hearings were conducted. When he became an unfriendly witness, an ordinance was passed to revoke his contracting license. The structures he had built were checked for sabotage. He had to leave town.) Exposure may exile him to Mexico, Canada or Europe to practice his art or profession. He may be forced to conceal or change his identity, or sell his skills or services on the black market.

If he loses one job, he may be hounded out of the next, like Lloyd Barenblatt, who lost four jobs because he resisted the Committee, or Jean Schudakopf, an unfriendly witness who was first fired from a teaching post and then from a social worker's job because the agency appropriation from the United Fund was threatened if she were retained.

The unfriendly witness must struggle not only for his livelihood, but for his mental balance and dignity. The damage to his emotional and personality structure is enormous; exposure is a wound that festers. The exposure victim is frequently overwhelmed by anxiety and depression. He considers himself a pariah. An unfriendly witness may acquire a deep self-contempt: he comes to accept the judgment of his accusers that he is subversive. A great many unfriendly witnesses cut themselves off from all forms of social action out of a fear either that they may be subpoenaed again or that their presence may invite attack on an organization or movement. They shun new friendships because of the harm they may bring to others. To them the exposure experience is a hair shirt which they must wear all of their lives.

The Committee wants the exposure to be as penetrating and permanent in its consequences as possible. It exerts continuing pressures to force discharge. After the University of Illinois voted to reinstate unfriendly witness Edward Yellin to his teaching post, Walter pointedly wrote to the University for a transcript of the proceedings. If the exposure doesn't take—or if the victim gets another job—the Committee may expose him all over again in a new proceeding.

To preserve the impact of the exposure, the witness' testimony is printed. The hearing is also indexed with the witness' name.

When the Committee publishes the annual report, it again lists all of the witnesses in the body of the report and in the index. These annual reports are widely circulated among Network members. Current reports squeeze out less than a hundred names. This is quite a comedown from the thousand-name years of 1952 and 1953. If the witness has particularly aroused the ire of the Committee, a Committee member may see to it that his name is again mentioned in a speech on the floor of Congress.

Finally, the witness' name is entered in the Committee's huge file and is printed in the next edition of its cumulative index—a permanent condemnation of his loyalty to dog him for the rest of his life. How many criminal punishments are as severe as this?

6   THE RIGHTS OF THE WITNESS

While there are a growing number of Americans who are concerned with HUAC's usurpation of law-enforcement powers, there are many more who condemn its procedural abuses. A host of the Committee's critics are ready to take at face value its assertions of legislative purpose. But they still sense that the witness is no different from a defendant in a criminal case.

Violation of the constitutional requirements of separation of powers is a concern of courts and legal scholars— but everybody who reads the newspapers, looks at television or goes to the movies knows about the rights of a criminal defendant. These critics say, in effect, to the Committee, "We do not challenge your claim to be acting legislatively—we know nothing about that. However, we insist that before you punish the witness as you do, you give him a fair trial. You can't have your cake and eat it too." This concern for the rights of the individual is deeply embedded in our folkways. We care less about where power is located than we do about how it is used—or abused. It was not primarily McCarthy's betrayal of his legislative responsibilities but his "methods" which undid him.

Thus, the demand has mounted that even one accused of Communism is entitled, before he suffers the very real punishment imposed by the Committee, to all of the procedural rights of a criminal defendant. These include indictment by a grand jury (or its Committee equivalent, a secret hearing); or the right to be informed in advance of the nature of the charges; the right to cross-examine the accusing witness; the right to compulsory process for obtaining defense witnesses; the presentation of evidence; the right to be represented by counsel; the right of the witness to testify in his own defense; and the right not to be exposed twice for the same reason (double jeopardy).

The Committee affords the witness none of these rights as they are conventionally understood and enjoyed. And, indeed, it cannot do so without admitting the truth: that it is exercising law-enforcement functions. Thus, as its procedural abuses mount, it renews its insistence that a legislative committee is not required to afford a witness from whom it only seeks facts the procedural rights of a criminal defendant. (When in the course of the 1955 Newark hearings a pilloried witness demanded the right of cross-examination, Chairman Walter replied: "There are no accusers here. This is a Congressional inquiry. This lady is not charged with any offense. This is in no sense of the word a trial and there are no witnesses against this witness at all. We are merely asking this lady some questions.")

But HUAC's justification for its procedural abuses is simply an extension of the same fraud by which its exposure operation is masked as a legislative investigation.

The most illuminating analysis of the procedural shortcomings of an exposure-type hearing is that of William T. Gossett, vice-president and general counsel of the Ford Motor Company:

Congressional investigations which are launched for

the purpose of inquiring into questions of personal conduct, closely resemble the inquisitorial functions of our grand juries. As all lawyers know, in any investigation or grand jury proceeding, it is inevitable that many fruitless lines of inquiry will be undertaken. And so some false leads must be pursued. The inviolate rule of secrecy in a grand jury proceeding is predicated upon the urgent necessity of protecting the good name of the many innocent persons who must be questioned and who, through no fault of their own, might be under suspicion before a determination is made as to which, if any, of those under investigation will be subjected to indictment or other action.

But no such protection is accorded to those who are so unfortunate as to be required to testify before many of our Congressional committees. Not only are witnesses interrogated in public, but they are denied basic constitutional safeguards which in a court proceeding are granted as a matter of right, even to one who, after investigation, has been accused of a crime. The constitutional safeguards to which I refer, of course, are the rights of the accused to be informed in advance of the nature of the charges against him; his right to be confronted with the witnesses who testify against him, and to submit them to cross-examination; his right to compulsory process for obtaining witnesses in his favor; his right to be represented by counsel; and his right to testify then and there in his own defense.

Congressional investigations which delve into matters of personal conduct assume the aspects of a trial and thus abridge the rights of individuals, guaranteed by the Constitution. And there have been cases in which, as a result of the publicity of committee hearings, witnesses have been exposed to such penalties as dismissal from their jobs, loss of pension payments, character assassinations and injury to their reputations.

• • • •

The practices of investigating committees thus are without proper standards. Persons are now subpoenaed before such committees and afforded no right to counsel. Although they often are subjected to the most searching cross-examination themselves, they are denied the right to cross-examine those who testify against them. If they are so-called hostile witnesses, they often are not even accorded the right to make a statement—prepared or otherwise; and if the behavior of the witness is such as not to please the committee or some of its members, he can be summarily punished.

Some committee members seemingly have viewed the committee as a final court of justice sitting in judgment on the conduct of individuals appearing before the committee. Thus they usurp the judicial function. On the other hand, committee members can and do slander witnesses with impunity, secure in the knowledge that there can be no retaliation in court.

. . . .

In such an inquiry there is no assumption that the individual is innocent until proved guilty. There are none of the safeguards of a trial to which, by the Constitution and the law, each man is entitled. Instead, there is a type of trial by public opinion, a pillorying of individuals not accused of crimes—of individuals only suspected of being engaged in or knowing something about some improper activity. And the rules are the same whether the witness is innocent or guilty.

Elmer Davis has trenchantly written on the subject of double jeopardy and exposure:

The Founding Fathers wrote it in the Bill of Rights that no person shall be subject, for the same offense, to be twice put in jeopardy of life or limb—and thought that they had taken care of that. If a man was acquitted in court, that ended it. They did not foresee that congressional committees would take over a considerable part of the judicial process, and would hold that they are not bound by the limitation which the Constitution imposes on judicial agencies. Technically this contention is no doubt correct, since a hearing before a congressional committee does not put a man in jeopardy of life or limb. The only penalty he can suffer, ordinarily, from congressional condemnation, unless he is foolish enough to perjure himself, is the loss of his reputation and standing in the community—a deprivation which the average senator or representative seems to regard as trivial, at least when it happens to somebody else. The victim may also of course suffer the loss of an opportunity to make a living, at any occupation that he knows; but the Constitution says nothing about that.

In any case, Congress seems to have established the principle that no man is ever acquitted, so long as a single influential member of either House is out to get him. If a committee—or three or four committees— have investigated him and found him innocent, that only means that they keep on setting up hearings before other committees, until they have found one that will pronounce him guilty. Double jeopardy has been ruled out in the courts; but before Congress any man may be in multiple and perpetual jeopardy for the same offense, actual or only unconvincingly alleged.

Even if the Committee's procedures were tested by the standards which it insists are appropriate—those of a legislative investigating committee—they would earn very poor marks for fairness. Indeed, HUAC's conduct of the hearing flouts the essential precondition of fairness—equality of treatment.

The Committee treats friendly and unfriendly witnesses in sharply contrasting ways. The friendly witness is greeted with warmth and respect. He is encouraged to testify at length and the Committee is gratified to hear his opinion on every subject. He is assisted in his testimony by a series of leading questions. He is invited to make charges and cast aspersions on others. His answers to questions may be rambling irrelevant or stupid—but they are always welcomed and lavishly praised.

In the 1953 hearing of Reverend Jack R. McMichael, the Committee left no stone unturned in its brutal drive to ruin him. It refused to permit him to explain his answers, put words in his mouth, and used highly questionable evidence against him. But it showed an extraordinary tenderness toward Reverend McMichael's accusers, a husband and wife team of FBI agents.

Mrs. Edmiston: Sir, may I point out——

Mr. Velde: I am sorry, Mrs. Edmiston; there is no question pending.

Mrs. Edmiston: Oh.

Mr. Velde: Not because we don't want to hear what you have to say——

Mr. Scherer: May I ask a question?

Mr. Velde: but because of the regular rules——

Mr. Scherer: May I ask a question?

Mr. Velde: Yes.

Mr. Scherer: What were you going to say, Mrs. Edmiston?

Mrs. Edmiston then explained that in her and her husband's present testimony, their affidavit and their previous testimony before the Committee in 1950, they could not "say that we sat with Mr. McMichael in any closed Communist meeting where party action was taken, nor were we put on assignment with him by a party superior as a Communist Party member, nor was he identified to us as a Communist Party member, . . . but our question then—and it has been to the groups of people we have talked to since—is: Who is doing the most damage, the Communist Party member who rolls the poison pill or the person, who, under the guise of religion, shoves it down our throats?"

After this volunteered testimony she apologized disarmingly: "I'm sorry—it's a bit of editorializing there."

The unfriendly witness, on the other hand, is stringently limited in his answers to the precise information sought. If he tries to defend himself, he is invariably charged with "making a speech" or "using the hearing as a forum." Of course, Arens, the friendly witness, and the Committee members make speeches and use the hearing as a forum to destroy the witness from the moment the hearing begins to its close. But that is another matter.

The unfriendly witness is compelled to give a yes or no answer to questions which cannot be answered in this fashion. He is forced to sit in silence while the Committee members abuse him; when he tries to defend himself, he is told, "There is no question pending." The prepared script by which the hearing is conducted contains no lines for him except those of collaboraton in his own exposure. If he manages to smuggle into the record some statement in his defense, he is hurriedly cut off. A favorite technique is to blackmail the witness into silence with the threat that persistence will result in unleashing Arens. In the 1959 Chicago hearings, a witness was falsely accused of Communist Party membership. After receiving the right to make a statement at the conclusion of his examination, he was cut off with this comment by Congressman Willis: "I would not enter that field if I were you. It will not do you any good and counsel will perhaps have to re-examine you, and if I were you I would not pursue that." And often, when adverse testimony does get a chance to be stated, it may simply disappear from the printed record.

The Committee has never troubled to justify its double procedural standard. In fact, it complains that it is limited by procedural requirements "which when formulated were meant to apply only to law-abiding citizens of this country." The Committee regards procedural protections as something to be granted or withheld at its own discretion. As Chairman Thomas put it, "The rights you have are the rights given you by this Committee. We will determine what rights you have and what rights you have not got before the Committee." The Committee regards it as only fair for it to promise the witness protection on condition that he cooperate. As HUAC once soothingly put it, "This Committee has no desire to persecute anyone, certainly not those who see fit to cooperate with the Committee." A witness who refuses to cooperate and still insists on such protections as the right of cross-examination is merely using the "Commie line." HUAC is hardly troubled by the fact that only uncooperative witnesses need protection.

Each witness receives a copy of the Committee's rules. The Committee regularly flaunts them as though they were a Magna Carta for the witness. Actually they are framed and interpreted to make things as easy as possible to carry on the exposure operation. They, too, are a deception.

There are 17 rules. Of these only four (advice of counsel, executive hearings, statement by witness and relationship of husband and wife) have any meaningful significance. But the Committee treats them all, not as protections of the witness, but as a means of harassing him.

Rule IX permits the witness to file a statement with the Committee, provided it is in writing and submitted 24 hours in advance. This is supposed to substitute for any oral comment the witness may care to make in his own defense at the hearing. Usually, even when a written statement is filed by an unfriendly witness, the Committee rejects it as an attack on the Committee. Sometimes it promises to incorporate a statement in the record if the witness will be cooperative. It has, on occasion, withdrawn previously granted permission to read a statement because the witness' testimony was too uncooperative. Of course if the witness cooperates from the outset, he can file any statement he pleases.

> Mr. Pressman: I believe my statement, which will be very brief, will answer the question, as well as indicate precisely what my position will be before the Committee today.
>
> Mr. Wood: Then will you be prepared to answer questions asked you?
>
> Mr. Pressman: That is correct.
>
> Mr. Wood: Proceed.

Like every "right" given a witness, the right to file a statement is merely another device to help his exposure. Congressman Scherer startled his colleagues and the witness at a hearing in Detroit in 1956 by moving for admission into the record of a statement filed by a witness who had declined to answer certain questions on Fifth Amendment grounds.

> Mr. Scherer: Now, madam, you can't possibly refuse to answer that question on any constitutional grounds.
>
> At your insistence, this statement of yours has been admitted to the record. And you tell us in here that you are under an order of deportation and a lot of other things.
>
> Now I have a right then to certainly ask you with reference to statements you have voluntarily submitted to this Committee. And if you refuse to answer those questions of mine on any grounds, I assure you that you are in contempt of this Committee. And I, for one, will recommend and move that the Committee cite you for contempt of the Congress because it is obvious you are in contempt.

Rule VII gives the witness the right to counsel. But—and it is a very large "but"—counsel can only advise his client and cannot speak for him. Counsel cannot address the Committee directly or try to persuade it that it is proceeding improperly against his client. The only lawyer the

Committee likes is a silent lawyer. The impact of this limitation is nightmarish. When his cilent is abused and vilified by the Committee, the attorney is gagged. An attorney seeks to protest Arens' rudeness to his client: "Mr. Chairman I ask that counsel be admonished to exhibit courtesy to the witness."

> Mr. Arens: I suggest counsel be admonished that if we have one more outburst he will be forcibly ejected from this room. . . .
> Counsel was ejected.

The frustrations which beset counsel in a hearing are well illustrated in the following colloquy:

> Mrs. Hart: May I make a statement on behalf of the witness?
> Mr. Doyle: No; I am sorry.
> Mrs. Hart: If the court please——
> Mr. Arens: Your sole and specific prerogaitve under the rules of the Committee is to advise the witness.
> Mrs. Hart: I can speak almost as loud as you can. I know what the rules are.
> Mr. Arens: You know you are in violation of the rules of the Committee when you address the Chairman of the Committee except to——
> Mrs. Hart: This is still the United States of America. I am going to ask the Chairman if I may address the Chairman. If he says "No," I won't.
> Mr. Doyle: Counsel, we do not permit counsel to get into discussion and get into argument with the Committee. I read the rules, and insist on all counsel complying with the rule of the Committee which limits you to talk to your client and not to the Committee.
> Mrs. Hart: That makes it very difficult, Mr. Chairman.
> Mr. Doyle: We are both lawyers, and we realize that you have the privilege to address your client on constitutional rights. We are glad to have you here for that purpose.
> Mrs. Hart: I am here as a matter of right, not as a matter of privilege, Mr. Chairman.
> Mr. Scherer: No, you are here on a matter of privilege.

The Committee tries in every way to strip the right to counsel of all effectiveness. A witness who appears without counsel is praised for having "come here without benefit of counsel to whisper in his ear the answers that he should give to the Committee. I think it is very commendable." The Committee has each consultation with an attorney noted in the record. These notations do not contribute to the Committee's store of information and are only made to discredit answers given after such consultation.

The Committee will count the number of times the witness consults with counsel and impatiently tell the witness that he doesn't need advice. A witness who answers after consultation is frequently charged with being coached—especially if the answer is unwelcome to the Committee.

> Your counsel has just told you that. Now I ask you is your answer you just gave the result of your conference with counsel? Or is it your own independent opinion?

Witnesses are asked, "What did your counsel advise you?" "I want to find out whether your lawyer told you that the Chairman's question was pertinent." "Did your lawyer tell you that the Chairman's question was pertinent or not pertinent?"

When counsel objects to the charge that he is coaching witness, he is admonished that he is forbidden to address the Committee and that "one more outburst like that" will result in his forcible ejection from the room.

The Committee has inevitably turned the exposure weapon against those lawyers who have fought hardest to protect their clients from its efforts. In February of 1960, the Committee issued a report, *Communist Legal Subversion,* charging an "elite corps" of "Communist lawyers" with everything from misbehavior before the Committee to espionage. This report followed an earlier charge by Congressman Walter that certain lawyers were a part of a subversive plot to persuade their clients not to cooperate with the Committee.

In the 1956 Youngstown hearings, Stephan Young (now Senator and formerly a member of the House) represented a witness who was denounced by Congressman Velde as "a very dangerous character." He added, "I am very sorry that the witness happened to be represented by a former colleague of ours. . . ." Young snapped back that ". . . all persons accused have a right to be represented by counsel. . . . I repudiate any assertion attacking my Americanism and my patriotism."

In a great many hearings the witness is asked whether the Communist Party supplied his lawyer: "How did you contact your counsel?" "How long have you known your counsel?" "Do you know your counsel in any capacity other than the capacity of attorney and client?" "Tell us all the capacities you have known him in since the first capacity in which you knew him." "Do you or have you ever known your attorney as a Communist?"

In the 1956 Youngstown hearings, the Committee, without any information to support its questions, tried to make it appear that there was a subversive relationship between counsel and client by asking the witness: "Was your counsel assigned to you by persons known by you to be members of the Communist Party?" When the witness pleaded the Fifth Amendment, Mr. Velde—apparently embarrassed by the questioning—hastened to add that these questions by Arens in no way implied criticism of counsel. But Arens wasn't so sure:

> There has been no suggestion on the part of the Committee that we have any information respecting the activities of counsel. But it certainly, it seems to me, would raise a query in the minds of any listener to this testimony for counsel to sit by a witness and permit her or advise her . . . to invoke the Fifth Amendment with reference to any relationship she may have had with counsel.

According to Arens, counsel should have drawn an inference of his own guilt from his client's plea of the Fifth Amendment and interrupted her testimony to "protect himself from this inference," even though there is no evidence that the lawyer advised the client to plead the privilege in response to this question. This is outrageous. No inference of guilt can properly be drawn from the Fifth Amendment plea: if counsel had intervened to prevent the plea, he could have discredited his client's use of the plea in response to other questions. Besides, he would have been rebuked by the Committee for coaching the witness. And, of course, if he had remonstrated against Arens' attack, he would have been rebuked for violating the rules and "making a speech." It is hardly surprising that this incident led the Civil Liberties Committee of the Cuyahoga Bar Association unanimously to recommend the censure of both Velde and Arens.

In the same Youngstown hearings, a lawyer briefly objected when his client was asked whether she had ever "served the Communist Party with him." Arens answered, "Counsel will have an opportunity to be sworn in a little while. We want you to be just as vociferous, to be just as fluid, and talk just as forthrightly in a few moments when you are under oath as you do now when you are not under oath." Counsel was then called to the stand and asked whether the client who had just testified was a Communist and whether his representation of this and other clients was at the direction of the Communist Party.

In the 1956 Los Angeles hearings, Arens' lawyer-baiting reached its climax. His tactics were censured in a historic statement of condemnation by the California State Bar in March 1957. The bar's board of governors concluded after reading the transcript and hearing the tapes of the sessions that "the proceedings of the Committee and the conduct of the Committee's counsel" were "improper" and lacking in "dignity and impartiality"; that they were characterized by "grossly offensive" tactics "directed at counsel for witnesses" and that they posed a threat to the right to counsel and the independence of the bar. The board of governors pointed out that lawyers were gagged and repeatedly told that they could not address the Committee. Arens was singled out for asking several witnesses whether they knew as a Communist one of the lawyers, despite the fact that the Committee had not intended to call or interrogate him. Arens, the statement points out, interrupted a witness in order to inject testimony of an informer to the effect that he knew the lawyer for another witness as a Communist. He thereafter referred to this lawyer as "Comrade." The governors also censured the bodily ejection of four lawyers from the hearing room, solely because they tried to protect their clients by appropriate objections.

Another witness protection which, like the right to counsel, is handled by the Committee in strange ways is the executive session. Such sessions of Congressional committees, where witnesses are sworn and a record made in private for the use only of the committee, is essential in situations where damage may be done to the reputation of the witness and others. Since the Committee wants to damage the reputation of its witnesses, the reader may well be puzzled as to how this protection of the witness against the public invasion of his privacy fits into the exposure system.

The Committee's executive session is really a parody of the conventional legislative executive session ingeniously adapted to the Committee's main task of destroying the unfriendly witness. Thus, the executive session is used to coach and rehearse the friendly witness and to shape his testimony for the most headlines. It is also a means of determining in advance whether a witness will be unfriendly, and which questions he will answer and which he will not, thus offering the Committee an opportunity to ask the most damaging questions in open session. Since, as we have seen, the Committee likes to expose the witness by asking "loaded" questions which it knows he will not answer, a dry run is useful. Similarly, the private session is a means of accumulating a reservoir of testimony so that the Committee can draft a script for the public hearing—sequence of witnesses, confrontation, etc.—for a maximum total impact.

Witnesses who fear public exposure and loss of jobs sometimes apply to the Committee for an executive session. These requests are usually denied unless the witness agrees to name names, or unless the Committee's exposure purposes will be better served by privacy. The Committee feels that the individual who seeks the cooperation of the Committee must himself cooperate. Indeed, the Committee has a standing offer to hear a witness in executive session if he will give it names. There are attorneys who specialize in arranging such sessions; Congressmen also collaborate with the Committee thus to ease the burden of subpoenaed constituents.

HUAC's explanation of this interpretation of its rule is revealing in its simplicity. Rule IV-A provides that a majority may grant an executive session if it believes that a public hearing of the witness might "unjustly injure his reputation. . . ." The Committee does not think that to expose publicly an individual identified as a Communist who refuses to inform is an "unjust" injury to his reputation.

But the inducement to name names in executive session

on the premise that the named individual will thus be spared exposure is deceptive to the witness. Those whom he names are not only subpoenaed; the testimony of their accuser is quoted and the accuser himself identified by name when they are exposed. After the event, the witness frequently realizes in bitterness and humiliation that the executive session was used to gull him into betrayal and injury of others.

The executive session also permits the friendly witness to shield those whose political involvement does not, in his view, warrant exposure:

> Mr. Arens: Do you have other names that you want to give the Committee in executive session?
>
> Witness: Yes. There are names of several people that I know beyond a shadow of a doubt to have turned against the Party. Many of them entered the Party at my urging and I feel sort of personally responsible for them. I know them to be anti-Party and to have nothing to do with it in any way, shape or form, and I would not want to mention their names in a public hearing.

The same witness referred to students in classes that he taught, whom he influenced to join the Party, as "mixed up and confused." Arens asked, "Are you going to give the Committee the names of those students in executive session?" The witness agrees, "I would never want to mention names like that in open session where they could be kicked around. I think they had better all live it down and forget about it."

HUAC cannot afford to acknowledge that the fear of exposure or the shame of informing drives witnesses into executive session. It has devised the fiction that political coercion or fear of Red vengeance compels the witness to refuse to cooperate. In its view the executive session is a sort of sanctuary which protects the witness from subversive pressures against cooperating. Having helped the witness thwart the Reds, its responsibilities are ended.

As a routine matter, HUAC leaks executive-session testimony to the press as well as to interested individuals who may help in the exposure process. Of this practice an American Bar Association Committee has said, "The most insidious misuse of the executive session has been to take testimony in private and thus elicit matters which the witness might only have been willing to disclose there, followed by the leaking of this supposedly secret testimony to the press." These leaks frequently misrepresent what actually took place in the executive session, but there is no way of checking the Committee's version of what occurred against the record until long after the Committee's version is released. In some instances the Committee holds up release of executive-session testimony for years.

But it must not be thought that the hostile executive-session witness is exposed only by publication of his private testimony. When the Committee learns in executive session that the witness will refuse to answer questions, it promptly summons him to a public session for a repeat performance. If he remonstrates against this exposure maneuver, he is overruled on the incomprehensible ground that "the executive session was taken as a matter of protection to the witness." When the witness declines to answer "on the same grounds relied upon in answers in executive session," he is directed to spell out his grounds.

The executive session is also used as an aid in the investigative process—almost precisely like a police inquiry into the commission of a crime. For example, in 1957 and 1958 the Committee questioned 13 former Government employees in executive session regarding their alleged involvement in a spy ring. No evidence was turned up, but the Committee nevertheless released and printed the testimony.

The Committee rules erect another dubiously protective bulwark: the confidential relationship of husband and wife is to be respected and "one spouse shall not be asked about the activities of another." This is based, the Committee piously tells us, on "reasons of public policy." But the Committee does ask one spouse about another. (Your husband was convicted for violating the Smith Act?") When the witness protests against this, the Committee points to a clause which cancels this rule "when a majority . . . shall determine otherwise." How fragile are "reasons of public policy"!

Even the protections which the Supreme Court has granted to the witness are used to expose him. The court ruled in the *Watkins* case that a witness who was in the dark about the purpose of the hearing or the pertinence of the question had a right to be enlightened by the Committee. When a witness seeks enlightenment, he is assaulted by one of Mr. Arens' highly prejudicial explanations, freighted with seditious rhetoric to stoke the exposure fires.

The short of the matter is that the most meaningful procedural protections (notice of charges, confrontation, cross-examination) are withheld from the witness. Even the puny concessions that are formally granted him are turned against him.

It is quite true that Congressional investigating procedure is generally not lavish in its concern for the witness and his rights.

But where the probe is of a hostile character, the witness is sometimes granted the rights of confrontation and cross-examination and is frequently permitted to submit written interrogations to the examiner. In addition, the bona fide investigation is held in check by the minority members of the probe. A subpoenaed witness can try to blunt the attack through the intercession of a sympathetic Congressman or Senator. If the investigator unduly harasses the witness, the press may attack; public sympathy for the victim may defeat the ends of the investigation.

But none of these restraints moderate the assault on HUAC's victims. The hostility to the witness is bi-partisan. No Congressman or Senator could be induced to shield the unfriendly witness. The Committee's procedural barbarism is largely unchallenged by the press and while there is much public criticism of its abuses, this hardly matches in volume the chorus of support.

The most important difference in the treatment of witnesses between a bona fide investigation and HUAC's is, of course, the exposure system. An ordinary probe is disciplined by the needs of the legislative process, but HUAC wields its powers with fanatic zeal against the witness in complete disregard of the legislative process and its needs.

The logic of the exposure system leaves no room for procedural fairness. It simply does not make sense to the Committee to grant the witness, whom it is trying so hard to ruin, the opportunity to defend himself and thus to spoil everything. They must unremittingly show its hostility to the witness. A fair hearing would confuse the community and possibly enable the witness to prevent hostile local action against him.

7 FRIENDLY HEROES AND UNFRIENDLY VILLAINS

The long train of HUAC hearings when reviewed retrospectively give the flavor of a hardy theatrical vehicle—a plot simple but rousing, a dauntless hero (the friendly witness), and a stock villain (unfriendly witness) at whom the fanatically loyal audience can always be counted on to hiss when properly aroused. There is even a claque to stir things up a bit when they get too dull. True, the performances tend to lose their freshness with the passing years and require more and more "business" and "gags" to stimulate excitement. But where in all the history of parliamentary government can one find a run to match it?

It is time to go backstage to meet the principals and to learn about the mechanics of this extraordinary dramatic production.

A Voice: The friendly witness has a few names he hasn't put in.

Second Voice: Why don't you tell him to put them in executive session and give him a trip to Washington?

The first voice in this exchange is that of Committee member Edwin A. Willis. The second is that of Committee member Gordon Scherer. Both voices were picked up by tape-recorder microphones of Station KPFA of Berkeley, California, on Saturday, May 14, 1960, at the conclusion of the Committee hearings in San Francisco which gave rise to student demonstrations. "The friendly witness" was Karl Prussion, an FBI informer planted in the Communist ranks who had, in the course of the three-day session, named 40 individuals as Communists or former Communists.

A grateful Committee did not let Prussion down. He got his "trip to Washington," where he shook the last few apples from the top branches of the tree. This testimony, with its additional harvest of names, was duly released along with the record of the earlier hearings.

A trip to Washington is a small price for the Committee to pay for a list of names. The Committee's capacity to function depends on the availability of names—the raw material of the exposure process.

A witness may be "friendly" and offer the Committee no factual information at all; he may be unfriendly and still offer a storehouse of information. The test of a witness' friendliness is his readiness (1) to answer the question, "Are you now or have you ever been a member of the Communist Party?"—enshrined in the jurisprudence of exposure as the "$64 question"—and (2) to act as an informer by naming others. If the witness is willing to admit present or former membership in the Communist Party but to go no further, he cannot escape the Committee's disapproval (and contempt citation) as an unfriendly witness. There are a few witnesses who answer the "$64 question" in the negative and are therefore not asked the second question, and there are some who are asked only about their membership in organizations suspected of being "fronts."

Friendliness and unfriendliness are descriptions not merely of testimonial behavior, but of loyalty. A friendly witness is a hero whose patriotism is certified by his cooperativeness; an unfriendly witness has the status of a subversive—until he becomes friendly.

There are two kinds of friendly witnesses; the paid undercover agent who has been planted by the FBI in the Communist ranks, and the ex-Communist—the defector or renegade. HUAC's primary target is suspected concealed Communists or ex-Communists. Informers are needed to "ferret them out," to use a favorite term of the Committee. The Committee hearing is an engine which is powered by a fuel blended of betrayal and revenge.

The typical prehearing staff work consists of conferences with the friendly witnesses to check the list of names. The names are examined not merely to determine which ones are to be subpoenaed as unfriendly witnesses; the informer may also know of possible friendly witnesses on the list: the inactive, the disillusioned, the doubting. The likely prospects are interviewed. If they talk, new names are placed on the friendly list and new prospects added, to be caressed or coerced into friendliness.

Certain names are selected from the lists to be subpoenaed; the rest will be named at the hearing and saved up for future subpoenas. For example, of the 40 San Francisco Bay area residents named by Mr. Prussion, only six were subpoenaed. The others—according to both Prussion and the Committee—will be subpoenaed on the Committee's next (already promised) trip to San Francisco.

A witness may sit on the fence at the time the subpoena is served, but the continuing pressure of the subpoena—the fear and the anxiety which it creates—sometimes brings him into line. Quite frequently the subpoenas are announced in advance and employment discharges result or are threatened. The victim may run to the Committee's door in order to square himself with his employer.

The friendly sheep are not wholly separated from the unfriendly goats until the hearing is over. There may be a straggler, a witness who has previously withheld his cooperation or been marked down by the staff as a recalcitrant who cracks at the hearing and turns friendly.

But surprises are extraordinarily rare. The Committee almost always knows in advance which witnesses will be friendly. Besides, the Committee's subpoena invites the witness to get in touch with HUAC's staff director (his telephone number is printed on the subpoena) if he desires to cooperate. Indeed, Chairman Walter has admitted that the Committee knows that a witness will be unfriendly by the identity of the lawyers representing him. The acid test of friendliness is an appearance without a lawyer; a great many friendly witnesses have no counsel.

The Committee's staff could, of course, interview the presumptively unfriendly witnesses and save time. A bona fide investigating committee might have doubts about calling witnesses knowing that they would not be helpful. But HUAC cherishes them; they are precisely the ones who must be exposed.

The HUAC practice of deliberately calling silent witnesses is built into the exposure system. At every hearing, there are many more unfriendly witnesses than friendly ones. In the 84th Congress (1955-1956), the Committee called a total of 529 witnesses. Of these, 464 were unfriendly and gave the Committee no information. The remainder were either Government officials (15), former

FBI agents (22), or persons who had left the Communist Party (28). In the 85th Congress (1957-1958), of a total of 402 witnesses, 331 were unfriendly, silent witnesses. The friendly witnesses included 11 former undercover agents and 18 ex-Communists.

The quantitative preponderance of the silent witnesses is apparent from almost every hearing. In the Committee's 1958 Atlanta hearings, there were 16 witnesses (not counting the Governor of Georgia, who welcomed the Committee). Of these 16, 13 refused to give the Committee any information. The three remaining witnesses were a former FBI agent, a customs official and a Hungarian refugee.

In September 1956, the Committee held hearings for three days in New Haven and made a record of almost 200 printed pages. It heard from 16 witnesses. Of these only four were friendly witnesses; two of these witnesses— Worden C. Mosher and Harold Mosher, a father-and-son team—were FBI plants; the other two, Harold Kent and Rowena Paumi, were ex-Communists who rejoined the Party at the request of the FBI. The four friendly witnesses testified for about 25 pages, for the most part identifying their former associates. The remaining seven-eighths of the record consists of a familiar pattern of refusals to testify, and extended efforts by the Committee to put the witness in a bad light.

Undaunted by its earlier frustrations, the Committee returned to New Haven for another two days of hearings in February 1957. This time it heard from nine witnesses. One of them who had been identified as a Communist by Miss Paumi, a star witness in the earlier session, denied Party membership. Another witness, a committee investigator, testified as to certain technical matters. The remaining seven witnesses gave the Committee no information. One of these seven had been called in the earlier New Haven session and had refused to talk.

On November 16 and 17, 1959, the Committee held hearings in New York City on the subject of Communist activities among Puerto Ricans. It compiled a record of almost 100 printed pages, consisting of the contributions of 16 witnesses, of whom three were friendly: a State Department interpreter, a customs official, and an undercover agent for the New York City Police Department Red squad, Detective Mildred Blauvelt. The remaining "testimony," 67 pages long, is the usual composite of long prejudicial questions by the Committee and refusals to answer.

With unslaked thirst, the Committee renewed its hearings the next day, November 18, 1960, in San Juan, Puerto Rico. It opened its show with no less than three customs officials, who testified about the dissemination of Spanish-language subversive propaganda. During the rest of the three-day session it heard from 17 more witnesses. Of these, three were friendly: Detective Blauvelt, a staff investigator, and the United States Marshal who had served the Committee's subpoenas. The remaining 14 witnesses gave the Committee no information.

The value of the friendly witness to the Committee is measured by the number of names he can put on the hearing record. In 1950, Matthew Cvetic and Mary Markward, former FBI agents, blazed a trail when they identified hundreds of Party members and their wives. In 1951, screen-writer Martin Berkeley scored a record which still stands, for Hollywood, when he named 162 names.

In 1953, when an ex-Communist newspaperman on the West Coast named over 200 former associates, Representative Donald L. Jackson—an expert in these matters—hailed it "as one of the choicest crops of names the Committee has ever received." Friendly witnesses, especially the paid agents, rate their testimonial importance and effectiveness by their production of names. Even though the day of the testimonial giants—like Harvy Matusow (216), Mary Stalcup Markward (318), Matthew Cvetic (411), William Ward Kimple (1000)—is vanishing, still some friendly witnesses come forward with thickets of names which make their memories, at least, remarkable. One of the most friendly of the recent HUCA witnesses, Barbara Hartle, who was convicted under the Smith Act and recanted while serving her sentence, has ascended to the 400-name ranks.

In four days of testimony in 1955, Detective Mildred Blauvelt posted a score of 450 names. A more recent (1959) Committee star witness, Armand Penha, has achieved what seems to be the acme of friendliness. According to an interview with Penha which appeared in the *Providence Sunday Journal* for March 20, 1960, "By his own count, he named 482 persons as Communists."

The availability of a list of names is a precondition of holding a hearing. The pattern of the hearings in any particular area simply mirrors the emergence of new identifying witnesses with a fresh stock of names for that area.

In 1954, Barbara Hartle, the recanted Communist already referred to, provided the Committee with the sinews of a ten-part, 200-page hearing on "Communist Activities in the Pacific Northwest." The very next year the Committee held another lengthy hearing in the same area, not because it found new problems, but only because a previously unfriendly witness had become enthusiastically friendly. In December 1956, the Committee returned to Seattle for a third time and the exposure machinery was once again oiled by Miss Hartle.

Miss Hartle belongs to a small group of chronic witnesses who appear again and again on the HUAC witness stand. She has already testified four times. John Lautner has testified many times, as have Matthew Cvetic and the late Detective Mildred Blauvelt of New York City's Red squad. The chronic witnesses (Elmer Davis called them "six-shot repeating witnesses") are valuable to the Committee not only because of their remarkable memories. They have had long experience in the Communist movement and are more at home with theoretical concepts than the run-of-the-mill ex-Communist or FBI agent.

The potency of informers in triggering Committee hearings is well illustrated by a series of area hearings held by the Committee in 1956. After the Smith Act prosecutions of the fifties had "surfaced" a large number of FBI agents as witnesses, the Committee recruited them to give virtually the same testimony in a round of hearings in the same cities where the prosecutions had taken place. The new hearings were made necessary, the Committee explained, because the witnesses had names which were excluded by the rules of evidence from the earlier prosecutions. In other words, they would give information to the Committee which would not be permissible in the trial proceedings.

The Committee thus held hearings in St. Louis in 1956 because a group of FBI undercover agents, who had "surfaced" in 1954 to testify in a Smith Act trial, supplied it with hundreds of names.

There are undercover agents who have never publicly revealed their identity in a legal proceeding or in any other way. These men are turned over by the FBI to the Committee and surface as Committee witnesses. They are particularly desirable witnesses since they have never been sullied by cross-examination, nor is the image of their patriotism clouded by prior disclosures of their earnings in undercover work. Besides, the triumphant announcement by such witness that "only last night" he met with the unfriendly witnesses adds a bit of derring-do to the proceedings and is good for a headline.

Usually an appearance as a friendly witness ends the FBI agent's usefulness (and income). But there are consolations. After Armand Penha had made his testimonial debut for the Committee, he was put on the Committee payroll for "perhaps a year or so," according to the Committee.

The Committee explained that Penha had been engaged to assemble his notes. Other friendly witnesses have benefited from this kind of largesse. In 1957 and 1958, John Lautner, a friendly witness who had been expelled from the Communist Party in 1950, was retained as a consultant to the Committee. Elizabeth Bentley also had a berth on the payroll for a while.

Legislative investigations are *ad hoc* and discontinuous, the exception and not the rule. The Rivers and Harbors, or the Education and Labor Committees do not launch investigations without a substantial public need. And the need arises quite rarely. But HUAC's hunt for witnesses to expose is not occasional or sporadic—it is regular and continuous.

Indeed, the Committee *must,* at frequent intervals, exercise its investigative powers. This operational continuity is vital because politics are dynamic; the challenge of new ideas is never-ending and must be met sharply and promptly. The Committee must find *someone* to subpoena and expose because its activity—in no matter what particular area—is intended to serve a generally repressive purpose. In short, this is a beat which the cop can never leave.

Besides, the Committee has become the leader and coordinator of the ultrarightist forces in the Nation. A slackening in the exposure process might weaken these forces. The dynamics of its leadership role thus require that it exercise continuing pressure against movements of protest, of difference, or of opposition—otherwise it loses its effectiveness altogether. The Committee is an active power or it is nothing. The Committee regularly justifies its existence by the claim that the country is crawling with subversives. A retreat from exposure might well be suicidal—a confession that the need for the Committee's existence has ended. The Committee must expose or die.

To keep going as a tribunal of exposure, the Committee exercises its powers in a curiously exhaustive way. With *cherchez les noms* as its battle cry, the Committee summons housewives, preachers, butchers, bakers and candlestick makers. The Committee thinks nothing of traveling to Charlotte, New Haven, Chicago or Buffalo, putting a witness on the stand suspected of Party membership long ago, asking him one question and then dismissing him. *Everyone* suspected by the Committee must be exposed. This is the technique of a criminal court; for example, the New York Court of General Sessions tries and punishes every offender found guilty—not just some. Law enforcement deals with every "case"; but bona fide Congressional investigations deal only with examples of a problem or abuse. The responsibilities of Congress are too broad and its staff too limited to permit microscopic scrutiny of a field.

The inescapable fact is that the Committee makes more sense as a kind of criminal court than it does as a legislative investigating committee. Like a court, it operates directly and with finality upon individuals. It has the institutional homogeneity of a court; it has exercised its power in the same way under Republican (Thomas and Velde) and Democratic (Wood and Walter) leadership. It thinks of itself as a continuing institution; as early as 1949 it informed Congress that "its work is part of an 11-year continuity of effort . . . . at no time in those 11 years has it ever wavered from a relentless pursuit and exposure of the Communist fifth column." Only recently, in the course of a hearing, the Committee took occasion to comment with satisfaction upon the fact that it was exposing the now grownup children of individuals who had been exposed in the forties and subsequently jailed and blacklisted.

The imperative need to maintain continuity forces the Committee to recall already exposed unfriendly witnesses. The practice has become increasingly common. Leon

Beverly and Francis W. McBain, two trade unionists, were called in 1952 and recalled in 1957; Elliott Sullivan, an actor, was called twice in a two-week period in the summer of 1955 and asked the same exposure questions. Hunter Pitts Odell testified as an unfriendly witness at the New Orleans hearing in 1958 and again at the Youth Festival hearings in 1960. In the 1957 Baltimore hearings, the Committee called nine witnesses who had previously been unfriendly in a 1951 hearing.

The Committee's name hunt drives it further and further into the past—when the Party's membership was far more numerous than it is today. The Committee is indifferent to how old or rusty its victims' ties with the Party might be. Although a man's past politics are a treacherous guide to his present views, for the Committee the more things change politically, the more they remain the same investigatively. The political enthusiasms of one's youth, even though long since revised or abandoned, may result not merely in one Committee appearance but in periodic appearances. To the Committee the passage of time is simply irrelevant; it lives in an eternal springtime in which a condemned association of today or 20 years ago is viewed with equal and unfading hostility. Similarly, an organization may be dead or defunct, but to the Committee it is timelessly sinister. In the world of the Committee, subversion is chronic, incurable and cumulative.

When HUAC's exposure effort is blocked by the witness' denials or a lack of available current material, it dons its deer-stalker and sniffs through his past with its trusty dossier at its side, to confront him with the political transgressions of his beardless youth. In 1953, HUAC exposed a number of revered religious leaders on the basis of activities which had occurred 30 years earlier. When Bishop Oxnam was interrogated in the same year, his associations as a theological student were exhumed to demonstrate how subversive he was. In the 1954 Dayton hearing, a witness was summoned from his teaching job in a Southern university to be asked whether he had taken an automobile trip to an American Youth Congress meeting in 1941. In the 1958 New England hearings, a witness who had denied Communist Party membership for a period of five years preceding his appearance was then asked: "Were you a member of the Communist Party five and a half years ago?" "Were you a member of the Communist Party January of 1953?" "Were you a member of the Communist Party February of 1953?" "After which date can you assert, while you are under oath, that you were not a member of the Communist Party?"

The only evidence which the Committee produced to justify this interrogation was a claim that the witness had signed Communist nominating petitions in the late thirties and early forties.

After it has exposed the witness by ventilating his remote political past, the Committee does not let matters rest. Years later it may issue a report rehashing the earlier stale material. This technique of freshening up an exposure and shielding it from the ravages of time was used in a Committee report on *Communist Legal Subversion.* Issued in 1959, it charged that certain attorneys were "an elite corps within the Communist Fifth column on American soil." The *Denver Post,* in commenting on the irresponsibility of the report, noted:

> Testimony regarding two of these lawyers was given in 1939, 20 years ago. Testimony on one was 19 years old; on one, 13 years old; on three, 11 years old; on two, 9 years old; on five, 8 years old; on twelve, 7 years old; on five, 6 years old; on one, 5 years old; on two, 4 years old; on one, 3 years old; and on four, 2 years old.

For HUAC the witness' past is simply a weapon in the struggle to perpetuate itself. It tirelessly beats the bushes for ex-Communists, depression radicals and antifascists of the thirties because—like the poor—there were so many of them. They swell the number of candidates for exposure. If they have joined any kind of meaningful social action group—non-Communist or anti-Communist, it does not matter—the Committee can use their participation to expose the organization as subversive. For every joiner there are thousands who hold off out of fear. When a man is not sure what association in his past will bring the United States Marshal to his door with a HUAC subpoena, he walks softly and shuns involvement in controversial matters.

In addition to the name-gathering methods already discussed, the Committee draws on administrative and court cases. It regularly subpoenas and exposes individuals who are involved in loyalty proceedings of one kind or another. In 1956, it subpoenaed passport applicants who were challenging the State Department's denial of passports on political grounds. In 1959, it subpoenaed a large group of foreign-born Americans who had successfully resisted efforts to deport them. In 1960, it called for an exposure hearing a number of applicants for renewal of radio licenses who were resisting an administrative loyalty test. It did the same thing to merchant seamen and marine radio operators who had attacked the Coast Guard's loyalty screening program. Government employees have been plucked out of loyalty proceedings for exposure hearings avowedly designed to ensure their dismissal. The fact that the Committee's actions might prejudice pending litigation furnished an added incentive for calling them. When a litigant wins a "political" case in court or before an administrative agency, the Committee frequently subpoenas him to prove that a miscarriage of justice occurred and that the court or administrative agency was soft on Communism.

It must not be thought that the Committee limits its exposure activities to suspected concealed Party members. The Committee constantly increases its reservoir of names by developing new chains of organizational kinship to the Communist Party parent stock. If a victim cannot be exposed as a member or former member of the Party, he can at least be exposed as a fellow traveler, an agent, a front, a dupe, a supporter of Communist causes, etc. When things get slack, the Committee is forced to call known Communists—such as Party functionaries. There is not much mileage in this; these witnesses cannot be hurt very much by exposure. Still, it is a reminder that the cop is on the beat.

It is no easy job to find new exposure victims; the pond has been fished pretty dry in the past decade. The number of undercover agents which the FBI can turn over to the Committee is obviously not unlimited, in view of the shrunken size of the Party. And the hope for defectors among current Party members is hardly promising: the Senate Internal Security Subcommittee has estimated that it takes three years for newly defected Party members to ripen into informers (ah, research!).

The Committee has always had trouble forcing ex-Communists to inform. The bulk of the ex-Communist friendly witnesses have been drawn from the entertainment field, which imposed the requirement of informing as a condition of clearance. The hearings resound with protests of American teachers, writers, artists and actors against the Committee's efforts to make them inform. One of the most moving is that of Dr. David Hawkins (Radiation Laboratory, 1950):

> . . . I feel very deeply—and I am sure you will will agree with this proposition—there are certain fundamental relations of trust which tend to distinguish American society from other societies in this world today; and, unless this kind of question is to your knowledge directly or indirectly related to the subjects you are investigating, I would very much like not to be asked such a question.
> If there is information of this sort that you would like to get, I would just ask whether there may not be more efficient and direct ways to get it, such as asking the question of the individual himself rather than of me.

Bernard Deutsch, a nuclear physicist, was sentenced to a jail term for contempt as a result of his refusal to inform. He asked the Committee, "I am perfectly willing to tell about my own activities, but do you feel I should trade my moral scruples by informing on someone else?" Deutsch explained in a press interview that he had joined the Party while a student at Cornell. "That part of my life was a period of experimentation and I don't feel that I should apologize for not being afraid to experiment." The coordinator of his Communist club was an FBI informer, Emanuel Ross Richardson, who drove students in his car to meetings at which he presided and then turned their names in to HUAC. He told the press, "I recognize the principle upon which Deutsch acted in refusing to name names. I think it has merit. I see a lot of merit in it." As to his own activities as an informer, he said, "Whenever you do that kind of work, you have some sort of qualms." He acknowledged that he sometimes had "regrets" about the morality of acting as a leader of Communists and then informing on them.

The demand that the witness who is ready to talk about himself name others as the price for escaping a contempt citation is a naked perversion of the investigative process. Congress has as little need to be informed of the names of the witness' associates as of the description and markings of each bird and beast in a census of vanishing wild life. No one has stated this more cogently than Congressman Walter before he became Chairman of HUAC. In the course of the interrogation of screen actor Larry Parks in 1951, he tried to support Parks' unwillingness to name names:

> How can it be material to the purpose of this inquiry to have the names of people when we already know them? Aren't we actually, by insisting that this man testify as to names, overlooking the fact that we want to know what the organization did, what it hoped to accomplish, how it actually had or attempted to influence the thinking of the American people through the arts? So why is it so essential that we know the names of all the people when we have a witness who may make a contribution to what we are trying to learn?

When Congressman Walter became HUAC's Chairman, he invoked the same rationale in justifying a private clearance hearing at which screen-director Carl Foreman was not required to inform. See Chapter 11, "Blacklist and Clearance."

What about the demand that the unfriendly witness state his own political affiliation? The Supreme Court has held that an inquisition into the witness' politics is unconstitutional if its purpose is solely to establish that he is a Communist or ex-Communist. There must be some pressing reason, an unavoidable necessity for invading his constitutional rights, and this reason must be germane to legislation. In 1959, the Court upheld the contempt conviction of Lloyd Barenblatt for refusing, on First Amendment grounds to answer the "$64 question." It recognized that the question invaded a constitutionally protected area, but ruled that the invasion was justified by the Committee's claim that it was necessary to find out whether Barenblatt had been a Communist in order to identify him as a person who was in a position to supply information the Committee lacked. The "$64 question" was merely what lawyers called a "preliminary" question to establish that the witness was qualified to testify about the matter under inquiry. If he had answered the question in the affirmative, the Committee claimed, it would then have asked him if the Party had taught and advocated the violent overthrow of the Government. Barenblatt's constitutional rights had to be subordinated to the national security. Barenblatt went to jail because a majority of the Justices of the Supreme Court were led to believe that his silence frustrated a vital concern of Congress: how to preserve the very existence of the Republic.

When an unfriendly witness demands a justification for the invasion of his constitutional rights, the Committee tells him (as it did in the 1960 San Francisco hearings) that "the reason why we want that information is that it is a necessary first question in order that we may undertake to elicit . . . information of which we think he is possessed respecting the operation of this conspiratorial force known as the Communist Party in northern California, of which we know he is a member."

This formula is a fraud on both the Supreme Court and the witness. If Barenblatt had answered the "$64 question" in the affirmative, the next question would not have been a demand for facts about activities, but only for the names of his associates. Barenblatt himself was "named" by one Francis X. Crowley. Crowley had been an unfriendly witness, but under the threat of a contempt citation, he returned to the Committee's witness stand as a friendly witness. He was asked no question on his second run about any of the matters which the Court thought so important as to outweigh Barenblatt's right to silence. He was not asked about what preparations the Communist Party had made for the overthrow of the Government, or even whether he had engaged in the advocacy of the overthrow of the Government. Apart from the questions about routine activities of the Party, Crowley was asked to identify a list of individuals as Party members.

In 1950, one David H. Levison of Cincinnati returned to the witness stand after an initial refusal to answer the Committee's questions. On his second appearance the Committee showed no interest in Communist tenets or teachings, but concentrated on the names of his associates.

Mr. Levison was asked some 185 questions, of which almost all called for names. About 20 of the 185 questions sought further details to establish the identity of those named. For example:

> Would you mind spelling those names?
> That is man and wife?
> Her first name is Vera?
> Do you know his occupation at that time?
> About what age person was he?
> One "p"? Do you know whether the name is spelled with two "p's"?

And so on. But whether this witness, or others, were planning to overthrow the United States Government, and if so, how, was information in which HUAC apparently had no interest.

Informing is deeply offensive to most Americans. But witnesses who plead with the Committee to waive the informing requirement so that they can be cleared as friendly witnesses are almost always refused. Thus the Committee may already know the names which it is attempting to force out of the witness; but that makes no difference. There is, it insists, an important principle involved: an ex-Communist who refuses to turn informer has failed to prove that he has made a "clean break." His patriotism is suspect.

As Congressman Jackson, the Committee's theoretician on informing, put it, ". . . the final test of credibility of a witness purporting to be a former Communist who has changed his opinions in the period which has intervened between his membership and the present time, would have to be primarily the willingness to name names, places and circumstances surrounding such membership."

It is not enough for the witness to identify some names and to shield others because he is convinced they are no longer Communists and are not in sympathy with the aims of Communism. Congressman Jackson wants every last name: "Then one who refuses for any reason to disclose members of the Communist Party, depending upon his own judgment, to distinguish between hard core Communists and simple dupes, is in effect and conceivably covering traitors."

The lengths to which HUAC will go to force the capitulation of the squeamish are boundless. The case of Larry Parks is legendary. Parks was originally subpoenaed in 1947, but was not called to testify. He was of a group of nine unfriendly witnesses who were subpoenaed with the "Hollywood Ten," but for some reason, were not put on the stand. Under the pressure of the Hollywood motion-picture industry blacklist, he reappeared in March 1951, the first of a wave of friendly witnesses. He believed that it would be possible to cooperate with the Committee without becoming forced to inform. He confessed to a fleeting and uncommitted membership in the Party which had terminated in 1946.

Shortly before Parks' appearance, the Supreme Court had ruled that once a witness had admitted Party membership he could not decline to name others under a plea of the Fifth Amendment. The admission of Party membership constituted a waiver of the plea as to all Party activities and associations. In the Parks hearing the Committee made clear for the first time that it intended to insist on names from admitted ex-Communists.

Parks pleaded, "I will tell you everything that I know about myself, because I feel I have done nothing wrong. . . . I would prefer, if you will allow me, not to mention other people's names." The Committee pressed hard. Parks wavered, but stuck to his guns and fought back. He denied that he had engaged in any subversive acts and charged the Committee with picking on him because he was a screen star. He conceded that his Party membership might have been a mistake in judgment. He went on to say: "This is debatable. But my two boys, for instance, I would rather have them make the same mistake I did under those circumstances than not feel like making any mistakes at all and be a cow in the pasture. If a man doesn't feel that way about certain things, then he is not a man."

The Committee refused to accept his assurance that the people involved that he knew of had left the Party and would be needlessly injured. Parks put his back up: "I don't think the Committee would benefit from it, and I don't think this is American justice to make me choose [to] . . . be in contempt of this Committee . . . or crawl through the mud for no purpose, because you know who these people are. This is what I beg you not to do."

The Committee recessed and met with Parks in executive session and indicated to his lawyer that it was "entirely possible" that he would be cited for contempt if he persisted in his refusal. His counsel urged the Committee to go easy in view of his cooperativeness in other respects. "It is only saving that little bit of something that you live with—you have to see and work in Hollywood with that—you have to meet your children and your wife with it and your friends. . . . His honest and sincere opinion is that what he is going to give you will only eat up his insides and you will get nothing, no more than you have today."

The Committee remained unmoved. Parks made a final futile protest and then proceeded to answer the question: "Who were the members of the Communist Party cell to which you were assigned during the period from 1941 to 1945, or the period when you dissolved your membership with the Communist Party?"

Late in 1953, Parks' executive-session testimony was released together with a letter to Chairman Velde which "clarified" the earlier testimony. "It is my conviction," Parks wrote, "that to assist your committee in obtaining information about the Communist Party and its activities is the duty of all who possess such evidence. Certainly if I were to testify today I would not testify as I did in 1951 —that to give such testimony is to 'wallow in the mud,' but on the contrary I would recognize that such cooperation would help further the cause in which many of us were sincerely interested when we were duped into joining and taking part in the Communist Party."

Robert Rossen, the screen director and producer, after refusing to name names in 1951, on the ground of "individual morality," capitulated in 1953 on the ground that ". . . no one individual can even indulge himself in the luxury of individual morality. . . ."

In Rossen's case, economic pressure forced a switch. Contempt citations reversed the previous unfriendliness of George Adams, a West Coast newspaper man, and Dr. Wilbur Lee Mahaney, Jr., a Philadelphia educator.

Adams reappeared before the Committee in September 1954, after having been cited for contempt for refusing to name names. As his Committee interrogators admitted, "In his previous appearances before the Committee [he had] testified fully concerning his own background, his own participation in the Communist Party, and his own opinion regarding Communist Party theories." He reluctantly complied with the demand for the names he had previously withheld, and protested that "the Federal Government is morally wrong to force me, under the threat of criminal prosecution, to do what you have forced me to do today." A great many of the names involved associations from ten to twenty years prior to the time of his testimony.

Dr. Mahaney, who first appeared in February 1954, discussed his own views and activities and refused to identify his associates before he left the Communist Party in 1946:

> It is a matter of deep and abiding conscience with me. . . . I have always believed and I have been told that to be an informer as to the friends that you might have or acquaintances you might meet along the pathway of life is contrary to every tenet of the American way of thinking.

He was cited for contempt. He reappeared after having been suspended from his teaching post in July of 1954, and was forced to identify a long list of persons—most of whom the Committee knew about already. All of them involved associations in the thirties and early forties. Among those he implicated were his former wife and another woman, both of whom had denied the charges in their own appearances before the Committee. He had previously refused to identify the individual who had made him a Communist in the thirties because she was dead. Under the prodding of the Committee he concluded that he had been "unduly squeamish about it," and turned in her name. He included in his list a woman to whom he had tried to sell an encyclopedia when he lost his teaching job.

Although, as we have seen, Congressman Jackson thought that the willingness of a repentant witness to name names on his reappearance was the supreme test of his good faith, Congressman Doyle was not so sure that the original sin of Party membership could be so readily expiated.

> Why didn't you get out [of the Communist Party] in 1945 when you began to have that impression

[that coexistence was not possible]. Why didn't you get out immediately? . . . You were blessed with more education and degrees than most. You were well read. . .

The Congressman was tortured by the thought that "not until after seven months had elapsed after you testified here, together with the fact that until you knew you were being cited for contempt did you ask to come back here and straighten out your conscience as a matter of public record." The offering of the names left the Congressman cold. "If a man has been in bad faith and a member of the Communist Party for 10 years, how can I know whether I can believe the good faith is true?"

Congressman Jackson took a different tack. He granted the witness that "giving names of people you knew a long time ago . . . is not an easy thing to do. . . . It is a very difficult ordeal." He wanted to be completely certain that the witness had turned in everyone he knew. He warned the witness of the folly of shielding "a close intimate friend" through a "false feeling of loyalty." How would it look for Dr. Mahaney—now seeking to purge himself of a contempt citation—if such a "close intimate friend" were in the future to be subpoenaed by the Committee and named Dr. Mahaney as a fellow Communist?

The Committee had obtained no facts from Dr. Mahaney, but it was entirely satisfied that he had completely purged himself of his "mistaken sense of loyalty." The contempt citation was dropped.

In writing of this episode, Alan Barth has asked:

What exultation did the members of Congress feel at using power to achieve this victory over a man's conscience. What manner of investigation is it that will stretch a human spirit upon a rack as cruel in its way as any of the torture chambers of the medieval Inquisition in order to wrest from him, not a confession of his own heresy—he had confessed that long since—but an accusation leveled at old friends, leveled even at the woman he had once promised to honor and cherish?

What service to security did the committee render by compelling this anguished outcry. The women at whom Mahaney's trembling finger pointed were hardly a menace to the state. What reverence did the committee accord to an honored American tradition by forcing this man to turn informer—to do what every American has been taught from childhood to abhor?

Since the witness who answers the Committee's questions about himself waives the right to invoke the Fifth Amendment, he will frequently plead this constitutional right because he does not want to be forced into the role of informer. The informing requirement forces the witness who might otherwise be ready to talk about himself to remain silent altogether.

A bona fide investigating committee would avoid frustrating the fact-finding process in this way. But the names (not the facts) are vital to HUAC's existence. A witness who is not ready to inform is not politically reliable enough to give the kind of lurid "facts" about the Red menace in which the Committee exclusively specializes. Under the circumstances, the witness' silence is more valuable to the Committee than the testimony. By forcing him to plead the Fifth Amendment, HUAC insures his punishment—his reputation will be smeared and he may lose his job.

Prior to the appearance in May 1952 of Lillian Hellman, distinguished American playwright, she wrote to HUAC's chairman:

I am not willing, now or in the future, to bring bad trouble to people, who in my past association with them, were completely innocent of any talk or any action that was disloyal or subversive. I do not like subversion or disloyalty in any form, and if I had ever seen any I would have considered it my duty to have reported it to the proper authorities. But to hurt innocent people whom I knew many years ago in order to save myself is, to me, inhuman and indecent and dishonorable. . . . I am prepared to waive the privilege against self-incrimination and to tell you anything you wish to know about my views or actions, if your committee will agree to refrain from asking me to name other people. If the committee is unwilling to give me this assurance, I will be forced to plead the privilege of the Fifth Amendment at the hearing.

The Chairman replied that "the Committee cannot permit witnesses to set forth the terms under which they will testify." Miss Hellman, in her testimony, invoked the Fifth Amendment privilege.

In 1953, the Committee subpoenaed a group of Philadelphia teachers. Several of them agreed to discuss themselves and their activities on condition that they not be compelled to testify about others. The Committee refused. When a witness offered to waive his right to challenge the proceeding on constitutional grounds and to answer any and all questions about himself if only the Committee would agree not to force him to identify others, the following colloquy took place:

Mr. Velde: We have already been through this harangue. Now are you willing to answer the question?

Mr. Margolis: What is your ruling, sir?

Mr. Velde: I asked you whether you are willing to answer the question. I have given you every privilege that any witness or any person deserves before this Committee [consultation with counsel].

Mr. Velde: Please show your patriotism. Show your love of country, if you have it, and answer that question either yes or no or refuse to answer it.

Mr. Margolis: I do love my country dearly and I would like to ask for a ruling.

Mr. Velde: The Committee does not make rulings. The Committee merely seeks out information from witnesses who are called before it [consultation with counsel].

Mr. Margolis: If you want information about me, I will give it to you, but not about any other individual.

Since the Committee refused to promise not to ask the witness about others, he declined to waive his rights under the Fifth Amendment as to most of the questions asked him about his own activities. His reason for refusing to name others is an interesting one:

My reason for refusing to answer questions about other people is that in answering questions based upon the imperfect and incomplete knowledge which one person has about another and without the right of that person to cross-examine anyone or to present evidence in his own behalf, I should be giving to this committee information which might be misleading. I do not wish to be a party to a proceeding which is contrary to the American concepts of fair play and those concepts of law which are characterized by the unfounded accusation and the big lie.

Sometimes a witness risks a jail sentence by admitting past membership in the Party without trying to make a deal. But the Committee disdains his offer to help—even when his testimony promises to be enlightening and fruitful. At the Committee's 1959 Chicago hearings, a witness who had been assumed to be unfriendly surprised the Committee by admitting his former Communist Party membership. A Communist teacher and functionary for about ten years, he appeared to be just the "hard core" type the Committee was looking for. But after he had testified almost eagerly for a long period of time about his Communist background, the Committee recovered from shock.

Mr. Arens first asked the witness who had been his immediate superior while he was a Communist functionary. The witness declined to answer that question, but insisted that he was "extremely willing to be cooperative and frank about my own activities." To the Committee his reluctance proved that the witness still harbored latent Communist sympathies. Arens reminded him that he was shielding the accomplices of Stalin, a "murderer who destroyed hundreds of thousands of his colleagues," of Khrushchev, "dripping in blood . . . of an estimated 8 to 10 million of the Kulak class," and of the Red Chinese who "are digging up the graves of their ancestors to use them for fertilizer. . . ." Arens bore down on the witness with: "The Communist operation in the United States today now is a more serious, more deadly fifth column on American soil than ever before in the Nation's history."

Again the demand for names was repeated: "Now, would you kindly tell us if you are opposed to Communism, if you think it is an evil force, would you tell us, please, sir, the names of persons who to your certain knowledge are now participants as members of the Communist Party in the greater Chicago area?" But the witness remained impervious to Arens' steamy diatribes: ". . . because I have been going through the unfortunate experience, very possibly losing my own job, by virtue of being summoned here because I was a Communist in the past, though I am no longer, and I am conscious while I have been freely willing to testify about myself, my own activities, in conscience I can't subject anybody else to the things I have been subjected to the past few days."

Further harangues about the wickedness of Lenin and the perfidy of Communists fell flat. The witness refused to be moved to the point of betrayal, although he begged to share with the Committee all the facts that he knew:

> Mr. Chairman, I would willingly stay here all day, all night, as long as the Committee wants, to give them all information in my possession about Communist activities, Communist techniques up to 1956 when I had knowledge of these things. However, when it comes to identifying persons whom I knew as Communists up to 1956, I can't evade the point that I might cause these people to go through the same thing I have had to go through for the past few days, including possible loss of a job. Most people who were in the Communist Party at that time, as the Committee well knows, have left the Communist Party, and are now opposed to it.

But the witness' pleading offer to stay all day and all night to give the Committee all the information in his possession fell on deaf ears. He was cited for contempt of the Committee on the theory that the witness' recalcitrance balked a quest for facts in aid of the legislative process! This apparently didn't make sense to the grand jury, for it refused to indict the witness.

The identification and exposure process so dominates the hearing as to leave little room for facts. But HUAC has to pretend that the hearings are about some theme or subject. If the witnesses are an assorted group from, let us say, Baltimore, the hearing is called "Communist Activities in the Baltimore Area"; it is known as an "area" hearing. If the informer has turned up with a clutch of teachers, the hearing is called "Communist Infiltration in Education"—an "infiltration" hearing. But except for the names, the transcripts of the "area" and "infiltration" hearings are completely interchangeable: the former tells us nothing about "activities" in Baltimore, and the latter as little about "methods of infiltration" in education.

The hearing is held not because some new problem requires it, or because some new facts might emerge from it, but because a "package" of exposable unfriendly witnesses has been assembled. This means not only that HUAC cuts the cloth of the problem to the witnesses, but that it deals with the same problems over and over again. A bona fide Congressional investigation would regard it as a waste of time and money to investigate and reinvestigate the same problem month after month and year after year. Why should it keep looking for information it already has? But HUAC endlessly rehashes a stock repertoire of problems, all of which involve not some evil requiring legislation—sabotage, sedition, espionage—but Communism as such, the "invented terror" of which Aristotle spoke.

From its inception to the present, the Committee has heard testimony about the Communist Party and how it operates in at least 25 hearings. It has issued a half-dozen reports on the teachings and organization of the Party. Most of the testimony which it has heard was publicly presented in Smith Act trials. The great bulk of it largely deals with such earth-shaking matters as the kinds of Party cells, how dues are collected, resolutions passed at conventions (none of them violations or any law), the use of mimeograph machines to reproduce statements, the Party's echelons of authority, etc.

Another subject of which the Committee never wearies is Communist fronts. This subject has dominated the Committee's hearings since the days of Matthews, Steele and Frey. It is surely legislatively the most sterile pursuit conceivable. We now have legislation on the books directed not only at Communist-dominated and controlled organizations, but even at Communist-infiltrated organizations. Many believe that these statutes trespass on areas safeguarded by the freedom of speech and assembly protections of the Constitution.

The Communist-front horse simply cannot be beaten any harder. Besides, it is by now quite a dead horse. Harassing legislation, the repressive political climate of the fifties, the Attorney General's list of organizations, and the activities of the Committee itself have disposed of most of the political, civic and "cause" groups which flourished a decade ago. The Committee is now reduced to charges that the Communists are by infiltration tactics subverting parent-teacher associations, the YWCA, the Protestant churches and similar organizations.

Another HUAC favorite is the alleged subversive infiltration of defense industry. It issued a full report on this subject in 1954, but that was hardly enough. It has held hearings on this subject in 1956 (St. Louis), 1957 (Buffalo, Baltimore), 1958 (Gary)—to name only a few.

One would hardly guess from the Committee's frenzied alarms that the whole of our defense-connected industrial establishment is subject to an intensive security clearance and control system. No more legislative life can be breathed into this investigatively exhausted subject, without trespassing on the Constitution.

The "facts" which emerge from HUAC's hearings invariably confirm its lurid version of the Red menace. The reason for this is simple: the only witnesses who are permitted to give testimony about facts are those who share HUAC's views. The testimony is little more than propaganda in question-and-answer form.

Despite the enormous numerical decline of the Communist Party, the weakening of the Party by criminal prosecution, its isolation and rejection by Americans in every area of our national life, the Committee insists that the Party was never stronger. HUAC asks each informer witness whether this is not so and they all dutifully agree. For example, in the 1959 Pittsburgh hearing, we learn:

> Mr. Arens: Is the Communist operation now more dangerous or less dangerous than it has been in the past?
> Mr. Golden: It is more dangerous, due to the fact that it is underground more and it can't be kept track of as good.

In the same year in Chicago, asked of a witness who had

terminated his relationship to the Party in 1949, ten years prior to the hearing:

> Mr. Arens: I should like to ask you . . . how serious is the Communist menace in this area to your certain knowledge as of now?
>
> Mr. Nelson: It is more serious now than ever before, because at this time almost all of the people are not formally in the party . . . still they maintain their Marxist-Leninist philosophy and they are in the leadership of various unions throughout the State of Illinois. I would say it is definitely in a better position today than they ever were. [This witness had left the Party in 1949, ten years prior to the hearing.]

And again in the Chicago hearings:

> Mr. Arens: . . . how serious is the Communist movement, the Communist operation at this instant.
>
> Mr. Poskonka: It is very, very serious. . . . Because of being undercover. They are using the scheme which instead of using openly the Communist Party, they are using front organizations and labor, and people think they are strictly a decent organization, fighting for labor. . . .

While the Committee runs no risks that the offerings of the informal witnesses will injure the cause, Congress obviously runs enormous risks of using this testimony for guidance in the legislative process. The problems of freedom and security in which the Committee deals are far too delicate and important to be entrusted to witnesses of this kind.

The volunteer for undercover political spying believes that he is doing his patriotic duty by plunging himself and his family into the milieu of a subversive. He inevitably tends either to distort the facts which he observes or, and this is the greater likelihood, to distort the meaning of the facts. Convinced of the existence of a sinister subversive conspiracy with its fangs at the throat of the Nation, he sees treason under every bed. For him everything that a Communist does—no matter how humdrum it appears— is smoky with sedition.

This kind of informer or undercover agent is primarily drawn from the ranks of the professional patrioteer. He expects the gratitude and admiration of his fellow citizens for his courage in unmasking the subversive menace. His psychological need to exaggerate the dangers which his victims pose to organized society is enormous. If he is to be a St. George, then the animal he is slaying needs to be a dragon.

The informer whose motivation is economic is likewise suspect. He knows that his economic usefulness depends on his readiness to report what he is paid to report. He is paid to spy on an organization in order to obtain evidence. He knows that if he fails to find such evidence, his value to his employer ceases. This economic incentive also serves to destroy his accuracy in the reporting of the names of subversives. Indeed, sometimes his compensation is directly dependent upon the number of names he produces. When the informer learns from experience that there is no effective check upon the data he turns in, he becomes bolder and more extravagant in his claims and charges.

Again, one cannot help concluding that a deep sense of guilt compromises the veracity of some of the informers. It would be a psychological miracle if a reasonably normal individual could engage in a systematic process of forming pretended friendships with others and then exposing them to loss of livelihood and criminal prosecution without suffering a profound guilt feeling. It is an elementary psychiatric truth that such a guilt feeling forces the individual into compensatory justification by the creation of elaborate phantasies concerning the crimes of his victims.

The informer who is motivated by a power drive is also a high credibility risk. Ambition forces him to lie about the activities of his victims in order to enjoy the sense of power which comes with exposing them and to achieve public recognition. He needs an endless succession of victims in order to get ahead in the informer world.

When the undercover agent or the police spy matriculates from undercover operative to public witness, his credibility does not improve. HUAC encourages him to draw the long bow in responding to questions. His testimony is privileged against defamation actions; there is no cross-examination, nor fear of perjury prosecutions.

The credibility hazard which informer testimony presents has been well described by Professor Zechariah Chafee, Jr.:

I want to make absolutely clear my position about spies as witnesses against men accused of political crimes. I am not saying that such spies will tell nothing in court except lies. Undoubtedly, some of them will do their best to tell the truth during their whole testimony while many others will mix a good deal of truth with falsehoods. What I do say is that there is a much greater risk of false testimony from spies than from ordinary men. Every witness, no matter how honest, is naturally inclined to make a good showing for his side. I know this from my own experience in will cases. But, in the case of most witnesses, any risks from this inclination are offset by several checks. Truthfulness is a requisite of most normal occupations from bookkeeping to the practice of medicine. An ingrained habit of telling the truth is carried on to the witness stand. And the ordinary witness knows that any lack of veracity may be detected when he testifies, as he usually does, about matters which are capable of objective proof or on which he can be contradicted by disinterested eye-witnesses of the facts.

But when spies appear in court, such checks operate in a much weaker way. The very nature of a spy's work requires lying. He has to deceive his associates into thinking him one of themselves. The longer he does spying, the greater the tendency for the boundary between truth and falsehood to be blurred. . . . And the subject-matter of a spy's testimony in political cases is often incapable of neutral verification. He has enormous power to imagine words which were never said. The only other possible eyewitnesses of the transaction he narrates are usually the suspected person he is helping to punish and other members of the alleged conspiracy. It is impossible to let in the light of day upon these dusky happenings.

The trouble is not that you cannot be sure a spy is lying. The trouble is you cannot be sure he is telling the truth. The risk of false testimony is tremendously increased.

The ex-Communist who is ready to inform is usually under heavy pressure to tell the Committee what it wants to hear. He may have fallen out with his former associates and sees the Committee as a vehicle of revenge. More commonly, he may be under pressure to "clear" himself for employment. Such a witness must be aggressive in his denunciation of his former views to qualify for clearances. He testifies, as one wit has put it, from his stomach, not from his convictions.

A talented FBI plant who combines a bent for the sinister with a large number of names is worth his weight in gold to HUAC. One of the most successful of such witnesses was Matthew Cvetic, who "surfaced" as a Committee witness in February 1950. Cvetic was the first of a long line of FBI underscover agents who had been planted in the Party in the forties who used the Committee as a forum. His testimony before the Committee is probably a record performance—six days in February and March of 1950, and four days in June, September and October of the same year. Cvetic's testimony was carefully prepared: he not only named names, but delivered himself of elaborate political commentaries on the evil machinations of his victims. He devised a cabalistic rationale to make the most innocuous document seem fraught with terror.

His story dominated the front pages of the Pittsburgh papers and filled the radio air waves for weeks. Headline articles carried Cvetic's recital of "Red Plots for the Violent Overthrow of the United States." "All Communists Must Be Ferreted Out" the Pittsburgh press proclaimed on March 5, 1950. An editorial entitled "Now Bring Them To Heel" charged the Communists with sealing defense secrets, preaching the violent overthrow of the Government, stirring up strikes, and concluded, "The Commies here will do worse unless they are brought to heel." An article in the *Pittsburgh Press* quoted Cvetic to prove that the "Communist Party is no more a political party than a gang of robbers is a political party." The *Pittsburgh Sun Telegraph* quoted Cvetic's testimony to the effect that Pittsburgh Communists were already laying plans for a war between the United States and the Soviet Union, and that Cvetic had been given detailed information about a plan of the Soviet Union to invade the United States mainland through Alaska. Stressed over and over again was

Cvetic's warning that the Pittsburgh area is the "chief concentration point for the Communist Party in the United States," and that the Communists' plan was to infiltrate Pittsburgh industries as the first step toward "overthrowing the Government."

It was in the setting of this testimony before the Committee that Cvetic named some 300 persons as either Communists or "Communist sympathizers." The names and addresses of these persons and their places of employment, when known, were printed in the Pittsburgh newspapers in heavy type with a summary of Cvetic's testimony about them. This was followed by radio and television broadcasts. As a result, nearly 100 persons lost their jobs. The mere mention by Cvetic as a Communist or a sympathizer was regarded as sufficient in the community to warrant discharge or other sanctions. As the *Pittsburgh Press* put it in an article on February 28th, "There has been no room for doubt at any time about the veracity of Matt Cvetic . . . the testimony, background and substance of Mr. Cvetic are too firmly established to justify any reasonable doubt about his story."

A man reported to have been employed by one employer for 20 years was given an "indefinite leave of absence" after being named by Cvetic. Another woman was likewise promptly fired by her employer after a long period of satisfactory service. A member of the Pittsburgh Symphony Orchestra was not only fired from the orchestra, but expelled by the American Federation of Musicians.

Other unions in the Pittsburgh area ordered named members either to deny the Cvetic charges or resign. The United Steel Workers of America were reported, in an article headed "Steel Workers 'Weed Out' Red Suspect," to have deprived one individual named by Cvetic of all union rights except that of paying dues. Another individual described by Cvetic as a "Croatian leader," was reported in the press to have been ousted from an American Federation of Labor union on the ground that he had "concealed his Communist ties when he joined the labor organization." A young war veteran was forced to resign a position with the American Federation of Labor because Cvetic named his father (not him) as a Communist. Two officials of the A.F. of L. Hotel and Restaurant Workers Union were ordered by the Executive Board to deny Communist charges or resign. One of them was forced to resign. Two other workers were faced with expulsion by the union because they were named by Cvetic as "Communist adherents."

The Pittsburgh papers of March 19, 1950, ran a headline story "Auto Workers Refuse to Seat Alleged Red," reporting that "members of a CIO United Auto Workers Local have blocked the installation of the new President of their union until charges that he is a Communist can be cleared up."

A "roundup" story in the *Pittsburgh Press* on March 19, 1950, is headed, "3 Fired, Others Jittery Over Cvetic's 'Red Label'." Its lead paragraph states: "Pittsburgh district persons named as Communists by Matt Cvetic have been having a rough time holding on to their jobs since the FBI undercover agent testified before the House Un-American Activities Committee." After referring to several persons who had lost their jobs or were threatened with job losses, the story goes on to say, "There were indications that other companies and unions are contemplating action against members of their organizations who were named as Communists by Cvetic." Five union members of long standing were reported in newspaper stories, complete with their pictures, to be facing trial by a steelworkers local union on charges by Cvetic that they were Communists. Cvetic's testimony against two of them was apparently based on the fact that they supported a Croatian newspaper said to follow the "Party line." He charged that "Their efforts for the paper were sufficient evidence for me to know that they were giving aid and comfort to the Communists."

A few unions went as far as to invite Cvetic to look over their membership lists and to pick out the "Reds." A Pittsburgh local of an electrical workers union staged a mammoth meeting at which Cvetic was reported as having been given a "hero's welcome." In the wake of the Cvetic revelations, there was a wave of firings of school teachers on every level of the school system. A former Pittsburgher who had worked as a librarian at Cornell University was promptly fired when he was named by Cvetic.

Expulsion from various clubs and associations also followed the Cvetic disclosures. The president of a mothers' club was forced to resign, a local newspaper headlining the incident, "Red President 'Poured Out' at Glen Hazel Mothers' Tea." The press also reported the expulsion of a member of the local board of trade as a result of his having been named by Cvetic—not as a Communist, but as a supporter of Henry Wallace and a delegate to the Progressive Party convention. Another individual named by Cvetic was expelled from a civic club with widespread publicity.

Cvetic designated one of his victims as "The Red Queen." The state at once cut her and her two children off relief, on the ground that she had violated an oath requiring relief recipients not to seek the overthrow of the Government.

A page-one article on March 16, 1950, declared "Deportation Faces 20 Reds Cvetic Named." It mentioned two pending deportation cases in which Cvetic was expected to be a witness. Under the headlines "Housecleaning Due—Red Lawyers May Be Ousted by Bar Association," the newspapers in May 1950 carried reports of a move to disbar lawyers in the Pittsburgh area who had represented politically unpopular causes and clients.

On March 9, 1950, Judge Michael A. Musmanno dismissed a grand juror whom Cvetic had named as a Communist. When the Judge recognized her on the panel, he took prompt action:

I withdrew to my chambers and made a quick call to the Federal Bureau of Investigation in Washington.

From the National airport of America's capitol an airplane took to the skies bearing a passenger who for the preceding months had been making first page news all over the country. Two hours later I was leading Matt Cvetic to a door from which he could see the grand jurors. I asked him if he recognized any among them. . . .

That afternoon I summoned the designated person to my chambers with Matt Cvetic, two county detectives and four other persons who had dealings with her . . .

The next day, in open court, the Judge dismissed her and denounced her from the bench with inflammatory grandiloquence:

One never hears or scarcely ever hears a Communist admit what he is doing. His directives proclaim the overthrow of Government by force and violence but he parades within the camouflage of societies, associations and programs, always striving for dissension and conflict. He stirs up class hatreds, he gets admitted into circles of high influence and then, when the opportunity arrives he betrays not only his Government but all mankind.

Need I tell you of the miserable wretches who accepted the usual pieces of silver for atomic secrets so as to bring on a race in atomic destruction which can conceivably lead to the end of all life on the planet itself? The appalling hydrogen bomb of which we have heard much is a bomb that can wipe Pittsburgh out of existence like one with a finger smashes a grape. . . .

The dismissed grand juror also lost her job; nor was she reinstated when Pennsylvania's Supreme Court, in an extraordinary action, condemned the judge for his arbitrary and illegal action.

The Pittsburgh hysteria fanned out in an ever-widening arc. Communist newspapers were banned; raids were conducted; Communist Party leaders on the basis of Cvetic's testimony, were charged with sedition under a Pennsylvania statute; and the bail of one of the defendants was set at $50,000. In September 1950, the Communist Party offices were padlocked. When the padlock order was reversed by the Pennsylvania Supreme Court, the lower court, on petition of Judge Musmanno, entered a new order directing the seizure of the entire contents of the offices. The documents which were seized were turned over to the Committee by Cvetic and Judge Musmanno.

In the spring of 1951, elaborate ceremonies were held in Pittsburgh to celebrate the premiere of "I Was a Communist For the FBI," a movie "based on the real life experience of Pittsburgh's own Matt Cvetic." The day of the premiere was officially proclaimed "Matt Cvetic Day." A special luncheon was held and a parade honoring Cvetic marched through downtown Pittsburgh in front of the courthouse where the sedition trial was being held.

Subsequent to Cvetic's Committee appearance, he appeared as a witness in various court cases. But courtroom testimony was not a métier suited to his extravagant, self-glorifying flamboyance. The Committee, the movie, and *Saturday Evening Post* authorship had spoiled him for the austerity of simple fact. Besides, cross-examination revealed a sordid private life. Despite these disclosures, he earned a substantial income from various anti-Communist enterprises. In 1955, a long history of mental disturbance and alcoholism, which he had previously concealed, was brought to light when he was hospitalized in Pittsburgh.

Two weeks after his last discharge from the hospital, he appeared before the Senate Internal Security Subcommittee, where he gave testimony alleging that John J. Mullen, head of the United Steelworkers Political Action Committee and a former Mayor of Clairton, Pennsylvania, was a Communist. Cvetic's mentor, Judge Musmanno, had inspired the charge and Cvetic tried hard to make it stick, but his attempts to bridge the inconsistencies in his story with politically sinister explanations no longer worked their old magic. Mullen appeared before the Committee, denied that he was ever a member of the Communist Party, and contradicted Cvetic's testimony in every particular.

Shortly thereafter, Cvetic left Pittsburgh. He now lives in California, where he lectures to organizations such as the John Birch Society on the Red menace—a long way from his Committee triumphs, when his mere word was enough to ruin a man. But Cvetic is now a full-fledged hatist and a speaker for Billie James Hargis' Christian Crusade Rally. He has expanded his talents for identification since his HUAC days and now includes in his act the leaders of the Fund for the Republic, SANE, and Cyrus Eaton ("a stupid, greedy, capitalistic pig").

8 THE ROLE OF THE PRESS

Any Congressional investigation, even when it has a legitimate legislative purpose, relies heavily on the press. It tries to create a public opinion favorable to Congressional approval of the legislation it wants passed. Good publicity can help re-elect an investigator, make him a national figure and advance his political ambitions. Just as the job of prosecutor frequently serves as a way station to a judgeship, so a Congressional investigation can be the precursor of bigger things. A good press is helpful, too, for renewed appropriations.

The importance of capturing the headline is underscored in the following memorandum on conducting an investigation which was circulated to the staff of a Congressional committee investigating the FCC:

> Decide what you want the newspapers to hit hardest, and then shape each hearing so that the main point becomes the fortress of the testimony. Once that fortress is reached, adjourn.
>
> Do not permit distractions to occur, such as extraneous bursts of would-be witnesses, which might provide news that would bury the testimony which you might want featured.
>
> Do not space hearings more than 24 or 48 hours apart when on a controversial subject. This gives the opposition too much opportunity to make all kinds of countercharges in replies by issuing statements to the newspapers.
>
> Do not ever be afraid to recess a hearing, even for five minutes so that you can keep the proceedings completely in control so far as creating news is concerned.

In a conventional legislative investigation, the wooing of the press serves to reinforce and further some legislative purposes. But HUAC's relationship to the press is sharply different. The public ventilation of the names of the unfriendly witnesses in the press is an integral part of the exposure process. Congress has no need to know the names; they are aired solely to trigger private action. The press—as well as radio and television—is indispensable to give exposure a community-wide resonance. The press does not merely mirror or report the hearing; it is an indispensable part of it—like a loudspeaker on a high-fidelity sound system.

A witness was told (before the advent of television):

> . . . you are now before the greatest open court in this country, I believe, beyond the confines of any limited courtroom in this country. You are now in the presence of probably 1,000 or more people in this committee room. You are in the presence of an invisible audience of millions of American people who

listen to the radio. You are in the presence of millions of American people who see moving pictures. You are in the presence of competent and able representatives of the American press, which is free.

HUAC holds its hearings at times and places which promise the most generous press reception. It arranges the script of the hearing for a maximum press coverage. Frequently a friendly witness begins and closes the proceedings. In the course of the hearing, it tries before the noon recess to create a good headline for the afternoon press and, before the close of the session, a new lead for the next morning's newspapers. It is equally adept at other publicity dodges. In order to "take the play away" from a Methodist minister who testified before it in August 1953, it released—in the course of his testimony—the testimony of another clergyman which was given two years earlier in executive session. Together with this stale testimony, it issued a special release to the press.

The logic of HUAC's dependence on the press drives it further and further into realms of invention and fantasy. HUAC must anticipate revelations of unparalleled treachery; promise blood-curdling confessions; call mystery witnesses and announce that it is finally on the trail of the master-plot to take over the country. This is the stuff of which headlines are made and this is the way the Committee makes headlines.

The Committee shamefully exploits the press. Alan Barth pointed out a few years ago:

American newspapers pride themselves on being impervious to the trick of press agentry. They have learned to detect the contrived handout, the planted story, the trial balloon. Yet they have found themselves in recent years sucked in as purveyors of gossip, and in some cases, of malicious falsehood put out in the guise of news—simply because it has been uttered on the floor of Congress, or under the auspices, and the protection of a Congressional Committee.

There is a section of the press which serves as a conscious collaborator and tool of the Committee in the exposure process. Newspapers in this group include the *Cincinnati Enquirer,* the *Baltimore Sun,* the *Miami Daily News,* the *New Bedford Standard Times,* the *Buffalo Evening News,* the *Chicago Tribune,* the *New York Daily News,* the *New York Mirror,* the *Newark Star-Ledger.*

Many of the Washington correspondents of these newspapers enjoy a close relationship with the Committee and its members. There is a junta of insiders, headed by radio commentator and news columnist Fulton Lewis, Jr., who are afforded generous access to the Committee's plans and files. Professor Robert K. Carr observed that:

> . . . the intimacy which has existed between the Committee and certain newspapers has at times been disquieting. With few exceptions the newspapers enjoying these close contacts have been reactionary journals, and the record makes it clear that they have aided and abetted the Committee in some of its most sensational and flamboyant undertakings.

These newspapers have cozy relationships with the Committee's field investigators, and pass leads to the Committee in exchange for "exclusives." This enables the newspaper to attack the witness long before he appears on the stand. When the decision to hold a hearing is formally announced, these newspapers proclaim it as a triumph of their journalistic vigilance. Their local reporters become, in effect, members of HUAC's staff. The hearings become their private journalistic fief. They spare no effort to make the hearing a success—screaming headlines, large photographs of the victims, interviews with Committee members, feature stories and personality sketches of everyone connected with the hearings.

The Committee's informers are pelted with roses by these dailies. There is hardly a major informer who has appeared before the Committee —Matusow, Budenz, Manning Johnson, Paul Crouch—at whose feet they have not sat and worshipped.

The role of HUAC's journalistic pets is not to mirror the news but to distort and exaggerate it and to lead the community in the hue and cry against the unfriendly witness. For example, HUAC decided to come to Buffalo in 1957, after the *Buffalo Evening News* had campaigned for hearings. For almost a decade it had been conducting its

150

own Red hunt in collaboration with the local Network—the Anti-Subversive Police Squad, the American Legion and private anti-Communist information services.

A week before the hearings commenced it announced that a three-man subcommittee would investigate Communist infiltration of industry in the Buffalo area and the distribution of foreign propaganda. The *Buffalo Evening News* disclosed that the addresses of the 34 subpoenaed witnesses were supplied to the subcommittee by the Buffalo Police Anti-Subversive Squad. On September 26, a front-page article by Fred Turner, the newspaper's Red specialist, headlined, "Efforts of Red 'Colonizing' Dramatically Shown Here." Turner wrote that the hearings would bare "Commy techniques of getting a job and worming their way into plants" in order "to bring about labor-management friction."

The stock feature of the road show is an opening-day press briefing by staff director Arens and the subcommittee Chairman. Arens gave the *Buffalo Evening News* his standard interview: "We regard this as a serious Communist operation." The Communist conspiracy is a "greater menace than ever" because it is now reduced to "a hard core of real revolutionaries." According to the *Evening News,* Arens went on to explain that "the Federal Bureau of Investigation is the 'finest of its type in the world,' but is outnumbered two to one by the Communists who respond to the will of Moscow." He told the press that "the Communist apparatus had given an all-out signal to its several hundred fronts and the several hundred fronts behind the fronts to discredit the House Committee. They are taking steps to abolish it."

The newspaper announced that while the public was invited to all nonexecutive sessions, "Priority ratings for admissions have been established, however, to guarantee certain individuals and groups such as the Erie County American Legion seating space in the courtroom."

The *News* gave all this the most prominent coverage. When the hearings began, it published the pictures of the witnesses as well as lengthy abstracts from their testimony. The hearings of the second day were likewise published in minute detail. The *News* carried a lead story under the heading "FBI Undercover Agent Tells of Peace Groups Set Up as Red Fronts." This story reproduces a long list of names as well as photographs of the witnesses and their counsel, together with a photograph headed "Dramatic Identification During Session of House Communist Probe." It is a classic picture of such a "confrontation," including the pointing of the finger by the informer and the hand-shielded face of the victim.

The same issue of the *Buffalo Evening News* ran a "dope story" that plans were afoot to instigate prosecutions of some labor-union witnesses for alleged violation of the non-Communist affidavit provisions of the Taft-Hartley Act. A story, headlined, "Red Probe Witness Removed as USW Local Delegate," announced that one witness, a Bethlehem Steel employee who had told the Committee under oath that he was not a member of the Communist Party, was nevertheless removed as a delegate from the local to the CIO Greater Buffalo Industrial Union Council. He had also been suspended from his steward's post at the Bethlehem Steel Company, pending the outcome of the subcommittee hearings.

The last day of the hearings received most sensational press treatment in the *Evening News*. The Committee had saved as a wind-up witness a local optometrist who, according to a huge headline, had been "Named a Top Red in Buffalo, Balks at Nearly All Questions." It became apparent in the hearing that this witness would plead the Fifth Amendment to all questions. He so pleaded in response to a question about a trip to Mexico. Arens then asked him a where-was-Moses-when-the-lights-went-out question: whether he had been in Mexico at the time of the attempted assassination of former President Truman in Washington, D.C., by Puerto Rican nationalists. The *News* did not think that these tactics were unfair—or if it thought so, it kept silent about it.

In order to do justice to the remainder of the last day's hearings, principally concerned with demonstrating Red infiltration of the YWCA, the NAACP, and parent-teacher groups, the *Evening News* devoted separately headlined stories, complete with photographs, to each of the eight "infiltrators," of whom seven were housewives:

SOCIAL WORKER AVOIDS REPLY ON
WHETHER HE WAS A RED

WOMAN INVOKES FIFTH OVER QUERIES
ON HOW YWCA WORKED

152

A *News* story of the same day, "Case of Ex-Reds in UAW's Hands," stated that production had been restored at a Buffalo plant where the men had walked out in protest over "having to work with former Communists" who had been witnesses at the hearing. A union representative charged that the company had instigated the walk-out.

Another story in the *News* of this day carries a large headline "Prosecution Here up to Washington." "Any contempt, perjury or Taft-Hartley Act violation prosecutions, as a result of the House Un-American Activities Committee Subcommittee hearings will be handled by the United States attorney's office in Buffalo but initiated by the Department of Justice." It recounts that the U.S. attorney had sat in as observer during the four days of hearings and that the Committee would deal directly with the Department of Justice in recommending any criminal action. The suboommittee members had indicated that they would recommend Justice Department investigations of the testimony of some witnesses. No such prosecution was ever begun. Thus a large metropolitan daily devoted the major portion of its news pages for four days to sensationalizing hearings which produced no meaningful testimony.

A few newspapers operate their own exposure mills. They train reporters who specialize in inside dope on the local Reds. In some cases they pick up an informer on the open market who has already testified before an antisubversive committee, or they buy his confessions before he makes his debut as a witness. Among the informers who have, at one time or another, found a journalistic outlet for their talents are Herbert Philbrick, Louis Budenz, Paul Cruoch, Harvey Matusow, Benjamin Gitlow, and William Teto.

One of the country's outstanding exposure operations was conducted for many years by the *Miami Daily News*. In 1948, the newspaper "covered" a public meeting addressed by Elizabeth Gurley Flynn, Communist leader. It printed pictures of the audience and told its readers that the center of subversion in the United States had shifted from California to Miami. In 1949, the newspaper repeated the tactic, this time in connection with a meeting of the Civil Rights Congress. Then it called upon informer Paul Crouch for a series of articles which elaborated the thesis that Miami was the hub of an international Red network covering Latin America.

The newspaper arranged with the Committee to have Crouch's material published *as testimony* in the hope of clothing it with immunity from libel actions. The Committee obliged, but the maneuver was ineffective. Crouch's charge that Armand Scala, a Pan-American employee, was a Communist courier between the United States and Latin America resulted in a successful libel suit. The jury found that Crouch had lied; the paper paid $5,000 damages.

But Scala's legal victory did nothing to lessen the fear and intimidation which by this time had engulfed a sizeable portion of Miami's permanent community. Liberal organizations purged themselves of "radical" suspects; liberals themselves retired from organizations which they thought might be vulnerable; many persons left the community altogether. The *Daily News's* expert on subversion, Damon Runyon, Jr., tirelessly listed individuals prominent in liberal movements as Reds or subversives. The *News* specialized in hair-raising political horror stories of espionage and sabotage. Paul Crouch told Miami readers that an espionage network was fanning out from Miami to spark South American revolutions. An agent named Joseph Mazzei—subsequently disowned as a liar by the Department of Justice—used its columns to inform Miamians that the Reds were plotting to take over the Opa Locka Naval Station as an invasion base for the Soviet Army. Another *Daily News* writer, Al Spears, a claimed ex-FBI agent, expressed the opinion that the Reds were bent on converting Opa Locka into a model Soviet village. The paper even printed a charge that the local Reds had infiltrated a million-dollar Miami Beach prostitution ring.

The *Daily News* coupled these scare stories with constant urging to readers to "repent" or "inform," preferably, of course, in the newspaper's own columns. In June 1954, Runyon collaborated with Al Spears in a series of articles charging that at least 300-card-holding Communists lived in the area, and complaining that all of them still seemed able to earn a living. Actually, about 50 alleged Reds were named, most of them on hearsay evidence. The series also smeared organizations which had never before been charged with subversion, among them the F.D.R. Club, a Miami Beach discussion forum, and the First Unitarian Church of Miami.

Runyon had a journalistic field day as the grand jury ground out subpoenas and indictments. "The Communist Party in Miami," he wrote, "already has complete plans of the stockade (the new police lock-up) which were obtained in anticipation that all would be rounded up when Soviet Russia attacks the United States." In another article, he wrote: "The Communist Party's method of preying on lonely people was described yesterday by a pretty German girl, a former atomic bomb technician, who said she unwittingly fell into Communist hands. . . ." The story was illustrated with a revealing photograph of the girl, bearing the caption, "I was lonely. . . ." The disbarment of a local attorney who pleaded the Fifth Amendment brought from Runyon the announcement: "The legal arm of the Communist Party [has been] smashed." When the disbarred lawyer moved away from Miami, the *Daily News* carried a huge front-page headline, "New Czar for Reds in Miami." Who the new "Czar" was, or where he came from, the newspaper never bothered to say.

Runyon's inventiveness was wide-ranging. "Reds' Safety in Jail Feared as Inmates 'Haze' Smolikoff," ran the headline over a story which reported that Charles Smolikoff, one of the men jailed for contempt of the grand jury, had been beaten up by fellow prisoners in an effort to make him sing patriotic songs "backwards and forwards." The *Daily News* ran the story for a full day after it had been denied by the sheriff.

In the winter (when else?) of 1954, the Committee finally succumbed to the campaign of Runyon and the *Daily News* for local hearings. But the three-day hearing only yielded 34 names—almost all of them already known. This was thin gruel for a community which had for years been fed on a rich diet of exposures served up by the *Daily News's* chefs. As a matter of fact, the hearing made the

Miamians wonder whether prior press accounts of subversion were not grossly exaggerated. The Committee tried to put on a good show, but it had poor material. Its chief witness was one Ralph V. Long, an ex-FBI agent whose testimony drew from Chairman Velde the comment that he was "one of the most outstanding witnesses to appear before this Committee." But his hometown newspaper, the Durham, North Carolina, *Morning Herald,* wasn't impressed. It wrote shortly before his appearance:

Long has a police record extending from September 11, 1949, through November 5, 1954. He has been tried twenty times for public drunkenness and each time has either served time, paid a fine, or appealed the judgment to the Superior Court. Several of the appeals are now pending. In addition, Long has been tried twice for disorderly conduct and twice for assault and battery. A nol pross with leave was taken in the first case of disorderly conduct, while Long paid court costs in the second. The first case of assault and battery was nol prossed; no disposition was recorded in the second.

The Miami papers apparently did not think Long's record newsworthy. Long's 21st conviction for drunkenness came on November 4, less than a month prior to his appearance before the Committee. Apparently his thirst overcame him again only a few days after he returned from Miami, for the records of the Recorder's Court in Durham, as printed in the *Morning Herald* of December 7, show that on December 6 he had again been found guilty of drunkenness and sentenced to 30 days. It was his 22nd conviction in five years.

In Seattle, too, the disclosures of the Committee were a journalistic anticlimax. After the Velde-led Committee came to Seattle in the summer of 1954, the *Post-Intelligencer* printed an editorial blazing with self-congratulations:

The names exposed by the Post-Intelligencer reporters from the forties on were the same as those exposed in the House hearings. So thoroughly had reporters for this newspaper done their work that hardly a new name came out of the exhaustive Seattle hearings—merely confirmation of the painstaking evidence that had been gathered and published over the last 10 years.

The editorial takes particular pride in its reporter, Traynor Hansen, who had got in touch wtih Mrs. Hartle after her Smith Act conviction and encouraged her to break with the Communist Party; "her decision might have been indefinitely delayed except for this reporter's initiative."

Sometimes a newspaper uses the Committee to hound a single individual, as a Scripps-Howard paper did in the case of a former union official whose conviction for filing a false Taft-Hartley affidavit was set aside by the Supreme Court and who subsequently received a fellowship from the Woodrow Wilson Foundation. After the newspaper attacks on him, he was called 3,000 miles from home to appear at a Washington hearing held to trap the witness into making statements which might be used for a second perjury charge.

The Committee permitted him to testify in executive session. However, when the witness emerged from the executive session, a Scripps-Howard reporter entered the room where the private hearing had taken place and was evidently told by staff director Arens what had occurred, for he immediately rushed to a phone and informed the Director of the Foundation how many times the individual involved had pleaded the Fifth Amendment. What did he intend to do about it? The Foundation refused to be blackmailed into revoking its grant.

The most fascinating journalistic experiment with the operation of a private exposure system took place in Cincinnati in 1950. In February of that year, the *Enquirer* published in its Sunday section the first of a series of six articles purporting to give the real lowdown on the menace confronting the city. Written by one James Ratliff, a reporter with a background of experience in army intelligence work, they were spread over a third of the front page of each issue.

The first installment was headlined: "Communists Mark 12 City Plants for Sabotage!" *"178 Reds in Cincinnati, Including Professor, Three Doctors, 16 from Labor."* But the story was coy about names: there were only three names in the text and none of the plants was identified.

The second article used equally large headlines to

charge Red control of two unions and infiltration of others. But still no names. The third article found Red penetration of the Democratic Party. In one primary election, "Two of them have been nominated and thus everyone in Hamilton County who voted the straight Democratic ticket in the November balloting where these Democrats ran, voted for actual members of the Communist Party." The article was not only silent about the names, but even failed to specify the year of the primary election.

As the articles rocketed across Cincinnati's Sunday breakfast tables, the demands mounted that the names of the comrades be disclosed. Employers wanted the names to make sure that their plants would not be blown up by their employees. Groups were demanding a purge of the University of Cincinnati; a lynch spirit was in the air. Some of the demands for identification came from labor groups who felt that they had been smeared by Ratliff's articles.

Early in March, before the publication of the final article in the *Enquirer* series, the two rival Cincinnati papers, the *Times-Star* and the *Post,* came to life. They exploded with stories relating that Ratliff and his informant, one Cecil Scott, a former FBI agent, had gone to Washington to enlist HUAC's aid. They attempted to get the *Enquirer* material, together with the names which the newspaper had withheld, into HUAC's records as "testimony." As such it would be libel-proof. But, the *Enquirer's* rivals reported, the Committee, after hearing the pair in private, refused to buy the package. Ratliff's information was hearsay; and as for Scott—he had a record of insanity. The *Times-Star* and *Post* subsequently published the fact that Scott was also a convicted forger. In addition, an important item of evidence submitted to the Committee turned out to be a forgery. The document had been altered to give it significance.

During the next few days, the two papers told of Scott's periodic confinements in a local mental hospital, and of his unsuccessful attempt to peddle his material to HUAC in 1949. The *Enquirer* had neglected to tell its readers (a) that Scott was the source of its disclosures; (b) that he was a convicted forger and a psychopathic personality; and (c) that Ratliff and Scott had gone to Washington to get the Committee to give them a libel-proof forum.

Instead of retreating quickly from its embarrassing position, the *Enquirer* charged in a lead editorial that its rivals had:

> . . . lent themselves to a publicity blitzkrieg that couldn't have been better organized if the Communists' own Committee for Agitation and Propaganda had planned it. Reporters descended upon the House Committee preparing to sit in executive session, demanding to see the "super secret agent" in such a way as to make the Committee counsel suspect the whole matter was a publicity stunt. . . . The *Daily Worker* scarcely could have been more enthusiastic than our afternoon contemporaries and their radio stations when a hitch developed in presenting the evidence to the Committee!

The *Enquirer* responded to the gibes of its rivals by urging its readers to sign a petition which had appeared on its front pages for a number of weeks demanding that ". . . the names of Cincinnati Communists be exposed before the proper investigating authority in Washington. . . ." When the total reached a claimed ten thousand, Mr. Ratliff made a second trip to Washington demanding action. No one questioned this strange use to which a legislative committee was being put.

This time the Committee acted. It held a three-day hearing in July 1950, but even the five friendly witnesses could shake out only about 70 names—most of them from the distant past. The Committee again heard Scott in private session, this time for five days, but refused to release his testimony despite the insistence of the *Enquirer*.

Perhaps the real reason for the passion of the *Enquirer*, an arch-Republican organ, and the reluctance of the Committee (then under Democratic control) to publicly back up this paper, was voiced by Scott himself, who ascribed his rejection by the Committee to the fact that he "had stepped on the toes of Democratic bigwigs when he testified that some of the Democratic candidates had been connected with the Communist Party." Chairman Walter rejoined that he was "inclined to believe that his whole story was politically inspired."

But in 1952, Scott and the *Enquirer* finally got their libel-proof forum: the Ohio Un-American Activities Commission which first heard his testimony in secret and then released it. During the course of the hearings before the Commission, in which four of Scott's victims denied his charges under oath, Congressman Velde, a Republican, who was about to assume chairmanship of HUAC, sent the Commission a wire that Scott in his appearance before HUAC "had presented creditable evidence of Communism throughout the State of Ohio. Some members of the Committee may have been disappointed with this testimony, but I wish to assure you personally that it was reliable."

Velde never explained why the Committee never printed the "creditable" testimony or what had happened to a recommendation by Congressman Walter that Scott's forgery be referred to the United States Attorney. What is brilliantly clear is that a powerful newspaper sought to stampede a community into a lynch spirit. It used the Red issue for crudely partisan purposes and in the process made a hero and patriot of a forger and psychotic personality. It then recruited HUAC and the Ohio Commission to shield itself from the consequences of its irresponsibility.

While there is a substantial section of the press which brings a special dimension of sensationalism and witch-hunting to coverage of the Committee, many newspapers do not permit ideological considerations to color their reporting of the Committee. They, nevertheless, give prominent coverage to its hearings because they believe that the hearings of a Congressional agency are news. The late Elmer Davis, one of the severest critics of our press, has observed that the press has become the collaborator of the witch-hunting committees because of the desire of reporters and editors to remain "objective" by running stories "as is" just because "somebody said it":

. . . . most American news editors have abdicated their judgment, and decided that news is what is said by somebody of importance—even if it is demonstrably and even notoriously false. . . .

Consider Senator McCarthy: not a single one of his charges has ever been proved, most of them have been pretty conclusively disproved in public hearings, yet he can repeat those same charges and still get space in the papers, sometimes on the front page . . .

very often in papers whose editors may know that this is old stuff, may know that none of it has been proved and much of it has been refuted, yet who feel that if a United States Senator keeps on saying it, it would not be objective to refuse to print it. . . .

The reader lays down his nickel . . . for the paper, in the belief that he is going to find out what is going on in the world; and it does not seem to me that the newspaper is giving him his nickel's worth if it only gives him what somebody says is going on in the world, with no hint as to whether what that somebody says is right or wrong. . . .

. . . .it makes a difference, a vast difference, to the health of the republic whether what is on that front page is what is so . . . or only what somebody falsely alleges to be so.

Many newspaper editors have become aware that the Committee has made them tools of its exposure operation. Some of them have accepted this role uncritically. They are content to stigmatize the unfriendly witness as disloyal without affording the injured individual an opportunity to reply. Nor do they register editorial protest against the abuses of the Committee.

But a growing number of dailies severely limit the publicity given to the Committee and its hearings. Included in the group are the *New York Times;* the *Washington Post;* the *Denver Post;* the *Hartford Courant* and the *New York Post.* A recruit to these ranks is the *San Francisco Chronicle,* which refused to print the names of a group of recently subpoenaed California teachers. These newspapers use their editorial columns to neutralize the harm done to those named in their news columns. They also carry the comments of the victims. A growing number of prominent and responsible newspapers have called for the Committee's abolition.

Perhaps the most serious shortcomings of the press is the failure to recognize *in print* the dangers in HUAC's abuse of the power of investigation. If newspapers have a duty to report what takes place in a hearing, they should also report what has not taken place. It is impossible to discover from accounts of Committee hearings what the purpose of the hearing is supposed to be and whether hearings conform to the purpose. Beginning with the Hollywood hearings in 1947, the press—even when critical of the Committee—has rarely bothered to explore the gap between the Committee's exposure activities and legitimate functions as an agency of Congress. Few newspapers have asked: Is exposure a function of a Committee of Congress?

Even moderate newspapers have acted as glorified press agents for the Committee's informers. An informer may fall on his face in public, but the press is either indifferent or silent. In the Owen Latimer hearings before Senator Tydings' subcommittee, one Larry Kerley, a former reporter for the *New York Journal American,* who subsequently became a staff member of the House Committee, was supposed to produce a witness who would swear that Latimer was a Communist. When the time came to produce this witness, John Huber, he "disappeared" from his hotel room. Kerley charged that he had been abducted and disposed of by the Reds and was probably "at the bottom of the Potomac." The simple fact was that Huber had "blacked out" and left town; whether or not under his own power, nobody knows. Few newspapers were curious about the backgrounds of either Kerley or Huber—although it was thought by many that Huber at the last moment had lost his nerve and refused to go along with what appeared to be a plot to "frame" Latimer. Instead, most of them printed Kerley's story about the Red abduction as though it were the truth.

While many newspapers generously report all of the Committee's doings, and unstintingly give space to its Chairman's most blood-curdling charges, few of them take note of criticisms of the Committee. The statement of Wisconsin Governor Gaylord Nelson calling for HUAC's abolition, the petitions of hundreds of university faculty members to the same effect, the spate of resolutions denouncing the Committee from all parts of the country, have been for the most part ignored by both the press and the wire services.

9 THE ROAD SHOWS

Legislative investigating committees usually hold hearings in Washington in order to give the committee access to its staff and files and to permit its members to discharge other responsibilities. But not HUAC. Since 1952, the Committee has divided its hearing days about evenly between Washington and the road. The Committee has never troubled to conceal the fact that these peripatetic endeavors are designed to extract a maximum response from the public—hardly a legislative end.

The Committee has made an institution of the "area" investigation. Other investigating committees concentrate on problems, but the Committee has an unquenchable zest for places (and, of course, the people in them). Since 1950, the following cities have received the area hearing treatment: Baltimore (1951 in Washington, and 1957); Boston (1951 in Washington, and 1958); Buffalo (1952, 1954); Chicago (1952, 1954, 1956, 1957 and 1959); Philadelphia (1952, 1953); Los Angeles (1953, 1955, 1956, 1958 and 1959); New York City (1953, 1955, 1956 and 1958); Columbus, Ohio (1953); Albany (1953, 1954); San Francisco (1953, 1955); Seattle (1954, 1955 and 1956); Portland, Ore. (1954); Newark (1955, 1958); Milwaukee (1955); Fort Wayne (1955 in Washington); Charlotte, N. C. (1956); Denver (1956); St. Louis (1956); New Haven (1956, 1957); Youngstown (1956); Atlanta (1958); New Orleans (1957); San Juan, P. R. (1959).

It may also be that the Committee travels so much to escape from the headaches and the responsibilities of the Washington scene. Why wrestle with real legislative problems when you can, without any effort at all, defend the country from the Reds and receive a crown of laurel from the local adoring patrioteers? Besides, on the road the living is easy. The Committee members have become enamored of the fleshpots of junketeering.

A series of articles by two reporters for the Knight newspaper chain published in the summer of 1950, based upon a study of expense vouchers, disclosed that members of the Committee figure prominently among a group of Congressmen who have charged as hearing expenses lavish bills for hotel, food and liquor.

In May 1958, Committee member Moulder ran up a nightclub bill of $90.38 at the Persian Room of the Plaza Hotel where he was occupying a $21-a-day hotel room. Congressman Moulder's total four-day stay cost taxpayers $282.17. His bill to the Government for a second four-day New York hearing in 1958 amounted to $255.66—his hotel room alone was $40 a day. A few months later, he and Chairman Walter, together with three staff members, ran up a $900.22 bill in Los Angeles. Walter and Moulder, again with three others, returned to Los Angeles in February 1959 and outdid their earlier performance; the bill was $1,187.64 for a four or five-day stay. Congressmen Moulder and Scherer, in March of 1959, managed, again with three staff members, to run up a bill of $973.66 for a four-day stay at the Waldorf-Astoria in New York. The Government was charged additionally the sum of $111.25 for the rental of Cadillac limousines.

Some of this extravagance is explained by the character and purpose of the Committee's road shows. When HUAC comes to town, it is surrounded by an entourage of police officers and members of the local security bureaucracy. Hospitality must be shown these people, for they are important adjutants in locating witnesses, keeping them under observation and developing testimony about them. Then, too, the friendly witnesses must be taken care of. Thus, on the floor of Congress, Congressman Moulder explained that he ran up one of his huge bills when he was host to "police officers, assistant district attorneys, FBI agents and sometimes two or three cooperative witnesses." Mr. Scherer told reporters that sometimes "a deputy marshal, a district attorney, a sheriff or a police chief" broke bread with the Committee in the course of "discussing evidence to be presented before the Committee the next day." Sheriffs and such undoubtedly never find their way to the tables and hotel rooms of workaday legislative fact-finders—but how appropriate that they should share the conviviality of the hunt with members of the Committee.

HUAC's drain on the public purse is further explained by another kind of hospitality which is rooted in the special role it plays in our national life. The Rivers and Harbors Committee has no followers who are raised to ecstasy by its arrival in town for a legislative investigation. But the Committee's arrival is *der Tag* for the zealots who look to it to save the Republic from Reds and pinks. The subcommittee panel is hailed as a liberating army; ceremonies are held; patriotic citations are awarded. The Committee is not indifferent to the ardor of its admirers. It makes special seating reservations for them and gives them inside tips on what is planned for the hearing. A select few—the praetorian guard, as it were—are invited to join or attach themselves to the entourage; they eat and drink with the sheriffs, the FBI agents, the assistant district attorneys and the friendly witnesses. As Congressman Moulder described them to the Knight newspaper reporters, they are "friendly people—you might call them fans of the Committee . . ." A road show, then, is an occasion for a reunion of the Committee and its "fans." This may not be an impressive function, but it is highly important in the exposure process: the Committee counts on its followers to carry through its propaganda and to execute its judgment and punishment of the unfriendly witness. The local hearing renews the faith of the faithful and invigorates their zeal.

These extraneous motivations rarely compete with a bona fide legislative purpose. HUAC's road shows assemble the same "facts"—over and over again. For example, many Americans learned, to their amusement and disgust, in the summer of 1960, that the Committee had carted around a New York customs official and put him on the stand in ten different hearings in ten different cities to give (at public expense) precisely the same testimony each time. Two more hearings along the same lines were held after the disclosures were made, bringing the total number up to twelve.

When the Committee travels, it does not neglect the home states and districts of its members. The Committee has already conducted investigations in the home districts or states of eight of its nine members. This enables the local man to shine at the local investigation over which he presides as chairman.

The Committee works up a particular concern with subversion in the home districts and states of its members in election years. In 1952, 100% of the hearings away from Washington between January and Election Day were held in the home states of members, and 27% in their home districts. In 1954, during the same period of time, out of 34 hearing days away from Washington, 26 (77%) were held in members' home states and 10 (29%) were held in their home districts. In 1956, during the same period, out of 23 hearing days away from Washington, 13 (57%) were held in members' home states and 6 (25%) were held in members' home districts. In 1958, out of 18 hearing days away from Washington, one-third were held in members' home states and 3 (18%) in members' home districts. From 1952 and 1958, between January 1 and Election Day in each election year, a total of 67 hearing days were held in members' home states and 25 in members' home districts —69% and 26%, respectively, of the total number of hearing days spent away from Washington.

Unless one is prepared to believe that the members of the Committee have particularly subversive constituents, one must conclude that, in part at least, politics has replaced legislation as a motivation for the hearings.

In recent years there have been three Committee hearings in the South: New Orleans, Charlotte, North Carolina, and Atlanta. The New Orleans hearing was conducted by Mr. Willis of Louisiana. The other two were conducted by Chairman Walter of Pennsylvania. This was no coincidence. The Chairman of the Committee is a close ally of the Southern Democratic bloc; he is grateful for their enthusiastic backing of his Committee; his personal participation in the Charlotte and Atlanta hearings, both held after the Supreme Court's desegregation decision, was simply a gracious expression of support in an hour of need.

The Committee has always been extraordinarily responsive to the needs of its friends and supporters and has not been averse to using its processes to help them. It has intervened in labor disputes on behalf of employers and permitted its powers to be used to aid a favored participant in representation elections, or a faction in an intra-union dispute.

Individuals of the proper background can put the Committee into action. As HUAC has stated,

The Committee has formulated the policy of investigating complaints received from American citizens who have the interest of the United States foremost in their hearts and minds. In each instance the Committee has undertaken an investigation only upon complaints by citizens.

When the Committee sought to investigate the radio broadcasts of certain news commentators, Congressman Landis explained, "As a public agency we are compelled to respect a reasonable request from substantial citizens." As we show later, individuals can obtain access to the Committee's facilities for clearance purposes.

Committee attacks on the social gospel movement of the Methodist Church in 1952 and 1953 were sparked by the Circuit Riders, a private religious grouping close to Chairman Velde and the Committee staff. The Committee even sent Circuit Rider literature to the Network organizations. Of similar origin was Congressman Walter's attack in June 1959 on the American Art exhibition in Moscow because of the alleged backgrounds and opinions of the artists. Walter's concern for the political purity of American art was believed to have been inspired by a small group of American sculptors who, as consistent recipients of Government art commissions, have a vested interest in confining and controlling Government art activities. This use of political weapons to entrench officially favored artists is, of course, a phenomenon made familiar by Fascism; but it is hardly impressive as an expression of legislative purpose.

Local road shows are more effective in stirring up hostility to the unfriendly witnesses and in forcing their discharge from employment than a Washington hearing. A Washington hearing is not televised, and because it is relatively remote, press coverage is seldom complete. Then, too, the local Network organizations are harder to mobilize.

For example, in 1951, HUAC held hearings in Washington on "the defense area of Baltimore." HUAC had an excellent witness, Mary Markward, an FBI undercover agent who named over a hundred names of Communists. In her career as a professional witness, Mrs. Markward has named a total of 318 names. In 1959, the Subversive Activities Control Board ruled that her testimony should be assayed with caution.

Somehow, her identifications did not procure a completely effective result. Numbers of people whom she named, as well as a large number of unfriendly witnesses, held onto their jobs.

There were two reasons for this: there was no telecast of her testimony, and the Baltimore press ran it on the back pages.

HUAC decided on a second try at Baltimore in 1957 to see if it could do better. (In fact the 1957 hearings were the fourth round. Dies had come to town in 1940, and a hearing was held in 1954.) This time it would hold its sessions on the spot and line up the press for sensational coverage. A second reason for coming to Baltimore was the need to stimulate support for an appropriation for the enforcement of the Ober Law, a Maryland antisubversive statute.

On April 24, the Baltimore papers reported a speech by one Louis Schmidt before the Minute Women of Baltimore, discussing the forthcoming House hearing. Curiously enough, Schmidt was not an agent of the House Committee, but an investigator for the special state unit in charge of the Ober Law. This agency was faced with extinction both because its entire budget had been wiped out and because a Supreme Court decision had ruled that Federal antisubversive legislation preempted the powers of the states. Schmidt urged an aggressive campaign by the Minute Women for the support of a bill in Congress restoring the dual sovereignty of the states in the antisubversive field and action in the state legislature to restore the budget cut. All this would be understandable enough, but what is striking is the way in which Schmidt used the authority of the House Committee to give weight to his plea. He announced in advance how many individuals would be subpoenaed for the House hearing and asserted that the foundation of the hearing would be the material amassed by the Maryland unit. This was nonsense, since the hearing was based entirely on the disclosures of FBI agents.

On the eve of the televised hearing, both Walter and Arens issued statements. According to Arens, the Baltimore hearings were of special importance because Baltimore was in the same organizational district of the Communist Party as the Nation's capital. Walter explained that "new techniques of conspiracy" had recently been adopted by the Party which required probing.

The *Baltimore Sun* of May 7, the day of the opening of the hearing, ran a screaming headline on the front page— "Undercover Agent Tells of Communist Cell Here." The story stressed the fact that the Committee's chief witness, an FBI informer, had met with Communist Party associates only the previous night. All those identified by the witness were listed, but there is nothing to indicate that they have engaged in any unlawful activity. A curious circumstance in connection with the testimony of the FBI agent, Miller, completely escaped the attention of the press. Although Miller was to be the star witness, he was placed under subpoena by the Committee along with the unfriendly witnesses.

A subsequent edition of the *Sun* ran a story with a new but equally large headline, "Three Bethlehem Workers Plead the Fifth at Red Probe." This story contained full identification of the witnesses, complete with photographs. The informer witness praised the Ober Law frequently and lavishly, its administration and effectiveness, how the law forced the Communists underground and how they emerged when a judge, whose ruling was subsequently reversed, held the law unconstitutional.

The *Sun* of May 8 likewise ran a large headline, "5th Amendment Is Invoked by 6 Sparrows Point Steel Workers at House Communism Probe Here," a piece of news which the paper thought deserved more prominence than Ex-Secretary Dulles' review of NATO's stand on atomic arms, or the conference between MacMillan and Adenauer, which occurred the same day.

On May 8, 1957, the *Sun* reported the second day's hearings with equal prominence. Its lead headline, printed in enormous type, "Red Probe to Quiz More Named as Reds Here." All of the witnesses who pleaded the Fifth Amendment were carefully identified and pictured.

On the evening of May 8, the *Sun-Post* ran a screaming headline, "Says Reds Infiltrate PTA, YWCA, Voters League Here," and the *Sun,* also in the largest type available to it, ran a headline "7 More Named as Reds Plead 5th at Probe Here." In this story, Chairman Walter deplores the ease with which those who plead the Fifth Amendment obtain new employment or hold on to their jobs. Walter said he "may recommend new laws requiring closer employment checks by industries handling government contracts." Mr. Arens, according to the *Sun,* interjected the observation that "a very significant amount of propaganda from behind the Iron Curtain arrives in the Port of Baltimore. It is part of the vast quantities arriving by the ton in the United States in violation of the law."

The *Sun* of May 9 thought the fact that "House Probers Name 3 as Red Leaders in Local Area" the most important piece of news which had occurred the day before. Its detailed story of the testimony identified seven more witnesses who pleaded the Fifth Amendment, gave their addresses and occupations, and the photographs of some of them. The testimony of a second undercover agent was liberally quoted and, again, no mention is made of illegal activity. A companion story indicates that some of the workers at the Bethlehem Steel Company had refused to work with one of the unfriendly witnesses.

The *Sun* of May 10 ran two front-page headlines summarizing the hearings: "Teacher, Lawyer, 7 Others, Plead Fifth Amendment"; "Unfriendly Witnesses Total 22 as House Unit Ends Its Hearings Here." This story quotes the Committee statement at the close of the hearing, expressing hope that the Ober Law enforcement unit "will be continued and strengthened in the splendid work it has been doing." A companion story bears the headlines "Bethlehem to Fire 6; Workers Took the 5th Amendment at Hearings."

The *Sun* of the same day (May 10) further deals with the aftermath of the hearings. The newspaper reports "Police Protection Ordered For 2 At Red Probe." The story describes how a lady FBI agent had received embarrassing telephone calls from a man who made improper proposals, while one of her victims had a brick thrown through her window. The *American* of May 12 describes more fully how two days after the brick was thrown, a "jeering, laughing crowd of about 75 persons demonstrated last night in front of the home of a woman who pleaded the Fifth Amendment when questioned by the House Un-American Activities Committee. . . ."

Probably the outstanding example of a road show which was conducted to serve private ends is the 1959 Chicago hearings which were held ostensibly for the purpose of investigating Communist infiltration of defense-connected labor unions. The Committee questioned eight officials of the United Packinghouse Workers, a labor organization, from a district director down to organizers—two Packinghouse office secretaries, a building manager, and two individuals who at one time had been connected with the union. All 13 of those subpoenaed swore they were not then Communists. Most of them swore they had not been Communists in the past five years. All 13 invoked the Fifth Amendment in response to questions, posed in various forms, as to whether they had ever been Communists. The three friendly witnesses included a member of Patrick Gorman's rival Amalgamated Meat Cutters. These witnesses admitted that they had left the Communist Party ten years ago, but asserted that the Packinghouse Workers was infiltrated by Communists.

The Committee never convincingly explained what all this political archaeology had to do with the Nation's security: how a meat packer's former membership in the Communist Party threatened our ramparts. But the true reasons for the hearing were barely concealed. The hearings sought to discredit and embarrass the Packinghouse Workers Union on the eve of crucial collective-bargaining negotiations with the leading employers in the industry. In addition, it gave Gorman a desperately needed reason for rejecting a merger with the Packinghouse Workers, widely sought by the rank and file of both unions. Gorman, who had denounced the McClellan probe of alleged Meat Cutters' corruption as "a putrid process of snooping," hailed HUAC's disclosures in these words: "As long as officials of the Packinghouse group hide behind the Fifth Amendment to keep secret their service to the Communist Party, our Union will never merge. We believe the House Committee proved our case for us."

The Committee had another private client on whose behalf it was conducting the hearings. A disgruntled Packinghouse vice president who was dropped from the union had filed charges with the AFL-CIO of Communist infiltration. It is well known in labor circles that the charges were kept alive by the pressure of certain officials in the Meat Cutters, eager to embarrass the Packinghouse Workers. Indeed, shortly before the hearings were held in Chicago, AFL-CIO President Meany announced that he was conducting an investigation of these charges to determine whether they warranted further inquiry by the AFL-CIO Ethical Practices Committee.

But these weren't the Committee's only private clients

by any means. Al Hayes, President of the International Association of Machinists, had long been embarrassed by a rank-and-file revolt against the business agents of Lodge 113, IAM, in Chicago. After the reformers forced the resignation of the business agents in 1956, they were required to accept a shackling trusteeship, over three years old at the time the hearing was held. Hayes and his International Union were prominent in the group of unions which had recruited the assistance of the Committee to solve their internal problems. As the labor reporter of the *Chicago Tribune*—a private Committee pipeline—put it in describing the investigation more than a month before the hearing, "The probe has received the full cooperation of a large number of large international unions, including the AFL-CIO International Association of Machinists which has been fighting a bitter and expensive battle with left-wing elements trying to take over locals representing tool and die makers." The rank-and-file revolt had to be quelled. The trusteeship had failed; what better instrument than the Committee?

The Committee's capacious security cloak, which had without difficulty enveloped subversive meat packers, had plenty of additional room for tool and die makers, a trade which has a natural security flavor. But obviously something more than a passion to perfect our defenses had led the Committee to concentrate on the very local with which President Hayes was having trouble and on the four individuals who were leaders in the rank-and-file movement to lift the suspension. Not even a stab was made at linking the four subpoenaed witnesses to security-sensitive posts. And the Committee's highly unlegislative aims were exposed from another quarter: it developed that the Communists had opposed the rank-and-file movement and had expelled one of the witnesses for favoring it! To make matters even worse, the chairman of the rank-and-file group denied a charge—apparently based upon information supplied to the Committee by his enemies in the International Union—that he had ever been a Communist or under Party discipline. (The witness, in the context of an interrogation about Communism, was asked whether "the figure E-88239" registered with him. By a peculiar coincidence, it turned out to be his union card number.) The rank-and-file leader put it mildly indeed when he complained to the Committee at the close of his testimony:

. . . I want to point out one fact, that I as a chairman of the committee to lift suspension of Local 113, which is the rank and file union in my union, feel that by being called before this committee . . . has served a purpose contrary to the objectives for which the membership of Local 113 or at least a very great segment is striving for, namely to lift suspension of their organization.

While the Committee was using its process to help the Meat Packers, the Amalgamated, the IAM, and Mr. Hayes in this strange investigation, it did not neglect its own interests. Despite its announced intention to confine itself strictly to the subject matter of the hearings, labor, it found time to subpoena and harass two individuals who were officers of a civil-liberties organization which had issued and distributed a pamphlet protesting the hearings as an interference in the internal affairs of unions and calling for the abolition of the Committee. Subpoenas were served on them a few days before the hearing and about a month after all of the other witnesses had been called.

In 1954, the Ohio American Legion called for a Committee investigation of Antioch College, long a citadel of midwestern liberalism. The demand was spearheaded by State Senator Lowell Fess, a Yellow Springs Republican, who saw in the friendly relations of Negro and white students at Antioch an example of "communistic subversion." His patriotism was particularly aroused by the campus performance of Othello in which Desdemona was portrayed by a Negro girl. Joining in the clamor for an investigation was the publisher of a dying local hate sheet, the *Yellow Springs American*, who ascribed the failure of his newspaper to a boycott, allegedly inspired by "left wing" elements. Committee member Scherer, a Republican from nearby Cincinnati, presided over the Committee hearing which, by a familiar coincidence, was held on the eve of a hotly contested election.

A local banker and a retired professor also swelled the chorus of requests for a hearing to rout the Antioch Reds, promising sensational testimony. They appeared in executive session, but their testimony was never printed—an almost certain indication that they had produced nothing

173

which the Committee could use. After all this fanfare, Scherer flushed only one Antioch faculty member. He testified that he had, for a few months, nine years earlier, belonged to a Marxist study group. But even this wan intelligence was further diluted by the admission of the Committee's informer witness that the group was "entirely open—advertised as such— and never conducted in any other way."

When the faculty member was retained by the college, the *Cincinnati Enquirer* urged that the inquiry be resumed. It claimed that it had discovered new evidence of subversion at the college. The Committee at first considered the possibility of reopening the hearings and then settled for an attempt to get the faculty member fired by citing him for contempt: he had refused on moral grounds to name the other members of the study group. The college refused to back down; the contempt indictment was dismissed, and thus ended the great Antioch subversive plot, a silly affair, perhaps, when viewed as a legislative investigation, but a sturdy reminder that the Committee does not let its friends down.

The Committee is partial to area hearings as a device to give the *coup de grâce* to a teacher or professor who is under fire. In March 1953, the Committee heard an Ohio State professor in Washington hearings on "infiltration into education." Thereafter the professor was suspended; he had told a university investigating committee, which was considering whether to recommend his discharge, that he was not and never had been a Communist Party member. Mr. Scherer promptly—in June 1953—brought a HUAC posse to Columbus, Ohio, to expose the professor for having made such a denial after having declined to answer before the Committee and, of course, to convert his suspension into a discharge. While Scherer was at it, he summoned the professor's wife and sister-in-law and subjected all three of them to a police-court grilling. When the record of this lynching party was printed, it was called, "Communist Activities in the Columbus, Ohio, Area."

10 SAN FRANCISCO

In June 1957, the Committee returned to San Francisco for the third time in three and a half years. In December 1953, it had held five days of hearings which had produced a crop of 326 names, supplied by a group of ten friendly witnesses, half of them FBI plants. A 1956 two-day hearing consisted of a foreign propaganda curtain-raiser and an instalment of the Committee's nation-wide hearings into the machinations of the foreign-born.

The June 1957 hearings are of more than routine interest. The hearings were held the day after the Supreme Court decision in the *Watkins* case. The newspapers of the community—with the exception of the Hearst press—had shown increasing coolness toward the Committee; prior to the Committee's appearance a subpoenaed witness had committed suicide; in March 1957 the board of governors of the California Bar Association had rebuked the Committee and its staff director, Arens, for their undignified and offensive conduct of hearings the previous winter and their abuse of lawyers appearing on behalf of witnesses.

A month prior to the hearings, the San Francisco *News* reported that subpoenas had been issued to 49 individuals in the area and commented editorially that, "The community has an obligation to its neighbors to insure that those who are called are not tarred before all the evidence is in."

The hearings were preceded by a series of advertisements signed by four individuals, appealing to area residents to consider for themselves whether the Committee was acting illegally and quoting comments on the Committee's abuses.

Shortly after midnight on June 16, a subpoenaed witness, William K. Sherwood, a Stanford University research scientist, killed himself. Before he went to his laboratory he left a letter declaring, "I will be in two days assassinated by publicity. . . . I would love to spend the next few years in laboratories, and I would hate to spend them in jail."

He added in a farewell letter, which had been addressed to a research colleague, "I have a fierce resentment of being televised." A statement prepared for submission to the Committee charged that the hearing was intended to deprive him of employment and of the opportunity to continue his research. He wrote that the Committee's interest in him stemmed from activities some 10 or 15 years earlier, prior to the time he had begun scientific work, and that the Committee's "trail is strewn with blasted lives, the wreckage of useful careers."

Sherwood had sought a three-day postponement of his hearing to enable him to read a paper at a Vancouver, British Columbia, conference. His paper, read after his death, was highly praised. He had been studying for a doctorate in biochemistry and had passed his written examination with the highest rating in his group. Described by his colleagues and superiors as a "brilliant" researcher, he had been working on a project which gave promise of establishing a link between cancer, some forms of heart disease and schizophrenia.

Sherwood's charge—echoed by his widow in a statement which she was not permitted to present on the opening day of the hearing—that his associations in the remote past had occasioned his subpoena, were confirmed in part at least by a Committee statement, offered when the local newspapers pressed for some explanation of the reasons why Sherwood was called. The Committee claimed that it was pursuing a lead arising from a 1955 hearing at which an individual with the same name was alleged to have been a "contact man" for a "Marxist discussion group" in 1938. At that time Sherwood was 22 years old. A Committee spokesman said that investigators later gathered "other information we are not at liberty to divulge." According to Sherwood's attorney, the only other "information" was the fact that a few months prior to his subpoena he had declined on three occasions to cooperate with the FBI. Other witnesses who were called had been similarly interrogated and at least one was told by an FBI agent that unless he cooperated by naming names he could expect a Committee subpoena.

There was a further indication that the Sherwood appearance was in reprisal for his refusal to identify left-wing associates and that he was to be subjected to exposure by the airing of stale material in the files of the

FBI. Some 15 years prior to the hearing, Sherwood had been interrogated by the FBI and cleared of "security risk" charges inspired by the fact that in 1934 he had worked in Paris as an expediter of medical-supply shipments to the Spanish Loyalists.

Rarely had the Committee's puitive purposes found so dramatic an expression. San Franciscans were shocked; at what point in life can a man find asylum from persecution for his past? What could the Committee have learned from this sensitive scientist that it or the FBI did not already know? What legislative need required that he be called from his laboratory, subjected to job-threatening pressures and even denied a postponement to enable him to read a scientific paper?

The Committee could not rest on its initially advanced reason of the witness' 20-year-old connection with a Marxist study group; the exposure purpose behind this justification was too close to the surface. When Walter arrived in San Francisco, he callously told reporters, "Well, it is certainly unfortunate that we couldn't interrogate him." Walter then added that Sherwood's death was "unfortunate" for the Committee, "Because we have every reason to believe that he had valuable information on the operation of the tax-exempt foundations and how they select the recipients of their grants." He denied that the Committee was responsible for the suicide which, in the language of the San Francisco *Chronicle*, Walter ascribed to "fear of going to jail rather than fear of exposure." But, as the *Chronicle* story points out, Sherwood's farewell letter had said, "My life and my livelihood are now threatened by the House Committee." Sherwood did refer in his farewell letter to "jail," but it was in a context of punishment by the Committee.

Walter's reason for calling Sherwood is no more impressive than his alleged connection with a Marxist study group in 1938. The Committee had already circulated detailed accounts of the matters under investigation in order to refute charges that the probe was in retaliation for the censure of the Committee in March by the California Bar Association. It had not even hinted at such a line of inquiry. No other witness was asked about foundations, nor did Walter particularize what "valuable information" Sherwood, who had been working at Stanford for ten years, possessed on this subject. Illegality breeds deception.

The suicide left the Committee with few friends in San Francisco. The local ACLU branch demanded the cancellation of the hearings; the Chairman said, "Those who were subpoenaed are going to be tried for their past associations and opinions. . . . I hope the ghost of this man appears at the hearings." Roger Kent, Chairman of the California State Democratic Central Committee, bitterly condemned the Committee: "It is the circus aspect of the hearings that drive people to this. The investigators are asking for information they already knew from FBI files. . . . This suicide is a new bit of evidence to awaken the people of the United States to the fantastic injury done to people by these things."

The suicide had more than a local impact. The reason for Sherwood's failure to appear at the Canadian conference was no secret to the international audience of scientists at Vancouver. Many of the Canadians present were all too familiar with the exposure-smear tactics of United States antisubversive Committees. On April 4 of that year, Canadian diplomat E. Herbert Norman had committed suicide in Cairo as a result of the smears of the Senate Internal Security Subcommittee. His death shocked the Canadian people and resulted in a protest against the subcommittee's vicious tactics.

Sherwood's death coincided with Supreme Court rulings curbing the Committee (the *Watkins* case) and restricting the application of the Smith Act (the case of the California Communists). But most British newspapers gave secondary importance to the decisions and featured Sherwood's suicide. The *Daily Mirror,* British multimillion circulation daily, printed a lengthy report of the suicide, to which it appended the account of the decisions as an ironic afterpiece. The *News Chronicle* devoted detailed attention to the Sherwood story on its front page and carried the court story on page two. Mexican newspapers likewise gave prominent coverage to the tragedy.

On the morning of the commencement of the hearings, June 18, the San Francisco *Chronicle* printed the first of a series of editorials critical of the Committee. It urged the Committee to conform its procedures to the limitations of the *Watkins* case. Of the suicide, it said that it "speaks eloquently of the terrible power which a congressional investigation exerts when operating in this particular field. The fact is that this committee has so aggrandized itself in the public eye that a mere subpoena has the look of guilt and can blast an innocent career or ruin a life unnecessarily."

When the afternoon session of the first day's hearings opened, Sherwood's widow, mother of four children, sought leave to make a statement; the Chairman brushed her aside and she left the hearing in tears. Her statement printed in whole or in substantial part by all of the San Francisco papers, said:

MEMBERS OF THE UN-AMERICAN ACTIVITIES COMMITTEE:

You have helped to kill my husband and make my four children fatherless.

That is our personal tragedy.

It is as nothing to the crime you have committed against the children of America and the children of the world.

For when you drove my husband to his death, you destroyed a man of bright promise, a talented fighter in the army of devoted men who are warring against disease.

My husband thought that he had found an important clue to the understanding of cancer and schizophrenia. Perhaps he was mistaken. Only time, and the opportunity to continue his researches could have supplied the answer.

This opportunity your Committee has denied him, and the loss is not only mine.

Throughout his lifetime my husband had but one goal—to ease the suffering of mankind.

It was this goal that drew him to support the Loyalists in the Spanish Civil War, that inspired his youthful identification with radical causes. It was this goal that led him, when greater maturity had mellowed and deepened his understanding, to abandon politics completely and devote himself single-mindedly to science.

Is it a crime for a young man in his twenties to dream of a bright new world?

Must the children of our country leave their idealism in the cradle so that their future careers will not be blighted by the Un-American Activities Committee?

And is it befitting, now that he is dead, that you insinuate he was a traitor to his country?

Is not his death enough for you?

Must you besmirch his honor, now that he is no longer able to answer you?

Members of the Committee, what you have done and what you are doing is an evil thing. Do not persist in it. Go away, go home, bow your heads in prayer, and ask forgiveness of your God.

After the rebuff to Mrs. Sherwood, her lawyer was served with a subpoena to appear and testify. It was later canceled, manifestly because the Committee had no convenient pretext such as tax-exempt foundations to conceal its vindictive use of its powers.

On June 20, the third day of the hearing, Sherwood's widow brought an action in the California Supreme Court against Walter and his colleagues, charging a "conspiracy to commit a wrongful death," and asking $500,000 damages as a result of the Committee's "malicious, oppressive and punitive" conduct.

The complaint alleged that the Committee had announced its intent to televise the hearings in "deliberate defiance of the rules" of the House of Representatives and that this announcement contributed to the suicide. Mrs. Sherwood charged that the Committee knew that at least 11 persons had committed suicide or died of heart attacks while under Congressional investigation. The Committee members thus had knowledge that an exposure hearing could produce fatal consequences and thus could not escape responsibility for the tragedy.

The suit stressed that the reasons for calling Sherwood were punitive; the Committee members knew that the plaintiff's husband had "not been engaged in any kind of political activity for more than ten years" and "had no information pertinent to any matter properly under inquiry by the sub-committee." The reason for Sherwood's subpoena, Mrs. Sherwood charged, was to "publicize his past beliefs, expressions and associations, to expose him for the sake of exposure alone . . . to subject him to public stigma, scorn and obloquy, to bring down upon him and his family the violence of public reaction . . . to cause him to suffer loss of employment . . . and to deny him the opportunity to continue his scientific career." As a further evidence of the Committee's malice, the complaint pointed to its denial of a requested postponement of the date of Sherwood's appearance and the deliberate advancing of the date to prevent him from attending the Vancouver meeting.

The lawsuit was reported in all of the San Francisco newspapers as prominently and sympathetically as the suicide itself. A tragedy had occurred; but as a result of it a community was learning about the abuses of Congressional powers. The Committee ignored the suit on the ground that their conduct was protected by Congressional privilege. Walter, true to form, attacked Mrs. Sherwood's lawyers as Reds.

He then read from a written statement. "The possible reasons for this action [the suicide] will be fully examined, particularly in view of the fact that the decedent expressed apprehension lest he be sent to jail for three years, and the statement by the plaintiff that her husband had worried for a long time over financial conditions."

Walter thus carried one step further the fear of jail theme of his initial interview; now the suggestion was that Sherwood feared a three-year jail term for some unspecified offense wholly unconnected with his Committee appearance. This was more than a conscienceless misrepresentation of Sherwood's words, linking his fear of jail with the Committee, but a vicious innuendo that fear of punishment for a crime was responsible for Sherwood's self-destruction. Sherwood had been plagued by financial difficulties and his widow *had* referred to them. But the fact is that Sherwood had not only blamed the Committee in two formal written messages, but had brooded about the Committee's threat to his livelihood and career from the time he received his subpoena. On May 22, he had written to his attorney, a personal friend, about his fears. Financial worries are hardly relieved by a Committee subpoena to an exposure hearing.

Walter's promise that the causes of the suicide would be "fully explained" appears to have been a way of using the Committee's authority to attack the lawsuit and Sherwood without answering the charges in court. A short time later, Mrs. Sherwood withdrew her action and said that it would "only bring more grief, pain and publicity to a family already overwhelmed with these conditions."

Sherwood's death and the lawsuit sharply focused attention on the Committee's use of television as an exposure weapon. The newspapers in San Francisco repeatedly called attention to Sherwood's tormented farewell letter, "I will be in two days assassinated by publicity . . . I have a fierce resentment of being televised." The *Watkins* decision had rejected exposure as a proper Committee end, and had emphasized that the publicity resulting from the Committee's procedures could seriously injure not only those called, but that "those who are identified by witnesses and thereby placed in the same glare of publicity are equally subject to public stigma, scorn and obloquy."

When the hearing opened, the Committee followed its customary practice of asking television cameramen not to focus on the witness if a request to that effect was made. The friendly witnesses, whose testimony took up much of the first two days of hearings, did not object. On June 19, the third day of the hearings, the Committee's television procedures were challenged in an unexpected quarter. Newsmen in Washington called Speaker Rayburn's attention to Sherwood's farewell letter. Expressing surprise that the Committee permitted such practice, he stated that he had specifically ruled in 1952 and 1955 against televising hearings, and that this was applicable to the Committee. He promised to put a stop to televised Committee hearings in Washington and out of town.

The San Francisco *News-Call-Bulletin,* which made the issue a crusade, ran an extra edition on the evening of June 19 with huge headlines across the entire first page:

RAYBURN BLASTS TV OF RED PROBE IN S. F.

The *News-Call-Bulletin* reported Rayburn's ban and quoted Walter's reply to a question whether the telecasts would continue: "I don't know any reason why we shouldn't." He admitted that he knew of the Speaker's rulings, but could give no reason why they were being violated. At the next day's hearing, a witness included among his reasons for resisting questions the fact that the hearings were being televised in defiance of the rules. The Chair replied, "The Chair is not aware that there is any such rule"—a direct contradiction of his statement to the *News-Call-Bulletin*.

According to Washington press accounts, Rayburn became furious on learning of Walter's defiance: "There will not be any more committee or subcommittee hearings in Washington, or anywhere else, televised or broadcast by radio. Period!" Walter's defiance of the Speaker had an unanticipated result: it persuaded many Congressmen that Chief Justice Warren's rebuke of the Committee in the *Watkins* decision was well grounded. A member of the Committee, Clyde Doyle, who, though he came from California, had stayed behind in Washington, agreed with the Speaker: "We're all familiar with the Speaker's ruling and we have no business permitting TV hearings"—a strange confession from the Californian who had permitted television not only as a subcommittee member, but as Chairman.

When Walter learned of Rayburn's second flat pronouncement that the televising of the hearings must be halted, he told the reporters, "I can't do anything about it. We are the guests at City Hall. I can't do anything about television, radio or the newspapers." If he received a direct order from Rayburn, he added, "The answer would still be the same." Walter's pretext for defying the Speaker is too ridiculous for comment; the television station told newsmen that it would abide by any order by Walter on the subject of television.

A further reason for disregarding the TV ban, Walter told reporters, was the fact that Washington attempts to halt the hearings were "backed by Communists." Since the Speaker had made it clear that he did not intend to communicate directly to Walter but expected him to abide by the ban which reporters had made known to him, Walter felt safe in refusing to prohibit television on the new ground that he had not heard from Speaker Rayburn, although he had previously said that a direct order would make no difference.

Walter's persistent defiance of the Speaker drew from Representative Cannon, House authority on rules and precedents, the comment that Rayburn's ruling was binding on Walter unless reversed by the House itself. Violation of pending rulings, he said, could be punished as contempt of the House or through censure proceedings.

The television controversy showed the people of San

Francisco that a committee of government could be arrogant, evasive and dishonest. The Chairman's determination not to sacrifice the exposure power of the hearing to the discipline of parliamentary government brought home to the community how ruthlessly the exposure purposes of the Committee are implemented. Most importantly, many realized that the Committee is not wholly without external restraints; it is an agent of the House of Representatives. The Committee has always sought to exploit the powers and prestige of the Congress both in attacking witnesses and in wooing community support. But people were beginning to ask, does the Congress really know and sanction what is done in its name? Chief Justice Warren, with long experience in government, shrewdly made this question the matrix of his *Watkins* opinion: "There is a wide gulf between the responsibility for the use of legislative power and the actual exercise of that power." In a completely unprecedented episode, the community learned that the gulf was far wider than the Committee would care to admit: that the Committee Chairman used the power of Congress only to aggrandize himself and was seeking to convert the Committee into an autonomous instrumentality.

The press dramatized this gulf in a truly remarkable way. The San Francisco newsmen acted as representatives of Speaker Rayburn in confronting Walter with the Speaker's ban and in reporting back his repeated defiance of it. Nor did they hesitate to lay bare the shabby shifts and dodges to which the Chairman resorted to prevent a curb on the Committee's lawlessness.

The vigorous handling of the issue by the press may only prove that it needs a Speaker to give it courage. But the role of the *Chronicle* proves something more. The newspaper published two editorials on this single issue. In the first, "When Conscience Is On The Rack," it examined the role of all forms of publicity in hearings invoking matters of conscience. It concluded that no special rules should be laid down for television, and that "where judicial and legislative enterprises are open to press and public, they ought also to be open to television."

However, the editorial insists, hearings involving matters of the kind inquired into by the Committee should be shielded from all forms of publicity:

When hearsay information and sketchy bits and

pieces of unsubstantiated evidence and rank rumors
are produced in the locked and guarded confines of
a Grand Jury room, little harm results. When paraded
amid the ballyhoo of an open, public, legislative inquiry, they may mean disgrace and ruin for innocent
or mildly censurable citizens. . . .

. . . Thus it feels that an overhauling of the technique of legislative inquiry may be in order; that the
protection of private hearings might well be accorded
persons under inquiry on matters of conscience and
belief. Where substantial evidence of guilt is developed, it will become public knowledge as it passes
through the established channels toward prosecution.
Where there is no such evidence, needless and tragic
injury will have been avoided.

A second *Chronicle* editorial on July 1 recounts that
after the hearing a conference between the Speaker and
Walter had resulted in an announcement that the hearings
would no longer be televised. Walter explained that he
was unware that the rules promulgated in 1952 and 1955
were still in effect. The editorial rejects this excuse:

. . . Walter's statement is not entirely in accord with
the facts. On the second day of the hearings here, the
local press carried a statement by Speaker Rayburn,
from Washington, that the televised hearings were
against House rules. When queried by reporters,
Walter said that he would go ahead until he received
an order to the contrary from Rayburn. That word
was carried by Washington reporters to the Speaker,
who said that he considered his press statement adequate warning to Walter. The show went on.

Why does Walter not deserve punishment for his contempt?

. . . The whole affair is being chalked up to a "mis-
understanding" of Rayburn's ruling, and hence no
punishment is expected.

Actually, Walter was in clear violation of House
rules, and proceeded with that knowledge. We have
(on television) heard and seen Chairman Walter
speak of the dignity of Congress and the necessity of
according it proper respect. Many people have been

indicted for contempt for their failure to do so. How now, Chairman Walter?

In the years since the San Francisco hearings, the Committee has continued to televise hearings with impunity. No reporters or editorial writers have raised their voices in protest. Maybe they are waiting for another suicide.

Prior to the hearing, there were persistent reports that the proceeding would be used to strike back at the California Bar for its censure resolution of March 1957. On the eve of the hearing, Roger Kent, the California State Democratic Central Committee Chairman, a San Francisco lawyer, who subsequently denounced the Committee for its circuslike tactics, issued a statement declaring:

> Chairman Walter can do nothing but injure the prestige of his committee if he comes to San Francisco, blasts the California State Bar and disregards its constructive criticism of his committee's outrageous actions in Los Angeles last year.
> Californians are more likely to put their confidence in the Board of Governors of their own State Bar than in one angry Congressman. I believe, too, that Californians would like to see committee procedures show respect for the constitutional rights of individuals, and I sincerely hope that the San Francisco proceedings will be conducted in that manner.

But Mr. Kent hoped in vain. When Walter arrived at the airport, he denounced "interested parties" in the state bar for the censure action. This seemed to be an attempt to question the representative character of the action, although it was overwhelmingly supported by California lawyers. Representative Scherer told reporters that he planned a "personal answer" to the bar censure resolution. The hearings opened with a televised blast by Scherer at the California Bar Association. His performance at the California hearings was in his best vein. As the San Francisco papers noted, it was "vitriolic" and "filled with bitter denunciations." He pictured himself and the Committee as the long-suffering victims of a plot by the lawyers. What was most "shocking" to Scherer—and richly amusing to lawyers who had long protested the Committee's procedural barbarism—was the fact that the Committee had been "censured without notice that any such action was contemplated, without any knowledge of the charges, without a hearing, without an opportunity to reply contemporaneously with the publication of the censure. . . ."

Scherer made his standard Red-plot charge against the lawyers whose abuse by the Committee had resulted in the censure. To the accusation of the California Bar that the Committee attacked a lawyer as a Communist who had not even been subpoenaed, Scherer replied, "Since when have lawyers who are Communists been immune from exposure or identification. Does the Board of Governors of the Bar Association seriously contend that this Committee, the Congress of the United States or the American people are precluded from attempting to detect and isolate traitors, even though they be possessed of a license to practice law?"

Thus, one day after the Supreme Court decision in the *Watkins* case forbidding the use of Committee powers for exposure purposes, Scherer was justifying such exposure activities in the context of the lawyer-client relationship. As the *Chronicle* pointed out in an editorial, "Scherer Takes On the State Bar":

> Scherer is here trying to justify a grossly personal reference to a lawyer representing his client before the committee. Unless the right of a person to have counsel is respected, even if and when counsel is a "Communist," our system is harmed. The role and function of the professional counsel is vital to the protection of individual rights, as Scherer—himself a lawyer—should appreciate.

Apart from unparticularized slurs against the censure resolution ("so biassed and erroneous that I wonder what influences were at work in its preparation and adoption,") Scherer made three specific charges. He insisted that the Bar Association was guilty of a "bold-faced misrepresentation of the facts" in referring to the purpose of the hearing which gave rise to the controversy as an investigation of "opposition to the McCarran-Walter Act." The hearing, insisted Scherer, was about "the activities of the Communist conspiracy in its program of political subversion." But the Bar Association's failure to use the Committee's special brand of anti-subversive Choctaw can hardly change the fact that the hearing did, as we shall see, probe opposition to the Walter-McCarran Act.

The bar association had complained that lawyers were not permitted to address the Committee or make objections. True enough, retorted Scherer. But this limitation on lawyers is based upon a rule of the Committee. It is hard to understand how the fact that all lawyers are gagged meets the bar association's complaint.

Finally, Scherer said, the "unwarranted and intemperate" bar action does not reflect the views "of the great mass of lawyers." The proof? ". . . we have received numerous letters . . . deploring and condemning the action of the Board of Governors." The bar association stuck to its guns, and the *Chronicle* wrote ". . . we ardently restate our belief that the censure was deserved."

Scherer's tirade had already suggested that the Committee was unabashed by the *Watkins* decision of the previous day and intended to persist in its exposure practices. The Committee met the problem of the *Watkins* case by announcing that the hearings were to be principally concerned with eliciting information to aid in keeping Congress informed as to the desirability of outlawing the Communist Party.

It is quite apparent that the Committee simply improvised a legislative subject matter comprehensive enough to justify its already prepared exposure proceeding against the group of teachers, doctors, lawyers, actors and members of other professions who had been subpoenaed. But this particular legislative justification was a most implausible choice. At a Committee legislative hearing in 1948, the Committee heard some 35 witnesses on the subject of legislation outlawing the Communist Party. There were few who would defend the constitutionality of an outlawry provision. Then Attorney General (now Supreme Court Justice) Clark contested the constitutionality of such a measure and, on the authority of J. Edgar Hoover, testified that such a measure would be unwise from a security viewpoint. And, in 1950, an array of witnesses expressed opposition to outlawing the Communist Party. Some were of the view that such action would be unconstitutional, while others thought it was dangerous because it would merely drive the Party underground.

In 1953, the Committee, in reviewing the determination

of the Subversive Activities Control Board requiring the Party to register under the Internal Security Act of 1950 as a subversive organization, noted that, "Further legislation to outlaw the Communist Party will await the final decision of the United States Supreme Court." In 1954, Congress refused to outlaw the Party and instead passed the ambiguous Communist Control Act. In 1955, the Committee reiterated that pending the Supreme Court determination referred to, "the Committee does not believe it advisable for the Congress to undertake any broad new legislative action against the functioning of the Communist Party."

In 1955, the Committee noted that the test case, the outcome of which it was awaiting, was expected to come to the Supreme Court for final disposition shortly thereafter. "Until final disposition is made by the Supreme Court of the issues raised, the Committee remains of the opinion that legislative recommendation in this specific field should be withheld." In 1957 (the year of the San Francisco hearings), the Committee in its annual report complained of "inadequacies in anti-Communist legislation," but none of these claimed inadequacies included the need for outlawing the Party. In its next two years' reports, the Committee likewise continued to wait for the Supereme Court's final disposition of the Internal Security Act's validity. (A final determination is expected this year.)

The internal content of the hearing reinforces the view that a legislative purpose was invented by the Committee. The hearing consists of the testimony of two friendly witnesses and 29 unfriendly ones. The two friendly witnesses were an ex-Communist, who left the Party ten years prior to the hearing, and an FBI plant who had left five years before the hearing. These witnesses between them named a list of 99 alleged Party members. All of the other witnesses were subjected to the exposure process. There were no substantive contributions by the friendly witnesses which could conceivably enlighten Congress on the need (or lack of it) for outlawing the Communist Party. There is no testimony by either of the witnesses about any illegal conduct, or indeed about anything which had not been aired in scores of hearings before and since.

The Committee received no legislative enlightenment. In its 1957 annual report it admits as much: "To evaluate the success of the Communist program and the damage done to the United States Government is extremely difficult," wrote the Committee of the San Francisco hearings. The reason? Almost no one was willing to admit Communist Party membership and "relate their experiences while members." But, as we have seen, this frustration has been built into the exposure process by the Committee itself. The Committee wants victims, not facts.

One witness who resisted the Committee's inquiries on First Amendment grounds was indicted and convicted for contempt, and given a six months' jail term and $100 fine. The Committee told the court that the refusal of the witness to testify deprived it of valuable information which was needed to help it determine whether the Communist Party should be outlawed. Illegality breeds deception.

11 SAN FRANCISCO REVISITED— AND OPERATION ABOLITION

The Committee finds the State of California simply irresistible. More than one-third of the total number of its road shows have been staged there. HUAC members respond with the avidity of the Forty-niners when the Golden State beckons. Its lure is so powerful that the Committee has, for the past 12 years, assigned a permanent investigator, William A. Wheeler, to comb the state for exposable victims.

The reader may remember that in the early part of June 1959, HUAC launched what was, even for it, a spectacular operation. It subpoenaed 110 teachers from Northern California and the Los Angeles area for hearings to be held later that month. The qualifications of teachers in a state school system are not primarily a Federal concern. For years California had screened its teachers through one of the tightest loyalty programs in the country. Could it be that the Red hordes had penetrated the classroom despite the state's vigilance, and were now poised to swoop down and claim the schools as a fief of Moscow?

The heroic number of subpoenas suggested a bold new tactic of direct, wholesale intervention by HUAC in the employment relationship. A dead giveaway to HUAC's strategy was the nature of the group of teachers sought out by the subpoenas. They were preponderantly teachers with only probationary and provisional status. Lacking tenure, they could be easily discharged on mere suspicion, without legal recourse and with no opportunity to defend themselves. As the St. Louis *Post Dispatch* editorialized: ". . . a vast dragnet operation. Obviously, the purpose is not to assemble information preparatory to drafting new laws. The purpose is clearly to expose for exposure's sake. It is to embarrass those summoned. Indeed to give them a kind of rough justice trial in the guise of conducting a congressional inquiry . . ."

HUAC did everything possible to make certain that the school administration knew about the subpoenas. School authorities were tipped off in advance that subpoenas would be served. HUAC representatives visited a university president two weeks before a subpoena was served on a member of his faculty to urge that the teacher be fired. HUAC did not merely put the teachers on the spot within the school system, it developed outside prehearing pressure as well. Time was too short to wait for the normal operation of the exposure process after the hearing: the school term would be over by then.

On the very day the subpoenas were served, newspapers in Northern California printed the names and addresses of most of the teachers subpoenaed in that area, identifying their teaching posts, together with brief biographies. Without a trace of supporting evidence, the teachers were stigmatized before students, parents, colleagues and the public at large. The Committee's official apologist, staff member Fulton Lewis, III, echoing an earlier statement by Chairman Walter, has explained to college audiences when questioned about the affair that the victims themselves released their names in a Red plot to embarrass and discredit the Committee. This is a remarkable example of HUAC's confidence in the potency of Red magic to shield it from criticism, for here are statements from some of the teachers themselves (from a questionnaire submitted inquiring into the time and manner of service of the subpoenas):

I was served June 5, 1959 at the elementary school. The two deputies told me they didn't tell the principal a thing while the whole story was just then reaching the newsstands.

I was served at 7:00 a.m. at home by a police officer. When I arrived at the school where I was practice-teaching, a press photographer and a reporter were waiting for me.

Police officers served the subpoena and advised me I could communicate with the HUAC. My name later appeared in all Bay Area papers.

On June 11, Chairman Walter embarked on a new tactic. He announced that the hearings were postponed until September 1, thus ensuring that the teachers' vacations would be ruined by the suspense and continuing suspicion. Nor did he leave this prospect to chance. He gave as the reason for HUAC's action that "ramifications of the Communist operations in California are so extensive and malignant that additional investigative work must be done before the hearings can be held." This cloud of characteristically portentous rhetoric drew from the San Francisco *Chronicle* the editorial comment that: "Forty northern California teachers (plus 70 in southern California) who are under subpoena and whose names have been made public (though not printed by this newspaper) stand accused, with no opportunity to clear themselves. This kind of procedure is hardly in accord with the best American practice, though it is not new with the House Un-American Activities Committee."

The timing, publication and postponement of the subpoenas fed widespread doubts that HUAC had ever intended to hold hearings in June— and certainly not with such a vast number of witnesses. Just as the hearings have become an exposure end in themselves, independent of the investigative process, so the subpoenas, independent of the hearings, were being used to mow down victims.

A storm of protest raged throughout the state. On June 19, the California Democratic Council denounced HUAC's hit-and-run tactics and urged Governor Brown and the California Congressional delegation "to employ all means at their disposal to bring about the cancellation of the existing subpoenas and to prevent any further maligning of the reputations of California citizens." A regional conference of the Methodist Church attacked HUAC for naming the teachers and leaving them "to suffer wounds before the whole state."

In July, the Friends Committee on Legislation urged HUAC's abolition and pointed to the publication of the teachers' names as typical of a train of abuses. Other church groups, individual ministers, and rabbis followed suit. On July 12, Mrs. Eleanor Roosevelt denounced the Committee tactics in her newspaper column. "I cannot believe," she wrote, "that Walter and his Committee are any more qualified to judge as to the qualifications of the loyalty of our teachers than those within our states who are responsible for the education that is given." She noted wryly that the inclusion of a teacher of retarded children among the victims "seems a little farfetched—since it is so difficult to teach retarded children anything, let alone communism."

In the same month, the San Francisco Labor Council and the Building Trades Council condemned the publication of the names and the postponement of the hearings. On August 13, the powerful California Federation of Labor, AFL-CIO, protested the teacher witchhunt. Many more unions joined the protest movement.

On August 13, the Committee again put off the hearings —this time from September 1 to October 14. This second prolongation of severe anxiety for the teachers, and the concomitant threat to their morale, caused many more groups to join the campaign to force the cancellation of the hearings. The community was learning that a HUAC subpoena is more than a formal summons to a hearing; it is in itself a form of punishment.

The next day, Bishop Pike, Episcopal Bishop of California, released a resolution calling HUAC's tactics "so threatening to the private welfare of countless innocent individuals that the public conscience is, and must thereby be, outraged."

On August 14, the San Francisco *Chronicle,* in an editorial, "Methods That Outrage the Public Conscience," called for the cancellation of the hearings. On August 21, the San Francisco *News-Call-Bulletin* said, "There is a peculiar emotional quality in the investigation on un-American activities. Anyone who has ever been in its inquiring spotlight is more than likely to bear its mark the rest of his life . . . this is why there are grave dangers of multiple injustice in the often-postponed House un-American Activities Committee hearings aimed at uncovering subversive teachers—if any—in California." The Washington *Post* also called for cancellation of the hearings.

The national convention, held in August, of the American Federation of Teachers likewise censured the Committee and called upon it to cancel the hearings. On August 18, the state executive secretary of the California Teachers' Association wrote Chairman Walter to question "whether or not these hearings have any recognizable relationship to legislation." He pointed out that the repeated postponement of the hearings "compounds the damage already done to individual rights and to the effective operation of many schools by earlier procedure."

On August 21, 1959, HUAC threw in the sponge and announced the cancellation of all 110 subpoenas. For the first time in its history an aroused public opinion had forced HUAC to turn tail and run. Said the San Francisco *Chronicle*:

> One of the most heartening victories for political decency and constitutional rights that it has been our pleasure to report in quite some time came in Friday's announcement that the House Un-American Activities Committee had canceled its scheduled inquisition of 110 public and private schoolteachers of California.

But HUAC did not just go quietly away after its drubbing. If the dossiers could not be communicated to the school authorities through the device of the hearing, another way had to be found to force the discharge of the teachers. Walter instructed HUAC's staff to turn over copies of its files on the teachers to local school boards for action. Suits were promptly filed to challenge this move. The threatened delivery of the files had no conceivable relationship to the only function that a Congressional investigative committee can lawfully perform. But Walter's vigilante posse quickly turned over the files of some 90 teachers to the State Superintendent of Public Instruction in order, as Committee investigator Wheeler admitted to the press, to "beat" the injunction action.

The State Attorney General advised the State Superintendent that the files must be kept confidential until the courts disposed of the challenge to HUAC's right to turn them over. The Committee then scurried around the state to place the copies of the files in the hands of local school authorities, outfoxing both the courts and the State Attorney General.

HUAC's desperate manhunt of the teachers might lead one to believe that it had information that its quarries were ready to mount the barricades. In point of fact, the material in the files turned out to be stale and monumentally innocuous, consisting, in the main, of a melange of gossip, rumor and hearsay attributed to unidentified informants, much of it more than a decade old. In many cases, the only "information" the school board received was the fact that the individual was under HUAC's suspicion. Chairman Walter announced that he was instructing his staff to turn over the files "and in cases in which information respecting the persons subpoenaed can be disclosed without jeopardizing sources of information or security procedures, to make such information available in confidence." He added, "I am advised, however, that most of the names reflect information which could not, because of the foregoing, be made available to the boards." In other words, the boards were being enjoined to ape the Committee, to make accusations in thin air and to assume proof of guilt on HUAC's say-so.

The state Attorney General released an opinion stating that the reports were worthless as evidence against the teachers involved. HUAC's assurance that the allegations stemmed from "reliable sources" could not substitute for evidence from identifiable witnesses. Only a few California school boards succumbed to HUAC's pressures and held hearings. The immediate consequence was that about six teachers were forced to leave the public schools—two by resignation—in the wake of the great "malignant" plot.

But HUAC's casualties cannot be written off so easily. A substantial body of teachers lived, for a period of ten months, in the shadow first of a subpoena, then of a twice-postponed hearing, and then of a threat of discharge and disgrace. It is hard to exaggerate the disastrous impact of these experiences on the quality of teaching both of the actual victims and of their colleagues—who were thus dramatically reminded that conformity is the key to security and peace of mind. As California Congressman James Roosevelt stated, HUAC might have triumphed even in retreat. It was possible quietly to ease out probationary teachers simply by not renewing their contracts.

"In the past," he said, "school boards have frequently let teachers go who have become the subject of controversy whether guilty of actual failings or mere victims of circumstance. If this happens, those who remain on the teaching staff will not miss the lesson. Anxiety lest they suffer the same fate, will inevitably stifle a part of their own intellectual curiosity and individuality. Their pupils will also be the poorer for this, for they may never know the mental stimulation which can be provided only by the teacher with an inquiring mind."

The abortive 1959 hearings contributed enormously to the Bay area's understanding—already enriched by the 1957 hearings—of what HUAC really is and how it operates. This was a naked attack on the security and tenure of over a hundred teachers, without even a pretext of legislative justification. It gave the community fresh insight into the arrogance and lawlessness of the Committee and its Chairman, and a realization that its vaunted dossiers and files were filled with trash, packaged in lurid wrappings and tied with irrationally sinister inferences.

The community learned, too, that while HUAC bites and kicks in the clinches, it can be outfought. The Committee was forced to turn tail because six forces in the community—the press, labor, religion, organized liberals, educators and students—closed ranks against injustice and cruelty. But the fight was not over.

HUAC had to return to San Francisco. There were too many unsettled scores. The California Democratic Council which had initiated the protest movement had to be brought into line. A widespread and highly effective movement had developed around the struggle to defend the teachers against the Committee's files. The campaign had achieved significant victories, not the least of which was the establishment of the principle that past, discontinued membership in the Communist Party was no disqualification for teaching.

Congressman Roosevelt's brilliant and witty speech on April 25 on the floor of the House, in which he arraigned the Committee at length, citing chapter and verse and demanding its abolition, gave the anti-HUAC movement of Protestant churches, labor, the liberal Democrats and the academic community a decided impetus. The conviction that HUAC should be abolished was widely held in the Bay area in the spring of 1960.

Early in May, HUAC issued 48 subpoenas for hearings to be held May 12-14. A number of the subpoenas were for teachers who had previously been served in 1959. Bertram Edises, the courageous lawyer who had been subpoenaed when he represented William Sherwood in 1957, was again subpoenaed. He had also been the lawyer for many of the teachers who were involved in the fight to retain their jobs after the 1959 HUAC foray. The rest of the subpoenas were for housewives, professional people, trade unionists, one student, a radio commentator, and a handful of Communist Party members. Several of the people in the group had been active in the picketing of Bay Area five-and-ten cent stores in support of the Southern Negro "sit-in" students.

Except for a small group of individuals whose names were published by ex-Senator Knowland's Oakland *Tribune,* the names of those subpoenaed were not printed in the Bay Area newspapers, largely because of the change in community sentiment. But HUAC found a way to accomplish the same destructive purpose as publicity would have done. It timed the serving of the subpoenas for 9 a.m., when the victims could not fail to be at work. Teachers were served at school, often in the presence of the principal and in his office.

Mr. Fulton Lewis, III, has again defended HUAC by claiming that the teachers were served at school only as a last resort, and after they had evaded earlier service at home. But here is a part of HUAC's letter to the sheriffs charged with serving the subpoenas:

> I am enclosing herewith a subpoena for service in your county. Some 45 subpoenas have been issued by the House Committee on Un-American Activities and forwarded to Federal and local agencies for service. Your cooperation in this matter will be greatly appreciated.
>
> It is requested that service be made at 9:00 A.M. on Wednesday morning, April 27th.

The Committee knew that the subpoenas would reach the victims at work. According to a speech by Congressman Scherer on May 5, 1960, the Committee in 1959 gave instructions to serve the subpoenas "at 7:30 A.M. at the residence of each teacher." The instruction to serve the 1960 subpoenas at 9 A.M., and the failure to designate the residence as the place of service, can only mean that the very service of the subpoena was planned as a form of discharge pressure.

But HUAC, in the case of the teachers, also applied direct pressure. There is evidence that a few weeks prior to the time of service, Committee investigators interviewed local school authorities and informed them that unless designated teachers' appointments were not renewed, they would be subpoenaed. Those with renewed contracts, or promises of renewal were subpoenaed. The same university instructor who had been subpoenaed in 1959 was again served. He was informed that his university president had been notified three weeks in advance of his pending subpoena and had been urged—as in 1959—to fire him. (He was finally told in May 1961 that his contract would not be renewed for the 1961-62 term.)

As the day of the hearings approached, the protest movement swelled. On the eve of the hearings, a large number of organizations and private persons, including the Central Labor Councils of San Francisco, Alameda, Santa Clara, San José and San Mateo Counties, 300 faculty members of the University of California, 165 faculty members of San Francisco State College, 200 of Stanford University and 100 of San José State College, the San Francisco Society of Friends, the Northern California Conference Board of Rabbis, the National Lawyers Guild, the Episcopal Diocese of California, the First Unitarian Church of San José, and the Berkeley YWCA, had all become part of the anti-HUAC group.

A formidable student protest movement, which began with a group on the University of California campus, Students for Civil Liberties, soon spread to the student body of Stanford University and San Francisco State College. The University of California group announced as its goal the cancellation of the hearings and the abolition of the Committee. In three days, 1,000 students—subsequently increased to 2,000—signed abolition petitions.

This time HUAC really needed its friends. It issued white cards for a specially invited group of guests. These guests were concentrated among the following groups: The Daughters of the American Revolution, the American Council of Christian Churches and local Baptist fundamentalists.

Staff Director Arens strove valiantly to meet the needs of the hour. The friendly witnesses agreed that the Communist Party had attained an unprecedented peak of strength and that America was in peril. Witness Karl Prussion, a bona fide ex-Communist and an informer for the FBI, solemnly testified that "never before in the history of the Communist Party of the United States has the situation been more critical for our democratic form of government." Because of the character of the friendly invited audience, Mr. Arens asked the friendly witness such questions as, "You have found your way back to God and patriotism; is that correct?" and, "Within the framework of the Communist operation, is there room for concepts of God and spiritual values as we were taught them at our mother's knee?" The relation of these questions to a legislative purpose is obscure, but the audience was delighted.

Arens lavished his most portentous rhetoric on HUAC's acquisition of documents—most of them of a public nature—dealing with a Communist Party convention in 1959, to the eye-popping horror of his claque from DAR and the Baptist Seminary. He repeatedly made it known that the documents were acquired "from confidential sources of unimpeachable reliability and integrity . . . an intelligence source of unimpeachable reliability and integrity." But: "It is a source concerning which we cannot make a revelation or a public record because of security reasons."

Mr. Arens curdled the blood of his audience with the testimony that the customers of an unfriendly ball-bearing salesman included a missile plant. The audience was invited to shudder at testimony revealing that a Communist had been expelled without a fair hearing from the Communist Party, that Khrushchev is a practitioner of "Communist semantics," and that Gus Hall, the head of the Communist Party, is a long-time member of it.

The testimony rehashed HUAC's standard formula—but with special emphasis on one theme: that in the realm of subversion, one may smile, and smile, and be a villain still. In order to force the discharge of more teachers,

Arens developed the thesis of *subversive nonmembership* in the Party. Even more dangerous than Party members, were those who were not members of the "formal entity," but who may have joined and left the Party in the distant past, or who were engaged in activities with a "façade of humanitarianism and do-goodism." This was a net fine enough to catch any form of meaningful social action.

The 1959-60 affair was a bold attempt to adapt to the teaching profession the discharge pressures and blacklisting techniques which had heretofore been confined to the entertainment industry. The strategy of the hearings was to bludgeon local school boards into acceptance of HUAC's theories of original sin, subversive nonmembership, nonconformist activity and dangerous thoughts as the tests of fitness to teach. The total haul as a result of HUAC's pressure was sizable. Some 25 teachers were forced out of the profession through nonrenewal of contracts, refusal to reissue teaching credentials, credential revocations, or resignation. Some teachers resigned because their health was so damaged by the long drawn-out 1959-60 pressure as to impair their teaching ability. In addition, the ball-bearing salesmen and a welder lost their jobs.

As in the 1957 San Francisco hearings, the testimony at the 1960 hearings is merely a footnote to another event which the hearings touched off.

On Thursday morning, when the hearings opened, protest action took place in two different areas. Students for Civil Liberties (SCL) posted pickets around City Hall where the hearings were being held. This picketing was policed and monitored by the students, and order was maintained throughout the three-day session. At noontime, more than 1,000 persons attended an SCL-sponsored rally at Union Square, where Canon Richard Byfield of Grace Cathedral (Episcopal) told the audience: "These unjustly conducted hearings not only damage individuals but also our society." Assemblyman Philip Burton said: "No legislative committee should have the power to place people in the calumny of the community without going through due process of law. . . . I am looking forward to the day when the resolution by Congressman James Roosevelt will abolish this Committee." Assemblyman

John A. O'Connell also called for the Committee's abolition. He added: "I do believe a Communist has a right to hold his political view and to say it aloud in public just as I am talking here."

Independently of the planned and organized picketing, several hundred students from local campuses, as well as faculty members and others, gathered in the rotunda of City Hall and sought admission to the hearings. Some of them had arrived as early as 7 A.M. Just before the hearings started, HUAC's special guests were admitted when they showed their white cards, which had been furnished to them in advance. (Committee investigator Wheeler: "I issued [the white cards] to keep the Commies from stacking the meeting. We wanted some decent people in there.")

After the holders of the white cards were admitted, some 75 members of the general public, largely students, were permitted to occupy the remaining seats and to stand in the back of the room. This was the largest number of general admissions in the course of the three-day session. Thereafter the number of students who were admitted steadily declined.

On Thursday, one of the subpoenaed witnesses was evicted from the hearing room after a number of them angrily demonstrated during a recess against the hearing and its lynch atmosphere. At the back of the hearing room, a group of students staged a brief protest against the restrictive admission policy, which was entirely unrelated to the ruckus in which the witnesses were involved.

At the noon recess, the hearing room was cleared on orders from Investigator Wheeler. Students who tried to remain in the room for the afternoon session were removed but promised that they would be allowed to return. It became apparent that the stacking of the hearing with HUAC's friends was to be a fixed policy when Wheeler refused to readmit the 75 students. Only about half were permitted to re-enter.

Some of the students who were barred joined the picket line outside the City Hall. The remainder joined a group in the rotunda fronting the Supervisors' Chamber, where the hearings were being held. Sheriff Matthew Carberry suggested to the frustrated students that they sing "to sort of break the tension," and they continued their spontaneous, unplanned protest with songs and chants.

At 2 P.M., Carberry called for quiet and suggested that

the students leave. Some of them did. At 3:30, 30 students outside the chamber were admitted in exchange for 30 students who had been in the hearings. The disappointment of the others led to a resumption of the singing.

On Friday morning, students, now aware of the white card system, queued up even earlier than on Thursday to gain admission to the hearings. They continued their picketing outside the hearings, and about 200 of them tried to get into the Supervisors' Chamber. Again the room was filled with card holders, who turned out in even greater numbers than on the previous day. About 20 students were admitted, while the rest cooled their heels in the rotunda, singing and shouting, "Abolish the Committee," and "Let us in."

On Friday, at about noon, Sheriff Carberry promised the crowd that if they waited quietly he would try to arrange for their admission on a first-come, first-served basis. He insisted that it was his job to maintain order and the students agreed to do so. They said that if he could not work out a relaxation of the one-sided seating arrangements they would stay there and shout or sing.

When the afternoon session started, the card-holders were again given preference and only eight students were admitted. Student leaders circulated in the crowd maintaining order. According to half a dozen eyewitnesses, the students engaged in no violence against the police or anyone else, but they kept up a chant, "We're still here!" When the police began to unroll fire hoses, the students sat down and sang. Suddenly the hoses were turned on. Investigator Wheeler helped the police by designating desirable targets: "There's a Commie." "That's a witness."

When the hoses failed to drive the crowd back, they were turned off and the police surged through the crowd swinging their clubs. They drove the students down a flight of seven stairs to a landing. The hoses were again turned on and then turned off again.

A new assault was made on the students on the stair-landing by club-swinging policemen. One student was dragged down the stairs by her ankles, her head bumping on each marble step. Others received the same treatment. Some who resisted attempts to push or drag them down the stairs by clutching the stair-railing were clubbed on the arms and hands. Several students who were charged by the police had their heads bloodied either from falling or being hit with clubs. Many students sat with linked arms on the steps to try to prevent being dragged down one by one. A number of students were kicked in the face and body by the police. One youth was beaten senseless by six police; another was clubbed by a policeman as he was held by two others. Above the shouts and screams and groans could be heard the chant, "We shall not be moved!"

But they were.

When the carnage was over, 64 persons (a number of individuals were swept up in the police haul who had nothing at all to do with the affair) were loaded into patrol wagons where they were charged with disturbing the peace, resisting arrest and inciting to riot. The charges against 63 were dismissed. The 64th, Robert Meisenbach, went on trial.

On Saturday morning the City Hall, normally closed for public business, was open only for HUAC witnesses, the press, white-card holders and a trickle of students. But outside, about five thousand people picketed and rallied in the City Hall area. About half of these were students. They remained until the hearings ended, at 5 P.M. The hearings were prolonged by HUAC's use of the investigation to blame the Reds for the demonstrations and the students for the violence. It heard the testimony of Sheriff Carberry, Inspector McGuire of San Francisco's Intelligence Squad, and Police Chief Cahill. It called no student witnesses. Only Maguire had been present at the hosing: he was not asked how it started.

A Baptist group of HUAC supporters castigated the demonstrators. The San Francisco *Chronicle,* in an editorial of May 16, 1960, blamed the students for setting back the cause of abolition. Some 85 faculty members at Stanford petitioned City Hall for a public probe of police brutality. The petition said, "At no time did more than a small number of demonstrators offer more than passive resistance to the police." Similar groups of university teachers and graduate students at the University of California and elsewhere demanded an investigation and condemned the police for their brutality; so did the California Federation of Young Democrats. The California Federation of Teachers passed a resolution which "publicly thanked the college students of the Bay Area for their dedication and for the courage to protest, even in the face of brutal and unjustifiable coercion and arrest."

The Mayor estimated the damage to City Hall at $250,-000, and suggested that the next time HUAC came to town it should meet under the protection of the Army in some Federal building. This led Congressman Scherer to charge the Mayor with "surrender to Communist-directed violence." Congressman Johansen grandiloquently added, "The Congress of the United States cannot and will not retreat under Communist attack."

The San Francisco *Chronicle* editorialized about the charges against the Mayor: "This twisting of meaning, this deliberate disregard of facts, this baseless tearing down of personal character and reputation explain in part the public's growing distrust and distaste for this expensive and outworn group. As for the Mayor, he may deem himself fortunate if he is not subpoenaed to explain a recent trip to Russia and photograph showing him in close conversation with some . . . hard-core Communists."

Congressman Scherer bluntly charged that the demonstration was "clearly planned at the highest Communist levels." J. Edgar Hoover, in a report circulated by HUAC, backed him to the hilt. He asserted that it was all part of a worldwide chain of Communist-directed subversion and that it was also "the best thing that happened for the benefit of the Communist Party in years. . . ."

We come now to a new and special phase of HUAC activity. Two days after HUAC left San Francisco it subpoenaed all films of the demonstration and hearings from two local TV stations—ostensibly for its own files. It promptly turned them over to a commercial film studio: Washington Video Productions. The studio converted the clips into a 45-minute film with the help of staff member Fulton Lewis, III, who also delivered the narration. The film, called "Operation Abolition," is a curious document and raises many unanswered questions.

It invokes the prestige of Government authority and invites acceptance as an expression of official views—an impression which is reinforced by the participation in the script of three Committee members, Walter, Scherer and Johansen. Yet, while carrying the unmistakable cachet of governmental authority, it is strangely coy about its origins. There are no film credits. Who is responsible for "Operation Abolition"?

Although HUAC is empowered only to investigate propaganda, not to originate it, the film was actually made part of a House Report issued by HUAC in October 1960, and given official imprimatur. But in a June 1960 news release from Congressman Scherer's office, the making of the film was credited to the National Coalition of Patriotic Societies, a federation of vigilante-style organizations.

Yet Washington Video Productions sells the film for $100 and is said to have sold more than 2,000 prints. Is someone making private profits from a film made out of clips taken free of charge from the television stations? Congressman Walter has stated in a WNEW-TV program of January 28, 1961, that the television stations were in no way exploited. On the contrary, the television stations "advised us if we wanted the film, we'd better do something about it because they destroy them; they don't keep them for any great length of time so we subpoenaed them to make sure they would be preserved. . . . They were very happy to turn them over to us as a public service."

In the course of this book it has been urged that HUAC distorts facts, draws crudely strained inferences, and reaches untenable conclusions. But nothing in HUAC's record of hearings and reports matches the film "Operation Abolition." Let us begin with the distortion and misrepresentations which HUAC and its agents have admitted.

In its determination to lay the demonstration at the door of Communists, the film narration states, "Among the Communist leaders who had an active part in the San Francisco demonstration were Harry Bridges [no court has ever upheld the charge of Bridge's Communism], who you see here being escorted out of City Hall *moments before the rioting broke out*." In the Hoover report on the occurrence the following appears: "Order had been restored when Harry Bridges, President of the International Longshoremen's and Warehousemen's Union appeared on the scene." Bridges, in point of fact, was at lunch at the time of the demonstration.

In a letter to the Washington *Post* of December 28, 1960, Walter admitted that the film was in error. He insisted that the error was "minor," but as the *Post* pointed out, "It contributed to the deceptive and distorted message of the film. . . ." In the 28-minute TV version of the film, this error has now been changed—to a new incorrect version— the narration now says ". . . moments *after* the rioting broke out."

Mr. Walter also admitted to three sequential errors in the film, but contends that they are "honest errors." But a frame-by-frame analysis of "Operation Abolition" shows that the film is heavily doctored throughout. Filmed scenes of the hearings which were supposed to have occurred on Thursday, May 12th, were photographed on Friday morning, May 13th. Two other scenes in this same series were shot on Saturday.

The most shocking distortions occur in the film's handling of the demonstrations of Friday (the day of the hosing and arrests). Scenes presented as occurring on Friday as *causal* events leading up to the police action were taken either on Thursday or Saturday. There are at least 13 scenes in the Friday sequences which did not occur on that day. According to a study by Russell Joyner, "There is evidence indicating that at least 20 scenes in the 45-minute version of 'Operation Abolition' were photographed on a day different than that stated by the announcer in the film."

The shortened 28-minute version of the film made for TV corrects some of the other errors in the film, but it retains the sequential errors. According to Mr. Joyner, "There is evidence indicating that at least 15 scenes in the 28-minute version of 'Operation Abolition' were photographed on a different day than on the day that the announcer stated."

The reasons for this tampering with sequences are hardly inscrutable: every bit of footage was organized and arranged to create the false inference of student aggression and to fit HUAC's Procrustean thesis of a Red plot.

Chairman Walter has defended the film's sequential errors as "honest" and accidental. According to the manager of TV station KRON, one of the two stations from which the film was subpoenaed, all footage turned over to the HUAC was carefully tagged as to place, date and sequence of exposure.

Fulton Lewis, III, has offered a different explanation for the garbled sequences. He does not claim that these sequential changes were errors; he asserts that they were deliberate. In a speech before an audience in Minneapolis, he stated that when HUAC lacked appropriate footage for a particular day, it borrowed "similar" footage from other days. This was done, blandly explained Mr. Lewis, so that "there would be no distortions."

"Operation Abolition" hammers two themes:
1. The Communists inspired the resistance to the Committee and exploited the mass of students as their dupes.
2. This planned resistance embraced the use and provocation of violence. This is the revolution in microcosm: this is how "it can happen here."

But the very entrance to this road is blocked by the facts. As has already been shown, HUAC came to San Francisco in the face of a hostility which pervaded an extraordinarily broad segment of the Bay Area. The film tells us that "the Communist apparatus activated its trained agitators and proponents in the San Francisco Bay Area months before the scheduled hearings were to begin." Yet, as a team of reporters point out in an article in the San Francisco *News-Call-Bulletin,* "no announcement of the Committee's coming was made until April 25, 1960, 18 days before the hearing." Do the Reds have an agent on HUAC's staff?

The film is HUAC's most ambitious exercise in the manipulation of the Red scare. It opens with a statement by Chairman Walter: "During the next few minutes you will see revealed the long-time classic Communist tactic in which a relatively few well-trained, hard-core Communist agents are able to incite and use non-Communist sympathizers to perform the dirty work of the Communist Party."

The exalted, taut voice of narrator Lewis explodes in a commentary giving new life to the scarewords which Arens works to death in the hearings. Every unfriendly witness is a "top Communist operator," "especially trained in agitation and incitement to riot." Over and over again we are told that we are viewing "Communist-inspired violence." As a scene unfolds, we are filled in with the sound track's unsupported explanations of the behind-the-scenes machinations which produced it: "The Communist agitators give new orders now to the students to sit down," etc.

Each of the three Congresmen who appear in the film brings hyperbolic support to the film's message. Congressman Walter concludes the harangue which introduces the film with this grim reminder: "We are all too familiar with the pattern of Communist-led revolution and rioting —in Venezuela, Cuba, and more recently, in Japan. Can it happen here on American soil? This film showing Communism in action will answer that question."

The writer of the script has given Congressman Johansen equally chilling lines. The students, he warns, are "toying with treason." Congressman Scherer has not been slighted. He concludes by telling us that we have just "seen Communism in action, the same Communism which is at this instant attempting to devour the world through subversion, revolution, deceit, sabotage and vicious propaganda. You have . . . seen Communism with its mask ripped off, with its sweet façade uncovered and its hard, bitter, and determined core revealed."

In this film we are at the center of HUAC's fearmongering world, an obsessive, hysterical world created by fiat, raised by bootstrap epithets, propped up by self-proving charges, and floating on hate. But the gap between what HUAC wants us to believe and what reason tells us, is as great on film as it was in the more familiar milieu of the hearing. A background of picketing, chants and songs is manipulated to preserve the "documentary" illusion. The narration, strident and endlessly reiterative, tries to bridge the gap between the truth and HUAC's vicious distortions. Lewis gives us commentary and photographic images instead of Arens' lurid questions. But what emerges is still a stranger to reason—guilt without fault, the Kafkaesque nightmare of the hearings. And something else. The events of the film are new to us, but the style and tone of the entire production have a puzzling sense of familiarity. Where have we seen this kind of thing before?

To be sure—the totalitarian propaganda newsreels of the thirties. The harangues of Propaganda Minister Goebbels eerily echo back to us through the years—in English.

At the beginning of the narration, we are told that the following "directive" (loyal Americans give orders or make requests, but Communists "issue directives") appeared in the *Daily Californian,* the official University of California student newspaper:

> The SCCL (Student Committee for Civil Liberties) plans to picket the hearings today. It has carried a call for students to attend the rally and hearings

and suggests that people "laugh out loud" in the hearings when things get ridiculous.

This "directive" was merely a suggestion made at an open meeting of the organization and was not adopted. The Oakland *Tribune,* where the account originally appeared, has retracted it as false, as has the *Saturday Evening Post* of October 1, 1960.

The first paragraph of the narration goes on to tell us that "Communist apparatus activated its trained agitators . . . months before the scheduled hearings were to begin." This paragraph is then followed by the statement: "The carefully organized protest campaign was climaxed with a student directive. . . ." This skillfully composed distortion first makes an unsupported charge of Red preparations; the unparticularized preparations are linked to the student group by "climaxed" and "directive." Without taking responsibility for a flat assertion, the narration makes the student group part of the "trained agitators" which the "Communist apparatus" had "activated." This shoddy innuendo appears in an official document of the United States Congress.

The film footage of the Thursday student demonstration inside the hearing room brutally distorts what happened. It suppresses the fact that it took place during a recess when the Committee was not in session and seeks to give the impression that the demonstration was a planned act of defiance executed during the course of the hearing. It conceals the fact that the demonstration resulted from the denial of a petition to move to a larger hearing room or to admit the students on the outside on a first-come, first-served basis.

To give substance to the Red-plot charge, the film asserts that "several students" were ejected from the hearing room on Thursday, together with two subpoenaed witnesses. Only one witness (and no students) was actually removed on Thursday. The student whose removal the film shows was in fact ejected on Friday, when she and several other students smiled at testimony given during the hearings.

The film's account of the Friday demonstration completely distorts its cause—the preferential white-card policy. The narration states the hearing hall's seating capacity was 400 and that "nearly 100" white cards were

209

issued on Thursday. It invites the inference that 300 seats remained for occupancy by the general public. But the full hall held only 75 outsiders on Thursday, the largest number ever admitted. What the narration suppresses is that up to six admissions were allowed for each card. A more direct misrepresentation is the statement that at Friday's hearing 200 from the general public were admitted. Observers agree that no more than 30 people were admitted on Friday morning and half that number in the afternoon. Communists did not plot to have HUAC bar almost all the students from the hearing room. The sit-down of the students, called as the hoses were being unrolled, was not, as the narration charged but never proved, a tactic of Communist agitators, but an attempt to assure the police that the demonstrators' intentions were peaceful and to prevent panic.

The narration states that on Friday morning "Police warnings are met with jeers and boos and renewed chanting and renewed singing." According to eyewitness reports as well as unedited tapes, when the police spoke to the students, they ceased demonstrating and paid attention. The film splices the request of the police with a shot of students taken hours later. (In a telecast over NCOP-TV on August 9, 1960, Investigator Wheeler admitted that the film sequence had been altered and that the shot of the singing and chanting did not depict the response to the police talk to the students.)

Plunging recklessly onward, the sound track gives the impression that the police notified the students that the building would have to be cleared. No films are shown of this alleged warning. As has already been noted, at about noon on Friday Sheriff Carberry addressed the students and, far from urging them to leave, promised to try to relax the restrictive admissions policy. The full sound tapes which were made of the day's occurrences contain no record of an order to disperse before the hoses were turned on.

The narrator tells us that, "One student provides the spark that touches off the violence when he leaps over a barricade, grabs a police officer's night stick, and begins beating the officer over the head. As the mob surges forward to storm the doors, a police inspector orders that the fire hoses be turned on." No films are shown of this stirring scene. It is pure invention.

The May 23, 1960, edition of *Life* magazine carries a photograph that was taken a split second after the hoses went on: some of the students are still partly dry. The students are either seated or moving away from the barricade. Robert Meisenbach, the student who allegedly stormed the barricade, is shown completely dry, standing against the side of the building watching the demonstration.

The officer involved did not claim, either in his official report, or in his testimony before the grand jury, that his attacker mounted a barricade or that he was hit more than once. He merely claimed that he was struck at some time during the confusion. At Meisenbach's trial for assault, *all* of the witnesses—prosecution and defense—agreed that no such barricade-storming assault occurred. The lurid claim that a "mob surges forward to storm the doors" is a figment of HUAC's overheated imagination. The film simply lies when it states that the hosing was triggered by a rush for the barricades which resulted in the beating of a policeman. (Professor John Searle has asserted that "there is considerable evidence that the hosing, clubbing, and subsequent arrest of the students by the police was planned in advance. It is, for example, an established fact that ambulances and paddy wagons assembled at City Hall prior to the hosing.")

"Operation Abolition," this document of the United States House of Representatives, is dishonest even about the simplest facts. It asserts that "four students suffered minor injuries, eight policemen are injured to the point where they require hospitalization." But the true casualty report is quite different: one student had his eardrum ruptured when a policeman deliberately aimed a hose at his ear; two suffered head injuries requiring several stitches; one student received a back injury which required an operation; one student's tooth was knocked out and several others required treatment for contusions. The police injuries were: two wrenched backs; a swollen finger; a head injury; a bitten thumb (the only injury that can justify an inference of intentional violence); and three cases of exhaustion (suffered by the older members of the force). The film tells us that "officer Dumphy, age 61, suffered a stroke when he was knocked down by student agitators." Police records show that he collapsed from exhaustion.

George Draper, of the San Francisco *Chronicle,* wrote on May 14, 1960:

I did not see any of the kids actually fighting with the police. Their resistance was more passive. They would simply go limp and be manhandled out of the building. . . . At this point it got very rough . . . I saw one slightly built lad being carried by two husky officers. One held the boy's shirt, the other held him by the feet. He was struggling, but he was no match for the two bigger men. Then, from nowhere, appeared a third officer; he went to the slender boy, firmly held by the other two officers, and clubbed him three times in the head. You could hear the hollow smack of the club striking. The boy went limp and was carried out. . . . Police were not clubbing the demonstrators at will.

The film steadily denies police brutality, and warns us that only Communist and pro-Communist propagandists will disagree with it—a true HUAC touch.

In a telecast of January 28, 1961, Congressman Walter, when asked whether "Operation Abolition" was doctored, replied, ". . . how anybody can doctor a moving picture is something that will remain a mystery to me. There couldn't possibly be anything more absurd than the charge that this was staged." The solution to this mystery is that you fake the sequences, telescope and splice unrelated film footage, use a sound track of falsehoods to assert what the film does not show, and tie it all together with a narration which is alternately dishonest, distorted or misleading.

Congressional documents are privileged under libel or slander actions. But the circumstances under which "Operation Abolition" was made, shown and distributed have caused many to question whether this privilege applies. It has been argued that those slandered by the film have legal recourse against the film's exhibitors and makers, and beyond them to the Committee and to Congress itself, in whose name the entire project was ostensibly carried forward.

The film's narrative relies heavily on a report by J. Edgar Hoover on the San Francisco affair. This report is a strange document, and like the film itself borrows heavily from the propaganda techniques of totalitarianism. As with the film, we are struck at the outset by the curiously novel form in which a representative of the Government has chosen to speak to us. Hoover's document, called "Communist Target—Youth," purports to be a report "illustrating Communist strategy and tactics" at San Francisco. But by what authority is the report made? It is not a report by the FBI about the results of an investigation into crime; it is not a publication of the FBI at all. It is a report of J. Edgar Hoover published by the House Committee on Un-American Activities. To whom is the report made? It is not a report to the Attorney General, the head of the executive department of which the FBI is a part. It does not claim to be a report to Congress. Nor is this the voice of Mr. Hoover speaking as a witness in a Congressional proceeding. The "report" is a transparent device to shield the film from defamation suits by providing its sound track with a "cover" of official utterance. The prestige and authority of its author have been used to lend respectability to the film's extremist views, sinister inferences and distorted facts. A factual "police" investigation has been made the pretext for a hatful of political propaganda, unproved assertions, unparticularized charges and bizarre inferences.

Like the film, the Hoover report suggests that there is a tie between the demonstrations of youth in Japan and Uruguay, and the San Francisco affair. We are never offered proof of the subversive nature of the activities of the Japanese and Uruguayan youth. Nor are we told how and why the California undergraduates were chosen as instruments of this assertedly world-wide movement. For reasons also only known to the author, there is no link between the demonstrations of youth in Korea, Turkey, Hungary and Poland, and the San Francisco demonstrators. Nor does the report see the connection which many sensitive observers of youth have noted between such protest movements as the Southern sit-ins in our own country and the demonstration against the Committee. We are by fiat required to accept the dogma that opposition to HUAC must be treason.

As in the film, the Hoover report tells us exactly how the demonstrations started: "One of the demonstrators provided the spark that touched off a flame of violence. Leaping a barricade that had been erected, he grabbed an officer's nightstick and began beating the officer over the head. The mob surged forward as if to storm the doors and a police inspector ordered the fire hose turned on."

As has been shown, this assertion is wholly without foundation.

The Hoover report, like the film, converts the entire protest movement both inside the City Hall and outside into a deep-dyed Red putsch. Like the film, it attributes to California Communists a diabolical omnipotence and omniscience. The entire report does not refer even once to the Students for Civil Liberties, the campus organization which had collected 2,000 signatures to an anti-HUAC petition prior to the hearing, and had organized the three-day picket line. The opposition of community organizations, and of hundreds of educators, is simply swept under the Red rug.

The enormously tendentious quality of the report can best be savored from its charge that the "grand climax" of the allegedly Red-planned anti-HUAC demonstration was to "have the demonstrators join a Party-sponsored peace march on Saturday, May 14, at the conclusion of the hearing." But the facts cannot be so easily stuffed into the Red mold.

A group of pacifists under the sponsorship of the American Friends Service Committee had, in January, planned a Peace March. It was held on the same Saturday as the conclusion of the hearing only by coincidence. When HUAC had originally announced that its hearing would commence on May 10th, the pacifist groups scheduled their march for May 14th. HUAC then changed its mind and postponed its hearing two days so that the last day of the hearing coincided with the day of the Peace March. Mr. Hoover offers no evidence in support of the claim that the Peace March, like the anti-HUAC demonstration, was "party sponsored," nor does he explain why the Communists would plan a demonstration and a Peace March on the same afternoon.

A detailed analysis of the affair made by Professor John R. Searle of the University of California's Philosophy Department, based on personal experience and numerous interviews, concluded both that the picketing demonstrations "were well monitored and orderly from beginning to end," and that none of the leaders of Students for Civil Liberties are Communists. "Nor was there any outside leadership of this group, Communist or otherwise." An article by Burton H. Wolfe in the *Californian* magazine for March 1961 concludes, as a result of personal interviews, that the student leaders "had taken particular care to reject overtures from the Communist Party made on two occasions. They made it clear that it was only to be a student demonstration with no interference from any kind of political party." Professor Searle has written, "On the afternoon of the first day, that's Thursday, Merle Brodsky, one of the subpoenaed witnesses, approached the monitors . . . on the picket line and tried to get them to cooperate with him in demonstrating inside City Hall. He was flatly refused."

And finally, on May 3, 1961, the last of the student demonstrators, Robert J. Meisenbach, was acquitted of assault charges. The San Francisco police, in presenting their case against the California senior, never even claimed, as did "Operation Abolition" and the Hoover report, that he or anyone else had leaped a barricade, seized a policeman's nightstick and assaulted him with it. The prosecution from the very beginning conceded that there had been no such incident, but argued to the jury that after the hoses were turned on, Meisenbach had become involved in a scuffle with a policeman and had attacked him with his own billy. The defense presented testimony that Meisenbach, far from beating the policeman, was himself brutally beaten by a group of policemen, including the officer who claimed to have been assaulted. The jury apparently believed the defense witnesses and returned a verdict of innocent in less than three hours.

The film and the Hoover report are thus twice discredited. There was no surge to the barricades and the assault on the policeman which is supposed to have triggered the attack on the students never took place at all. As Meisenbach's lawyer declared:

> This knocks the film "Operation Abolition" into the creek, and nails the lies in the original police department reports. Both are filled with falsehoods.
> It is a direct blow to the House Committee on Un-American Activities, given by 12 impartial citizens who finally heard all the facts.

The jury verdict can hardly inspire a thrill of pride in our FBI Director. A San Francisco State Representative, John A. O'Connell, a Democrat, said he thought FBI Director Hoover had "lied in attributing the disturbance at the House Un-American Activities Committee hearing in San Francisco solely to Communist-inspired opposition to the Committee."

There is, perhaps, nothing that can be done to correct the distortions and misstatements in the Hoover report, but will HUAC now make still another version of the film? Or will it simply discover yet another Red plot to overthrow the Republic—this time on the part of the film's critics?

HUAC must brand criticism as Red-inspired as a matter of sheer survival. It always puts its techniques of distortion and suppression to most ruthless use when it is under attack. "Operation Abolition" is a forgery on celluloid. It belongs to a long tradition of hoaxes and forgeries—the Popish plot, the Zinoviev Letter, the Bordereau (in the Dreyfus case), which are used as instruments of social and political leverage in periods of tension. Such frauds are frequently manufactured to support charges of subversion and betrayal.

But the making and circulation of this film is more than another attempt by HUAC to smear its critics. The film was produced at a time when HUAC's stock had fallen to a new low. It was losing its hold on the press and on public opinion. California, HUAC's favorite hunting ground, had taken it on and sent it packing. Congressman Roosevelt's speech had given hope to the growing abolition movement. The Committee was becoming the darling of fewer and fewer people—and these were concentrated on the far right of the political spectrum.

"Operation Abolition" was boldly conceived as a double-headed stroke—to whitewash HUAC activities by creating a wholly false impression of imminent danger from the Communists, and as a propaganda stroke to restore HUAC's failing fortunes. The subpoenaing of the footage, the decision to make a film, the commissioning of the Hoover Report, the ultimate release of the film with the official imprimatur of the Committee itself—all of these steps have the piratical and ruthless quality which has become Walter's trademark in his leadership of HUAC.

"Operation Abolition" is not merely a plug for the Committee. It introduces to our country the techniques of totalitarian propaganda. It is our first officially sponsored totalitarian style political propaganda film. Masquerading

216

in the ill-fitting disguise of a report to Congress, this fabrication is becoming a potent instrument in the arsenal of restraints on political freedom. In a speech on the floor of Congress, in March, 1961, Congressman Walter claimed that over 10,000,000 people have already seen the film since its release in July 1960.

Fulton Lewis III has shown and spoken on behalf of the film in more than 200 colleges. The John Birch Society, the newest and most active member of HUAC's Network of supporters, is a principal distributor of the film in many American communities. The society is particularly zealous in developing pressure campaigns for the showing of the film in churches. It, too, denounces as Communists all critics of its accuracy.

The film is a regular feature of American Legion Post meetings. Employers, such as the Allen Bradley Company of Milwaukee, espouse showings of the film for their employees. On many campuses the Young Americans for Freedom, a right-wing student group, have become the film's official sponsors. When the film is shown, other HUAC propaganda publications are frequently distributed.

Government agencies have bought copies of the film in quantity for "educational" purposes. Army posts book it months in advance. State police agencies show the film as part of a "security education" program. In Wilmington, Delaware, according to the Wilmington *Morning News,* the state police show the film as part of an 18-point program, "What You Can Do To Fight Communism." Among the points in this program are: "6. Be as cautious in sponsoring movements as you would be in signing a business contract. *Check with local intelligence agencies before you sign or join.* 7. Identify public officials and policies displaying 'softness toward communism.' *Demand a more patriotic attitude.* 8. *Check 'Peace' groups . . .* Communists are today promoting appeasement in the guise of peace."

And in Michigan, "Operation Abolition" and another film on Communism were shown in high schools and to private groups by the State Police Subversive Activities Squad—until the Governor ordered the discontinuance of such showings on the grounds that the films were ". . . inaccurate and distorted and thus harm, rather than advance, the purpose of an intelligent anti-Communist program."

But the racist, anti-Semitic and other crackpot groups

who form HUAC's grassroots support, endorse the film and exhibit it to complement their own programs.

"Operation Abolition" churns up the fanatics with an "authentic," "documentary" dress rehearsal for revolution. The enemy is no longer in the far-off Kremlin: he is within the gates, "rioting" before their very eyes as he vents his mad lust for power. After the showing, the meeting turns with renewed determination to the tasks of fighting integration, impeaching Justice Warren, keeping America safe for White Gentiles(or even White Protestants), abolishing the income tax and related problems.

The film has not lacked critics. Frequently, when it has been shown at schools, churches and factories, it has been denounced as biased, inaccurate and a contribution to a revival of McCarthyism. And despite the efforts of Fulton Lewis III, the response to the film on the campuses of American universities has been predominantly hostile. The *Protestant Christian Century* and the Jesuit publication *America* have both condemned the film, as have a number of other Catholic organs.

The National Council of Churches has urged Protestant ministers "not to exhibit the film unless a full and fair presentation" is made of all the facts. Editorial or news analyses condemning the film have appeared in the San Francisco *News-Call-Bulletin*, the San Francisco *Chronicle*, the *Capital* (Madison, Wisconsin) *Times*, the New York *Post*, the Washington *Post*, the Minneapolis *Star*, the New York *Times*, the *Nation*, the *Reporter* and the *New Republic*.

Nor has the film succeeded in blocking the abolition movement. On the contrary;, the spectacle of a Government-sponsored forgery sold for private profit, for exhibition to hate groups, has broadened the awareness of HUAC's degradation. Not the least of the reasons for the spread of the abolition movement is the California student demonstration which has become for youth everywhere in the United States, a symbol of resistance to HUAC.

12 THE EXPOSURE FORMULA— ITS OPERATION AGAINST ORGANIZATIONS AND GROUPS

The exposure of organizations and groups complements and nourishes the exposure of individuals. The Committee, of course, regards the Communist Party as subversive (but not the Ku Klux Klan, John Birch Society, or the White Citizens Councils) and documents its every move in an extremely sensational manner. The Committee also exposes organizations which it claims are adjuncts of the Communist Party. But a much larger number are exposed solely because the Committee disapproves of their objectives or because they are not sufficiently anti-Communist. To conceal these reasons for moving against organizations, the Committee characterizes them with a special discrediting vocabulary, inherited from its predecessors and constantly embellished: "Communist front," "arm of the Communist Party," "Communist satellite," "formed to advance Communist aims," "Kremlin-inspired," "bulwark of Communist protection," etc.

Thus, the technique of exposing an organization is simple: its aims are denounced as subversive solely because they have also been espoused by the Communist Party. The political dossiers of the organization's officers and sponsors are then offered as confirmation of the organization's subversive character. These dossiers sometimes charge that the individual was once a Party member (e.g., "identified in 1932 by Benjamin Gitlow as a member of the Communist Party"). But if this "corpus delicti" is lacking, the Committee scrapes together other affiliations and connections which it does not like (e.g., "Member Chicago Committee for Peaceful Alternatives," "signer of letter opposing renewal of the Dies Committee," "signer, *amicus curiae* brief in United States Supreme Court in support of Communist leaders," etc.). The Committee is a firm believer in the theory that while a person may occasionally lapse into liberalism, a consistent and active liberal is subversive— even if he cannot be shown to be a Communist.

The false inferences about the politics of the organization's leaders or sponsors are then linked to its condemned aims by a scaffolding of new inferences of conspiratorial tactics for which support is invariably found in the writings of Lenin, regarded by the Committee as an infallible prophet with millions of concealed domestic disciples. All that remains is to characterize the organization in a sinister way.

By a fascinating process of subversive cross-fertilization, a relationship to an organization which is exposed as subversive is in turn used to expose all the other organizations which its officers, directors or sponsors belong to or join. If, for instance an officer of the Emergency Civil Liberties Committee happens also to belong to a church group, this automatically gives the Committee a shooting license on the church group. If this structure seems somewhat jerry-built to the reader, it is only because he is insufficiently aware that subversion is "interlocking."

This chain exposure of organizations is an important end in itself, since it permits the Committee to intervene in group expression and opinion formation about the vital issues of our time, from racial integration to peace. It is also a means of replenishing the supply of exposable individuals—now seriously depleted after 23 years. Thus, nonmembership in the Communist Party will not prevent the exposure of an individual who belongs to an exposed organization or who fails to leave it promptly after it becomes suspect. An individual who retains his affiliation "after the organization has been publicly exposed" must be regarded as a secret Communist Party member.

The Committee exposes organizations in a number of different ways. Some of its reports deal exclusively with organizations: for example, in 1944 it issued a report exposing the CIO Political Action Committee; in 1947 it issued reports, among others, on the *Southern Conference for Human Welfare,* and on the *Civil Rights* Congress; in 1949, it issued a *Review of the Scientific and Cultural Conference for World Peace;* in 1950, the organizations denounced included the National Lawyers Guild, the National Committee for Defeat of the Mundt Bill, and the Honolulu *Record;* and in 1952, it issued among other attacks on organizations, a *Review of the Methodist Federation for Social Action.*

In the course of its hearings, the Committee questions witnesses concerning their relationship with particular organizations. It then puts into the record its own charges concerning the organization and its "subversive" nature. The most thorough form of exposure is to be "cited." This is an official designation of subversion, akin to a judgment of conviction, which is made, first in the Committee's annual report, and then in the form of a permanent blacklist in the Committee's *Guide to Subversive Organizations and Publications*.

The *Guide* is not a legislative document, nor even a report to Congress. It is the Burke's *Peerage* of organizational subversion. The last edition, published in January 1957, lists 628 organizations and publications cited as subversive by various governmental agencies on Federal and state levels. The citations are largely by the House Committee and its Senate counterpart. This is an increase of 180 organizations and publications over the listings in an earlier (1951) edition. Perusal of the *Guide* should cause no tremors of fear for the Republic—fully 80% of the organizations listed are defunct, many since the thirties. These listings—the Bronx Victory Labor Committee, Citizens Committee to Free Earl Browder, the Committee to Aid the Hearst Strikers, New York Tom Mooney Committee, to name a few—are primarily intended as a reference aid for blacklisters. Who knows how our security may be menaced by the infiltration of a former member of the Bronx Victory Labor Committee? If a functioning organization wants to be "uncited," there is a way of doing that too. It must purge its officers and staff of those objectionable to the Committee and obtain approval of its aims. A corrective press release will then be issued and its name deleted from the next edition of the *Guide*. Defunct or nonfunctioning organizations, no longer able to purge, must, of course, be condemned to a purgatory of permanent citation.

The *Guide* also includes the organizations listed by the Attorney General for use in the Government-loyalty program, although the Supreme Court has held that such listings are invalid when the organization has not been properly charged and heard. This does not trouble the Committee—nor does the fact that the organizations which it cites had neither notice nor charges nor hearing. But, then, the Committee explains such procedural niceties are not appropriate to a legislative committee. What the Committee does not explain is what legislative purpose the *Guide* serves.

It is time we took a closer look at how and why an organization is exposed. In 1956, the Senate Internal Security Subcommittee, in its notorious *Handbook for Americans,* cited the Emergency Civil Liberties Committee (ECLC) on the ground that not only had it defended "the cases of Communist lawbreakers" and offered a "bulwark of protection" to the Party, but that it made "special appeals in behalf of civil liberties and reaching out far beyond the confines of the Communist Party itself." Nothing further was offered in support of the charges of subversion.

In 1956, the organization conducted a vigorous campaign against political restriction on the right to travel—a campaign which culminated in a Supreme Court decision in 1958, completely vindicating ECLC's position. In 1956, the organization's director, Clark Foreman, sought an opportunity to testify on the subject of passport legislation in a Judiciary subcommittee hearing conducted by Walter. When Walter, as Judiciary subcommittee Chairman, received the request, he answered it in his capacity as Un-American Committee Chairman—with a subpoena.

In June 1956, Foreman and ECLC's general counsel were subjected to a typical exposure grilling. At the conclusion of the hearing, Foreman, who had answered all of the Committee's questions, was threatened with contempt for refusing to surrender his passport, which had just been obtained after onerous litigation. Because Foreman refused to comply with this wholly improper demand, the Committee voted to cite him for contempt—although this action was never carried through in the House. When Foreman subsequently received the transcript of the stormy hearing, there was a serious omission: his testimony linking HUAC with Aware, Inc., a New York group active in blacklisting, was edited out of the transcript.

In November 1957, the Committee issued a report "Operation Abolition" (not to be confused with HUAC's film of the same name) which charged a plot by ECLC and its Middle West and West Coast counterparts, with three traitorous objectives: the shackling or abolition of HUAC, the discrediting of J. Edgar Hoover and the FBI, and the crippling of Government antisubversive programs.

This, the Committee charges, "dovetails with the past program of political subversion inaugurated by the Communist Party."

This fiendish plot, the Committee charged, was inaugurated by a rally at Carnegie Hall in September 1957, following the decision of the Supreme Court in the *Watkins* case. It was followed by an advertisement on November 2, 1957, "You and the FBI," which discussed the rights which the citizen enjoys in his relationship to the FBI. Of this simple straightforward account, the report states that although it "avoids a frontal attack upon the FBI, it cunningly suggests that the FBI engages in tactics of intimidation."

This is the whole "case" of HUAC against ECLC—two and a half pages long. The following eight pages are taken up with a listing of the affiliations and activities of those of its officers and council members who boast dossiers in the Committee's files.

The House Committee's condemnation of the Emergency Civil Liberties Committee is pure reprisal. The charge that the campaign against the Committee was a tentacle of a larger plot against the FBI and "the antisubversive programs of Congress" reflects a new HUAC technique devised to make opposition to the Committee seditious. A similar technique is used by the Committee to protect the Walter-McCarran Act from criticism. The Committee's attempt to share the untouchability of the FBI as common targets of a subversive plot is ludicrous. Even stranger, because wholly undocumented, is the charge that the campaign against the Committee was somehow linked to a plot against security legislation.

Three recent cases dramatize the Committee's new *lèse majesté* thesis. In July 1958, Carl Braden, one of the witnesses in the famed "Louisville Seven" case, and the field secretary of the Southern Conference Educational Fund, was subpoenaed for an appearance in Atlanta later that month while he was visiting at the summer home of Harvey O'Connor, ECLC chairman. The trial record of Braden's contempt conviction leaves no room for doubt that the reason for Braden's subpoena was his activity in support of integration and in organizing a petition campaign against the Committee. This was embellished with

the Committee's customary embroidery about "coloniza-
tion of basic industry," "Communist techniques" and
"Communist propaganda," but the Committee did not
try too hard to conceal the retaliatory and purely political
motivations for the affair. As Arens put it: "He had something to do with the dissemination of petitioners [sic]
which were circulated in the Southland for the purpose of
precluding or attempting to produce a softening of the
very hearing we proposed to have here." The revealing
reference by Arens is to a petition by 200 Negro leaders
filed with Congress in opposition to the Atlanta hearing.

Braden had to be exposed for the additional reasons
that he was identified with the *Southern Newsletter*, an
integrationist publication, and had been served while va-
cationing with O'Connor, an ECLC official. (Two counts
in his indictment involve a refusal to answer a question
about his connection with ECLC, whether he and O'Connor had met to "develop plans and strategies" for ECLC.)
A purpose of the hearing, the Committee explained, was
to determine whether to "cite" ECLC. A final reason for
exposing Braden involved his organization's activities in
developing resistance to the states'-rights measures offered
in Congress, ostensibly to overcome the Supreme Court's
ruling in the *Nelson* case to the effect that Federal legislation in the field of sedition had superseded state laws
dealing with the same subject. These measures were of
special concern to Chairman Walter, who opened the
hearing (Governor Griffin of Georgia was an honored
guest); they beautifully cemented "security" and Jim
Crow.

Braden's one-year jail sentence has just been upheld by
the Supreme Court in a 5-4 decision. The Supreme Court's
ruling may well encourage the Southern bloc to use the
only too willing Committee to combat the movement for
integration through the Red smear—a tactic with which
legislative groups in Mississippi, Louisiana and Florida are
boldly experimenting. Indeed, three Negro ministers in
Florida have recently been cited for contempt for resisting
attempts to compel surrender of NAACP membership lists
to determine whether the NAACP is "Red-infiltrated."
J. B. Matthews, former research director of the Dies Committee, has informed the Mississippi legislature that he
knows "of no organization in the United States so heavily
infiltrated by Communists as the NAACP."

A companion case to Braden's is that of Frank Wilkinson, the director of the Citizens Committee to Preserve American Freedoms. Wilkinson had been subpoenaed to a 1956 West Coast hearing as punishment for his efforts in organizing a meeting protesting HUAC hearings. He had refused on grounds of conscience to answer any Committee questions, but was not cited for contempt only because the session terminated before a Committee quorum could be assembled. His role in the 1957 Carnegie Hall rally for the Committee's abolition marked him as a sure target for reprisal and smear. The Committee was lying in wait for him. Arens' explanation of why he was subpoenaed to the Atlanta hearings was, though spiced with his customary rhetorical flourishes about Communism, unusually frank. He said,

> . . . you were sent to this area by the Communist Party for the purpose of developing a hostile sentiment to this committee and to its work for the purpose of undertaking to bring pressure upon the United States Congress to preclude these particular hearings. Indeed it is the fact that you were not even subpoenaed for these particular hearings until we learned that you were in town for that very purpose and that you were not subpoenaed to appear before this committee until you had actually registered in the hotel here in Atlanta.

Wilkinson was subpoenaed three minutes after he registered. When the marshal was asked how he knew where to find Wilkinson, he replied, "I received a call yesterday afternoon from Washington. They said they were sending a subpoena down for you and that I'd find you at the Atlanta Biltmore early this afternoon."

The Supreme Court, in another 5-4 decision, also affirmed Wilkinson's one-year sentence. The Supreme Court's decisions in these two important cases give HUAC *carte blanche* to punish its critics. All that is needed is a *claim* that the purpose was to gather facts for legislation. What counts is what HUAC *says* it is doing—not what it is really doing.

Early in September 1958, Harvey O'Connor, Emergency Civil Liberties Committee's chairman, was subpoenaed as he arrived at a meeting held to protest Committee hearings in Newark. In declining to appear, he pointed out to the Committee that the subpoena did not conform to limitations on the investigative power imposed by the Supreme Court in the *Watkins* case, for its purpose was not legislative, but was an attempted exercise of the power to "expose for the sake of exposure."

How would the Committee respond to this challenge? It could say, as it did, in effect, in justifyng the Atlanta exposure of Wilkinson, "*Watkins* or no *Watkins*—a Congressional committee can use its power not only for legislative fact-gathering, but to 'protect' itself from hostile criticism from 'subversive' sources." The Committee decided that what worked in the South might fail in the North and that it needed the help of a carefully phrased legislative purpose to send O'Connor to jail. Legislative purposes gushed from Arens like a mountain stream: Both Congress and the Committee had pending before them measures to amend the term "organizing" in the Smith Act so as to include not only the initial organizing of the Communist Party, as the Supreme Court had restrictively interpreted the term, but also the subsequent organization of entities under the control of the Party. According to Arens, the Committee had "information" that ECLC had been "organized, grouped and regrouped" by the Communist Party; that Braden and O'Connor, both identified as "hard core" Communists, had met in Rhode Island where they "were planning strategies, tactics and organizational activities of the Emergency Civil Liberties Committee."

Besides, the Committee had "factual information and testimony" that "the Emergency Committee was created by the Communist Party for the purpose of discrediting the Committee on Un-American Activities, of hampering the security program of the United States, and of undertaking to tie the hands of the Federal Bureau of Investigation, and to discredit the Director of the Federal Bureau of Investigation." (The "factual information" referred to by Arens was apparently the Committee's own "Operation Abolition" report; but even that far from modest document made no such charges, and as for testimony none appears or is summarized in the brief text of the HUAC pamphlet. Of course, it is quite possible that HUAC has discovered informers pliant enough to expand the original charges with "testimony.")

In addition, Arens went on to explain, the Committee had high hopes of being enlightened by O'Connor in appraising the need to return to the states the power to deal with sedition. (Arens neglected to explain why O'Connor —never before known to be a champion of states' rights— would be helpful to the Committee in this endeavor.)

Finally, to round things out, HUAC had "factual information" that O'Connor and ECLC were disseminators of Communist propaganda. O'Connor's failure to respond to the subpoena had frustrated the Committee's hope to obtain "factual information" to help it appraise pending legislation and to "maintain a surveillance over existing legislation pertaining to Communist propaganda."

A hundred volumes could not tell us as much about HUAC as Arens' self-serving recital. The "factual information" which HUAC is supposed to have had about ECLC has never appeared in any of its publications, including the tendentious "Operation Abolition" report which was prepared for the purpose of demolishing ECLC. The purpose of the hearing, as announced and as printed, was, "Communist Infiltration and Activities in Newark, N. J."—not the "organizing" provision of the Smith Act and not the states' rights measures to neutralize the *Nelson* decision. Equally suspicious is the fact that not one witness at the hearings was asked about these subjects. O'Connor was not even a resident of New Jersey. The hard fact is that O'Connor's subpoena was an act of reprisal, just as Wilkinson's and Braden's were, masked by a false face.

The amusement with which one initially reacts to Arens' clumsy attempts to "make a record" soon gives way to disgust and concern that the rigging may succeed. Will the trial court believe, as the Committee would like it to, that waiting for O'Connor at the hearing was the grandmother of legislation, and not the wolf of exposure dressed in her clothes? And beyond the O'Connor case are the larger questions: how meaningful are our basic liberties and their judicial safeguards when the people's representatives deceive both the people and the courts in order to destroy the right of dissent? Indeed, how safe is democratic government when personal vindictiveness and dishonesty replace the ethical preconditions for the exercise of power?

227

The formal "citation" of ECLC came in the Committee's 1958 annual report. HUAC has used it precisely as though it were a judgment of condemnation made by an authorized tribunal under the law after due hearing. Who will ask by what authority HUAC sat in judgment on an organization, or in what way the "citation" furthers the legislative process? But ECLC attacked HUAC. ECLC stands condemned.

Another cow, which is almost as sacred as HUAC itself, is the Walter-McCarran Act. In 1956, the demands for amending the act were mountainous. There were no less than 78 bills in Congress amending or revising the Act. President Eisenhower, for the third time in three years, urged Congress to revise what he called its "discriminatory and inequitable" provisions.

The pressure on Walter, as Chairman of the Immigration subcommittee, to process these amending provisions was enormous. In response to this pressure, Walter as HUAC Chairman, launched hearings to discredit the entire movement for amendment as a Red plot. Ironically enough, in the hearings which he did conduct, he subpoenaed correspondence between private citizens and their Congressmen in which the latter complained of Walter's refusal to hold hearings or permit amendments to the law.

As the New York *Times* stated, the Committee "was collecting data for a counter-attack in advance of the prospective legislative battle. The Committee already has in its files bales of similar testimony from the same persons as it is now hearing and proposes to hear. The Committee's point, apparently, is to show again that many of those persons or groups favoring modification of the present immigration laws have been touched by Communism."

These hearings, held coast-to-coast for 13 hearing days, are published in a tome of almost 1,000 pages and are among the most remarkable ever held by any Congressional committee. The entire record consists of the exposure of about 120 unfriendly witnesses. For 1,000 pages these witnesses are attacked in a stepped-up exposure routine, jeered at, insulted, but asked nothing about the ostensible subject of the hearings, the Walter-McCarran Act. No less than seven lawyers were subpoenaed and harassed—solely because of their efforts in behalf of the foreign-born—but were not permitted to speak a word in criticism of the Walter-McCarran Act.

The immediate target of the hearings was the American Committee for the Protection of the Foreign Born. HUAC was entirely undisturbed by the circumstance that the Subversive Activities Control Board (SACB) had already conducted hearings and that the status of the American Committee for the Protection of Foreign Born was then pending before it. Indeed, HUAC introduced into the record much of the material which had already been introduced in the administrative proceeding. HUAC subpoenaed many of the records of the American Committee for the Protection of the Foreign Born, as well as of area committees which have the same objectives. These subpoenas called not only for documents, but correspondence. Out of these documents and correspondence, together with many others obtained independently by HUAC, a record was made which was subsequently printed as an appendix to the hearing, over 1,300 pages long, a grab-bag of materials dating from the thirties.

Many documents in the appendix were obtained through FBI plants who stole them from the American Committee. Cross-examination of one of the Department of Justice's witnesses in the SACB case against the American Committee disclosed that, as a paid plant for the FBI, the witness had become a volunteer worker for the Los Angeles Committee for the Protection of the Foreign Born and had taken from the Los Angeles Committee's files and passed on to the FBI numerous papers, including correspondence.

The proceedings of a banquet given by the American Committee appear in HUAC's appendix, as well as a seating chart and notes for the chairman on the agenda. These also were stolen by an informer. In addition, it appears that the text of the speeches at the banquet were taped by an FBI agent at the banquet; the transcription appears in HUAC's appendix. In short, the appendix is a good example of the beautiful teamwork which has developed between HUAC and the FBI.

Attached to the appendix are two indexes. One index of 115 pages contains nothing but names, over 2,000 of them; the other index, some 20 pages long, is an index of organizations. The 2,000 individuals are regarded as subversive by the Committee because of their support of the rights of the foreign born. They include Mrs. Eleanor Roosevelt, Arthur Schnabel, Yehudi Menuhin, C. Wright Mills, Emily Greene Balch, Zechariah Chafee, Jr., and scores of other distinguished Americans.

Apart from the usual roster of informers to identify witnesses, the hearings rely on the testimony of a single friendly witness—Colonel Archibald Roosevelt, who spoke for three Network organizations: The Alliance, the American Coalition of Patriotic Societies and the Sons of the American Revolution.

The nation-wide hearings, the elaborate appendix and indexes, according to the Committee, document a brand-new technique used by the Communists. This technique is described in a special report issued in August 1957, *Communist Political Subversion—The Campaign to Destroy the Security Programs of the United States Government.* Despite the comprehensively ominous title, the report deals almost exclusively with the American Committee for the Protection of the Foreign Born, with special emphasis upon that Committee's opposition to the Walter-McCarran Act.

A preliminary analysis (not even faintly supported by the rest of the report or the hearings) develops the thesis that the entire security system of the United States is menaced by a campaign of Kremlin agents to use political subversion to accomplish the political destruction of our system far more completely and effectively than "could have been achieved by the classic means of force and violence." According to HUAC, the Communist Party, acting through the American Committee for the Protection of the Foreign Born, is seeking to wipe out the Walter-McCarran Act, the Internal Security Act, the Smith Act and all other legislative and executive action "aimed against the Kremlin conspiratorial organization in the United States." In one sweeping smear, HUAC dismisses nation-wide opposition to the Walter-McCarran Act as subversive.

HUAC explains its equating of immigration control with security on the basis of the testimony of two "experts." The first, Colonel Roosevelt, testified that our weak immigration laws had permitted Red agents to breach our shores for many years. Furthermore, the Reds were determined to see to it that the army of Kremlin forces in this country, poised to seize power, could not be deported or denaturalized. The second authority, Louis Budenz, had testified before another committee that the Kremlin plots to get weak immigration laws in this country to make it easy for "political tourists" and "Comintern agents" to breach our shores for subversive purposes.

How simple it is—150 years of social, economic and cultural history swept under the rug in the name of "security." But HUAC still had to explain why so many individuals and organizations (indeed, the Eisenhower Administration itself), had opposed the Walter-McCarran Act. It had also to explain why the President's Commission on Immigration and Naturalization, in 1952, had thoroughly demolished the statute, after lengthy hearings in which virtually all sectors of our national life were heard in criticism of the law—teachers, lawyers, fraternal orders, religious groups (Jewish, Catholic, and Protestant), social workers, civic groups and experts in the field. This is simple, too. It is the successful outcome of the Kremlin strategy of political subversion against the entire security system of the United States. "By concealing its real purposes in fraudulently humane language," the Communist Party duped thousands of well-intentioned people into opposing the law. The Party's machinations were also responsible for flooding Congress, as well as the platform Committees of our state and national political parties, and the state legislatures, with appeals calculated to give the false impression that "popular sentiment exists for debilitating the nation's immigration and security system." Finally, the Committee darkly notes that the proposed changes in the Walter-McCarran Act, "and the other security measures," coincide with the objectives of the Communist Party.

The entire movement against the Walter-McCarran Act is thus an example of "political subversion" because (1) it includes Communists; (2) the Walter-McCarran Act is like a sedition statute because Communists who oppose sedition statutes also oppose this statute; (3) the Act is not an ordinary security statute but the one on which the safety of the entire Republic rests; (4) opponents of such a super-security measure must be either dupes or Kremlin agents; (5) the very size of the opposition to the Walter-McCarran Act proves the effectiveness of this plot to overthrow the Government by means more efficient than force and violence. If you are not convinced, maybe you, too, are a dupe of the Kremlin—or worse.

Reprisal inspired another HUAC attack on an organization in 1956—The Fund for the Republic. The Fund's president, Robert M. Hutchins, had courageously announced that in his view a qualified person should not be denied employment because he was a Communist. The Fund had gone so far as to hire an individual who pleaded the Fifth Amendment before a Congressional committee. Something had to be done about that—such a policy jeopardized the whole exposure system.

In 1954 and 1955, Fulton Lewis, Jr., HUAC's favorite spokesman and advance man, had persistently attacked the Fund. It was, therefore, with a note of triumph that he informed his radio listeners in November 1955 that his demand for an investigation of the Fund had borne fruit and that an investigation would be undertaken after the first of the year, when the preliminary staff work would have been completed. Lewis' prediction was confirmed by a Committee press release in December which promised an investigation of the Fund and its president, Robert M. Hutchins.

On the heels of the press release, a Committee investigator, Karl Barslaag, began to probe the Fund and examine documents in its files. Barslaag is a former employee of the McCarthy subcommittee and of the Americanism Commission of the American Legion, which he served as a leading theoretician. The Fund's counsel, Bethuel Webster, a distinguished New York lawyer, tried to see Walter about the proposed hearing. When Webster was finally granted an interview, Walter asked him whether or not the Fund was financing attacks upon the Walter-McCarran Act and whether it was becoming interested in immigration problems.

At the end of the interview, Walter personally served Webster with a demand for the production of a huge mass of papers dealing with the Fund's activities. On June 11, 1956, Walter startled the country with a press release that the Committee would begin hearings on June 27 to determine whether the Fund itself was a "friend or foe in our national death struggle against the Communist conspiracy." Walter added the disclaimer that he was not then passing judgment on the Fund, but was seeking only "objective facts."

Webster tried in vain to get a list of the proposed witnesses, to be assured the opportunity to cross-examine and, if necessary, to introduce witnesses for the Fund. Staff director Arens told him that no cross-examination would be allowed and indicated that the hearing might be adjourned after the Committee witnesses had been heard. When a promised list of witnesses was not received, President Hutchins wrote to Walter requesting equal time for each day scheduled for the hearing to present the Fund's witnesses in order to develop the "objective facts." Hutchins, a teacher of legal procedure and evidence before he became an educator, observed that if hostile witnesses were permitted to dominate the proceedings without an opportunity for explanation by those in possession of the facts, the likelihood of a smear would be great.

Instead of replying to Hutchins' request, the Committee suddenly announced through the press that the hearing scheduled for June 27 to probe the Fund itself had been indefinitely postponed because "new areas" and additional facets had to be probed. The urgent need to determine what side the Fund was on in the death struggle with Communism had suddenly vanished after seven months of investigation and a thorough examination of the files.

Having thus hit the Fund and run, the Committee returned to the attack in July, shortly after the publication of John Cogley's Fund-sponsored study of HUAC's blacklist in the mass entertainment media. Again, Fulton Lewis Jr. was used as an advance agent of the Committee's probe. When Cogley was subpoenaed, it was obvious that HUAC would make a flank attack on the Fund through the study on the blacklist hearings instead of hitting the Fund directly. Hutchins tried once more to get the Chairman's assurance that the Fund would have an opportunity to defend itself—again without success.

A subsequent request, made after the blacklist hearings were begun, was rejected on the ground that the Fund was not being investigated. At "an appropriate time" its representatives would be heard. They never were heard.

Cogley had been informed in advance that the hearing would be in executive session. In reliance upon this assurance his counsel did not think that a lawyer would be necessary. When he came into the Committee room without counsel, he discovered that the hearings were to be open indeed. The press, television and radio were all on hand in full array.

The blacklist hearings illuminate the sharply polemic way in which the Committee uses its powers. Cogley was subjected by Arens to a sneering, hostile cross-examination. He was the only witness to be asked exposure-type questions ("pick up the thread of your life and give us a chronology of the principal employments which you have had since the completion of your formal education"). Arens applied a brush soaked in smear. He charged that the Catholic magazine, *Commonweal,* of which Cogley had been Executive Editor, was not a bona fide Catholic publication; that the Fund's president approved of the employment of Communists; that an anti-Communist member of the blacklist study staff had been a member of the Young Communist League (more than twenty years earlier); that a second staff member, also strongly anti-Communist, was a Socialist ("You, of course, are aware of the fact that Lenin, the key philosopher of Communism, has said that socialism is only one transition toward Communism. . . . And Socialists are only people who are conducting the transition from Socialism toward Communism").

A third staff member was attacked because she had arrived in this country in 1945 and had been a member of the Social Democratic Party in Austria. In addition, Arens charged that Cogley had failed to consult with the FBI, which, one is surprised to learn, "has an accumulation of information which is available to such organizations as the Fund for the Republic and other such groups upon solicitation."

The cross-examination of Cogley disfigured his study on HUAC's blacklist by selecting from it a few cases, ignoring scores of others, and shaping the record to Arens' rather special needs. Apart from two carefully chosen blacklist victims, almost all of the other witnesses were fanatic Committee partisans (James O'Neill of the American Legion, Vincent Hartnett, Roy Brewer, Francis McNamara, etc.). These witnesses were simply used as instruments to discredit the Fund-sponsored study. In contrast to the treatment given Cogley, they were glorified and congratulated on their patriotism, humanity and objectivity. For example, when McNamara, then involved in

Americanism work for the VFW, former editor of *Counterattack*, and publisher of *Red Channels,* a blacklister's bible, left the stand, Congressman Kearney lauded his testimony: "It contrasts to some of the other testimony we have received." And the Chairman added, "Yes, it is very refreshing to receive the testimony of those who have no axes to grind." Mr. McNamara is now a $12,000 a year Committee "research consultant." Not one "security officer" from the advertising agencies of the mass entertainment fields (movies, radio, TV), in which blacklisting is a structured part of the hiring process, was called to testify. The hearing, combining the techniques of a prosecutor driving for a conviction and a high-school debater scoring "points" over his adversary, turgidly develops the following notions:

1. There is no evidence of "blacklisting" and no "blacklist"—words which the Committee invariably surrounds with quotation marks or prefaces with "so-called."

2. Anyway, there is no physical list.

3. Certain individuals are "precluded" or "disassociated"from employment because they are "controversial." These individuals are without exception "hard-core Communists." This state of affairs is true of the movies, television and radio, but not entirely true of the Broadway stage.

4. The inability of the Committee to drive its victims off the Broadway stage demonstrates that: (a) The Cogley study is exaggerated; (b) the Communist propaganda line against blacklisting has "completely falsified" the true facts, and (c) Broadway is subversive because it hires actors who "are part and parcel of a treasonable apparatus."

5. It is subversive to apply to this state of affairs the "odious term," "blacklisting" which is used by the Communists to create sympathy for their adherents.

6. There is no such thing as "clearance" or clearance agencies because there is no blacklist; how can an individual require relief from an injury from which he has never suffered?

7. There are certain patriotic and humanitarian individuals and groups who help "rehabilitate" or "recreate a climate of employment for" the repentant, the dupe and the unjustly accused.

8. The real blacklist, ignored by the Cogley study, is directed against the friendly witnesses and is Communist-inspired. There are also individuals who, as a result of being "named," cannot find work despite their readiness to cooperate by naming others. These people deserve the Committee's compassion and will receive a hearing on request, "not," of course, "to the end that we either clear or convict, because we do not have that authority," but so that the testimony may be officially received under oath.

Many newspapers denounced the hearing, an undisguised attack on a publication solely for the purpose of discrediting it, as censorship. They may have become convinced by the Chairman's explanation: "We called on you for the purpose of ascertaining what your sources were in order to determine whether or not your conclusions were the conclusions that we would have reached had we embarked on this sort of project."

The Fund enraged Congressman Walter when, in 1955, it made an award to the Plymouth Monthly Meeting, a Quaker group, because of its support of its Library Committee in refusing to dismiss a librarian who had, prior to her employment, pleaded the Fifth Amendment before a Congressional committee. The fact that the Plymouth Monthly Meeting had acted out of religious conviction did not spare it or the Fund from Walter's wrath. What would happen to the entire exposure operation if asylum were offered to Committee victims who refused to act as informers?

HUAC "investigated." The Fund witness was Mrs. Maureen B. Ogden, not a Fund officer but an employee who had merely investigated the facts surrounding the award to the Plymouth Monthly Meeting. Although she obviously was not responsible for the award, she was made the target of the Committee's attack on the Fund. Mrs. Eleanor B. Stevenson, the Fund director and committee chairwoman who had recommended the award, flew from a vacation in Mexico to the Philadelphia hearing to refute the charges, but she was not permitted to testify.

The challenge to religious principles posed by the hearing was emphasized by the Plymouth Monthly Meeting when it refused to comply with a Committee subpoena for its records and minutes on the ground that it "is a

236

religious society and its records protected by the First Amendment from subpoena by a government body." But it must not be thought that the Committee was hostile to Quaker beliefs: Arens championed the "Quaker principle of unanimity" and arraigned Mrs. Ogden for having disregarded it in reporting to the Fund!

Although Mrs. Stevenson was forced to return to Mexico unheard, the Committee did not, even after the hearing, relax in its efforts to discredit her and the Fund. About a month after the award hearings, Fulton Lewis Jr. read to his radio audience a handwritten letter of Mrs. Stevenson to an officer of the Fund concerning the Plymouth award, dated March 14, 1956. This letter had been subpoenaed from the Fund by Walter, together with other files about the Plymouth Meeting award. When the letter was read, the Fund's counsel sent a wire to Walter protesting making available to the radio commentator documents obtained under subpoena that were never made a part of the record. Walter never answered.

The Plymouth Meeting affair drew from a group of leading Philadelphia Quakers the charge that "We regard such inquiries as a serious transgression upon the complete division between church and state which is one of the important foundations of our democracy."

Walter's charges and insinuations about the Fund's "political subversion," as the Fund pointed out in reviewing the affair, "would have been proven false if the Fund for the Republic had been given the full hearing demanded by the American tradition of fair play, due process and common decency."

In an intensely personal sense, Walter loathes the Fund and all its works. His refusal to take on the Fund frontally hardly spells finis to his vendetta with the Fund. There was more exposure mileage in hitting at the Fund selectively and running. Walter still vows that the showdown, "friend or foe in the struggle against Communism," hearing will be held as soon as staff investigation is completed. There may never be a full-dress exposure hearing; there doesn't have to be. Walter, a master of the cat-and-mouse game, knows that properly timed press releases threatening a probe are potent blackmail to keep an organization in line. In the meantime the Network has been alerted to the pursuit of a new witch—a "multi-million dollar propaganda machine."

To those who may be puzzled about the legislative justification for investigating the Fund, the Committee has
a ready answer: it operates with tax-exempt funds. The
fact that the Committee has no jurisdiction in this field
would only occur to coddlers of subversion.

13   HUAC AND RELIGION

The Committee has long been convinced that many
American ministers and clerical groups are engaged in un-
American activities. Constitutional separation of church
and state and the guarantee of religious freedom have not
prevented the Committee from using its powers of propaganda and exposure in the field of religion. The target of
the Committee has, over a decade, been the social application of Christianity—the theory and practice of many
of the Protestant churches in this country that whatever
concerns man and his welfare is a concern of the church
and its ministers. The social and ethical demands of religion have involved many church groups in the important
public questions of our time: peace, foreign policy, integration, the rights of labor, social-welfare legislation,
the United Nations.

The repression of the fifties confronted the church with
new challenges: jail terms for political offenses, loyalty
oaths, violations of right of conscience; the abuses of
McCarthyism; the glorification of informers; the attacks
on dissent; book-burnings. Of all groups in American life
who traditionally have contributed to the process of
opinion-formation, many of the Protestant churches spoke
out most effectively against the witch-hunters.

By the early fifties, the churches felt the impact of the
repressive movement which gripped our entire culture.
The threat of Communism and the intimidation of church
leaders had silenced large sections of the church in matters
of the application of the social gospel to contemporary
issues. The excesses of the witch-hunt, too, won a troubled
acquiescence from many churchmen.

The confusion and division in the church placed in a

vulnerable position the ministers who refused to abandon their responsibilities. Equally important, this schism jeopardized the social-action groups of the great denominations who had committed themselves to programs which brought them into conflict with HUAC. Finally, this division stimulated the growth in power and influence of a number of reactionary splinter religious groups. These include the Circuit Riders, The American Council of Christian Laymen, the American Council of Christian Churches, the International Council of Christian Churches, the Christian Crusade and the Church League of America: all are opposed to modernism in religion and liberalism in the interpretation of the Bible; they proclaim various versions of the "old time religion," all of which view Christianity as irrelevant to the problems of social welfare or justice. They bitterly oppose the policies of the National Council of Churches of Christ, the dominant cooperative church body in the United States, and especially its 1952 revision (Revised Standard Version) of the King James translation of the Bible.

Many of their leaders are self-seeking demagogues with a talent for sensationalism—the McCarthys of the pulpit. Some of them have been driven out of the major denominations; others have organized movements catering to the rankest bigotry—anti-Catholicism, anti-labor, racism, and anti-Semitism. The Red issue afforded them an ideal opportunity to convert charges of apostasy into subversion in their theological warfare. Today these groups are drawing increasing support and subsidies from the South, and are playing a vigorous role in resisting church-centered movements in furtherance of integration.

These fundamentalist groups became an important HUAC weapon in the fight against the social gospel. They fed into HUAC's files material seeking to discredit church leaders and church groups. In turn, these dossiers—now bearing the Committee's official imprimatur—were used to conduct theological and political warfare against the church leadership. The extremist religious groups are an important segment of the Network. They give religious sanction to the entire movement of the ultra-right and are highly successful in carrying its message to the grass roots. Their fanatic zeal enabled the Committee to attack the loyalty of churchmen without assuming responsibility for its actions or appearing to invade the doctrinal autonomy of the churches, and it gave the theological critics of the churches an effective means of sowing mistrust of church leadership. There were many victims of this undercover smear tactic, including Bishop Henry Knox Sherrill, Bishop Henry W. Hobson, and hundreds of others.

A notorious example of this technique was a file report issued by HUAC in the early fifties on the National Council of Churches, which said:

> The Committee on Un-American Activities has never investigated the National Council of Churches of Christ in the United States of America, nor has it made any finding concerning the activities of the group. However, public records, files and publications of this Committee contain the following information.

This was followed by 21 pages of smear material attacking many of the most distinguished religious leaders in the country.

The Committee's master strategy in moving against liberal Christianity is to exploit the theme of Red godlessness. The church is invited to join the Committee as a partner in a struggle against "Communistic atheism." Ministers and church movements which fall under the Committee's disapproval are not only subversive but betrayers of their faith to the powers of darkness.

HUAC first gave tentative expression to its thesis that certain forms of religious expression are un-American in a 1948 publication, *100 Things You Should Know About Communism and Religion*. This pamphlet, reprinted in a 50,000-copy edition in 1951, is one of a series (others deal with labor, education and government) and was written "to help you protect your religion and faith from Communist attack by showing you exactly what the Communists are up to." The pamphlet attacks the social gospel by charging that it is a cover for the spread of Communist ideas—the Committee's favorite theme. The basic assumption of this pamphlet is that HUAC is an authoritative judge of what is true religion and what is not. Its underlying thrust is that religion, as defined by HUAC, requires Christians to enlist in a holy war against the Reds.

Two of the questions in the pamphlet dealt with the Methodist Federation for Social Action, which was characterized as "a tool of the Communist Party . . .; it is trying to use the prestige of the Methodist Church to promote the line of the Communist Party." No proof was offered of this charge. The Committee subsequently admitted that it had made no investigation of the Federation. The only support offered for the charge was that the Methodist Federation had been "denounced by numerous loyal American Methodists." These loyal denouncers were, of course, the fundamentalist groups in the Church who had turned to the Committee for help in their crusade against the social gospel.

In 1952, the Committee published a *Review of the Methodist Federation for Social Action*. The Committee explained that "a careful and studied review" was required "because of the many inquiries about the organization." HUAC was under pressure to get a report out as quickly as possible. The "careful and studied review" turned out to be, not an objective study, but a hasty scissors-and-paste compilation of the tendentious material in the Committee files, concluding with a clumsy attempt to equate the social gospel with Marxism.

The *Review* was one of the early fruits of the collaboration of the Committee and the Circuit Riders, Inc., an organization of Methodist laymen formed in 1951 to fight liberal trends in the Methodist Church. One of its initial goals was to liquidate the Methodist Federation. Congressman Velde, himself a Methodist, had ties with the Circuit Riders and subsequently boasted that he had personally worked on the *Review*.

The *Review* was ordered printed in February 1952. Its release date and its contents were known in advance to the Circuit Riders. This fundamentalist group obtained enough copies of the review to mail to each of the delegates to the Methodist General Conference, which held its quadrennial session in May of that year. Thus, the authority of the Government was brought into the deliberations of a church body for the sole purpose of obtaining conformity to the Committee's interpretation of Methodist religious teaching. This was a historic step. But there were few to protest.

The *Review* was only a curtain-raiser to a large-scale Committee attack in 1953. In the spring of that year, Velde, who had long been anxious to take the clergy to the Committee's woodshed, announced that he was considering hunting for Communists among the clergy. The proposal was greeted by a storm of protest. Church groups were fed up with the Committee's sniping, its alliance with individuals discredited and deposed by the great denominations, its release of slanderous and uncorroborated charges, its meddling in religious affairs. Rarely in its entire history had so much bitter criticism of HUAC been stirred.

Thus, the May 1953 issue of the *Outlook,* the official journal of the National Council of Churches, attacked the proposed investigation because it "would raise a serious question about the relation of Church and State and the constitutional guarantee of freedom of religion." The *Outlook* went on to deplore the confusion of a " 'liberal' Christian or honest advocate of social reform with Communists. This is something which is now happening in an alarming and inexcusable degree."

The account points to the case of the Rt. Rev. Henry Knox Sherrill, presiding Bishop of the Protestant Episcopal Church, whose loyalty was attacked on the basis of material in the Committee's files. "The allegation against him is that he was a sponsor of a Congress of Soviet-American Friendship, and the reader is left to assume that this means a reprehensible pro-communist attitude. But now note the facts which the document of the Committee on Un-American Activities wholly omits. The date of the sponsorship was 1942, when the U.S.A. and the U.S.S.R. were allies in arms, and when it was a patriotic duty to support the war." The *Outlook* article goes on to state, "The case of Bishop Sherrill is not an isolated one. There are hundreds of other clergymen who have been treated with similar unfairness and similar un-American procedure."

On May 17th, the Very Rev. (now Bishop) James A. Pike preached a sermon on social action in dealing with attacks by Congressional committees, in the course of which he said:

How can churchmen best counteract the present unwarranted assaults, threats and fulminations of the Un-American Activities Committee? They can of course quite properly protest the Un-American character of this committee's procedures, its trial by press and television, its reversal of the principle that a man is innocent until proven guilty. But important as this approach is, it is negative. A positive counter-assualt should be launched. One reason why it has been possible for these congressional smearers to highlight particular Christian leaders is that the church as a whole has been increasingly silent in recent years about the social application of Christianity, leaving those still so concerned in a conspicuous "exposed" position. The church has been in retreat from the confusion which has been engendered by the world communist threat. Let the church rise to its responsibilities to bring a critique on unrighteous conditions in our land, and we will demonstrate that there is a healthy ferment that is by no means communistic and in fact is the best defense against communism, because it addresses itself to the conditions that breed communism. We will thus so surround our brethren who are smeared (like Bishop Oxnam and Sherrill) that there will be confusion in the smearers' camp—for they will know that they cannot investigate us all, and if they try to smear us all they will be made ridiculous in the public eye.

Other church groups and religious periodicals deplored the repression, the slander, the accusation and distrust fostered by HUAC. The *Christian Register* of May 1953 stated in an editorial "Whom Do The Congressional Committees Fear?": "The internal threat to this country is the misappropriation of the investigating rights of Congressional committees. Instead of doing their proper task of investigating for the purpose of making law, they take on the coloring of judicial and executive procedures."

The churches had recognized that the Committee was threatening the very values by which they lived. Nor were they intimidated by a warning from Velde that criticism of the proposed Communist hunt was itself evidence of subversion. And they were equally unimpressed when Velde gave assurances that only some ministers might be called as individuals. But the use of Congressional power as a weapon against religion took on a new dimension when Senator McCarthy, on June 22, appointed J. B. Matthews (see Chapter 2) as chief aide to his Committee.

Matthews had written an article for the July issue of the *American Mercury,* "The Reds in Our Churches," charging that "The largest single group supporting the Communist apparatus in the United States today is composed of Protestant clergymen." Matthews claimed that this group numbered 7,000.* Their subversive taint was ascribed in part to the "vogue of the 'social gospel' which infected the Protestant seminaries more than a generation ago."

The May reaction was as nothing in comparison to the wave of protest which greeted the article and the appointment of Matthews. Scores of ministers communicated directly with Congressmen. Heads of denominations made a point of publicly denouncing the witch-hunters. All over the country, Protestant clergymen delivered sermons against the new inquisition. One of the country's leading Protestant theologians, Dr. John A. McKay, president of the Princeton Theological Seminary and moderator of the Presbyterian Church in the U.S., said:

> We have come to a moment when in certain circles in our country, you can be anything you want, if you are anti-Communist. You may be a liar, a rake, or a Fascist: everything is condoned so long as you vociferate against Communism.
>
> I am not ashamed of any document I ever signed or any cause I ever sponsored, whether it was in the interest of Republican Spain, or in favor of Spanish refugees from Fascist tyranny, or to advocate repeal of the McCarran Act. . . .
>
> We confront the Twentieth Century American version of the Sixteenth Century Spanish inquisition.

On July 9, President Eisenhower, after vigorous objections had been lodged by the representatives of the three leading faiths, spoke out against indiscriminate attacks against the clergy. On the same day, McCarthy dismissed Matthews. All of these developments confronted the Committee with a serious dilemma: should it confess error or try to prove a case? At stake was not merely a single investigation, but the entire campaign against the social gospel. Matthews might still be vindicated and the army of his critics routed.

---

* This same figure was repeated in April 1961 by Robert Welch, Jr., leader of the John Birch Society. And no wonder. Matthews is now associate editor of *American Opinion,* the Birchers' official organ.

The Committee knew that religion was dangerous territory; it decided to reconnoiter first in secret sessions. At these sessions, held on July 6, 7, 8, 13 and 14, 1953, the Committee heard from six witnesses. Five of them—Philbrick, Kornfeder, Gitlow, Manning Johnson and Leonard Patterson—were ex-Communist informers and professional witnesses. The sixth was Colonel Archibald Roosevelt, who, as in the case of the Walter-McCarran hearings, was called to give brief endorsement to the Committee's aims. He adjured the clergy to "save souls—not to save forms of government or advocate alien doctrines."

The remainder of the hearings were taken up with the testimony of the five informers. These witnesses were not only asked to name names, but also to testify as experts. It is quite plain that they had been commissioned long in advance of the hearing to make a case against the clergy and that they had made elaborate preparations. No one has ever discovered who footed the bill for this venture and how much was actually paid out. What is perhaps more important is that the Committee had gone to great lengths to bring together five informers who not only denounced ministers and rabbis as untrue to their faiths, but testified as experts about the nature and programs of religious organizations.

The Committee's resort to informers usually bears a direct relationship to its probative requirements: as the probative need increases, so does the reliance on informers; the more far-fetched the charge, the greater the perjury. The application of this formula to the clergy involved peculiarly offensive irony: Witnesses notorious for their conscienceless pliancy testified attacking ministers of the gospel as betrayers of their faith.

This vicious use of informers was made clear from the hearings themselves, which had as their purpose a massive attack on long-established, well-understood and widely recognized ethical demands of religion, and on the exclusive right of the churches to act as judges of the religious conduct of their members and ministers.

Herbert A. Philbrick, FBI spy in the Communist Party, was the Committee's first witness. Philbrick admitted that after nine years as an FBI plant, he had no "legal evidence" that there were any Communist Party members among the clergy. He testified that he had been told of two clergymen who were members. Neither of these men had been named as Communists in Philbrick's book *I Led Three Lives,* and only one of them had been named by him in an earlier appearance before the same Committee in 1951. Pressed for more names, the informer said that he had heard of seven or eight ministers who were Reds, but that the furtiveness of their operations had prevented their detection. He finally identified three ministers as working "with the Communist Party" or "operating under Communist Party discipline." All three of these ministers denied Communist Party membership and were ready so to testify under oath.

One of them, Dr. Donald Lothrop of the Boston Community Church, pointed out that the pulpit of the Community Church had been occupied by men of all political beliefs and faiths. Philbrick later told a Boston audience that Dr. Lothrop might demonstrate his loyalty by admitting to his pulpit such anti-Communists as Roger Baldwin. In point of fact, Baldwin *had* spoken at the Community Church.

Desperate to justify its attack, HUAC made public Philbrick's evidence. He was furious, and charged that HUAC's release of his testimony had been premature and "a bad mistake." He explained that his evidence had been "in the nature of leads and tips to be followed for further facts," and that he had not expected the Committee to release testimony, including names, that he had given in executive session. "The Committee has played right into the hands of the Communists," he added.

The Committee then turned to the veteran ex-Communist, Joseph Kornfeder, a professional witness with a memory sensitively attuned to the prosecutive needs of each particular case. He recently performed as an "expert" in aid of a Louisiana legislative committee which needed "proof" that the NAACP is a Red-tainted organization. (A number of courts have refused to credit his testimony.) He testified, but not "from first hand," that 25 or 30 years ago the Reverend Harry F. Ward had met in Moscow with important leaders of the Soviet Union. "I am fairly certain in my mind," he said, that Dr. Ward "saw . . . Joe Stalin." Kornfeder gave it as his personal opinion also that there were about 600 secret party members among the clergy, an estimate based on "knowledge I have in this field." When Representative Scherer expressed surprise at the smallness of the number, the witness conceded that it "might be an underestimation." He added that there were "three or four thousand fellow-travelers."

The third witness, Benjamin Gitlow, entered a sweeping condemnation of the social-gospel movement. Without offering any substantiating evidence, he charged that among the ministers who "carried out the instructions of the Communist Party or collaborated with it" were John Haynes Holmes, Irwin St. John Tucker, and the late Rabbis Judah L. Magnes and Stephen S. Wise. Gitlow was expelled from the Party in 1929. Gitlow also charged that the Reverend Jack R. McMichael was a "leader of the Young Communist League." But when Gitlow was expelled from the party in 1929, Reverend McMichael was 11 years old.

Manning Johnson spent three days on the stand. Johnson was an ex-Communist and professional witness who admitted having perjured himself on the stand and vowed that he would "do it a thousand times" in the interests of the FBI.

Johnson had been one of the witnesses in the second Harry Bridges case, in 1949, who testified that Bridges attended a 1936 Communist Party convention meeting in New York City. Bridges' counsel demanded that Johnson be charged with perjury and asked that he be held in custody for grand jury action. The trial judge refused to do so, but directed him to hold himself in "readiness for the processes of this court until the conclusion of the trial." The Court of Appeals for the Ninth Circuit commented on this testimony (199 F. 2d 811, 841):

> Considerable doubt is thrown on this aspect of the case by reason of the fact that it was established, apparently beyond controversy, that at the very time the 1936 convention was being held, Bridges was in Stockton, California, making a speech at a union meeting. If he was there he could not have been present at the 1936 convention. . . .

In 1954, Johnson and another informer, Leonard Patterson, who also testified against the clergy, had accused Dr. Ralph J. Bunche, a U.N. official, of Communism. This testimony was refused credence by the International Organization Employees Board. After Johnson had appeared as a witness in the Communist Party case before the Subversive Activities Control Board, the lawyers for the Party attacked his testimony in the Bunche case as perjurious. The Government did not deny the charge, and his testimony was stricken from the record in the Communist Party case pursuant to a Supreme Court decision. After 1954, Johnson was stricken from the rolls of Government witnesses. But in 1953, HUAC heard Johnson link the clergy to espionage and sabotage. Equipped with photostats of various public pronouncements by the clergy, Johnson developed an elaborate chain of organizational relationships from which it would appear that almost every manifestation of liberal Christianity in the last several decades stemmed from the Communist movement. He declared that the United Christian Council for Democracy, whose executive committee was headed by one of the country's most astute anti-Communists, Dr. Reinhold Niebuhr, followed a policy "based upon the program of the Communist Party for the infiltration of the various Protestant denominations on the basis of conditioning them mentally and organizationally for the overthrow of the Government of the United States."

Johnson and Leonard Patterson identified the Reverend Jack McMichael as having been a member of the "New York District" of the Young Communist League in 1934 and 1935, although, in fact, McMichael was enrolled at that time as a freshman of Emory University in Georgia. During the 1950 hearing on Communism among New York school teachers, trial examiner Kiendl rejected the testimony of this same Patterson as unworthy of belief. During the same year that Patterson was recruited to testify against Reverend McMichael, the Government Immigration Appeals Board on three occasions found his testimony so contradictory on its face that they officially rejected it as unworthy of belief.

Shortly after these hearings, Bishop Oxnam was heard by the Committee in a stormy ten-hour session. The subject of these hearings, requested by the Bishop, was the Committee's files which, for a period of seven years, had been used to pillory him. The Committee's file and reference service, charged the Bishop, "gives rise to a new and vicious system of Ku-Kluxism in which an innocent person may be beaten by unknown assailants, who are cloaked in anonymity and at times immunity and whose floggings appear all too often to be sadistic in spirit rather than patriotic in purpose." Although Bishop Oxnam proved that the Committee's files were inaccurate and slanderous, he found himself attacked and traduced all over again. There was no reparation or even acknowledgment of wrong.

In the course of the Oxnam hearings, a Committee member informed the Bishop that the earlier secret hearing had produced testimony that two Methodist ministers—the Reverend Harry F. Ward and the Reverend Jack R. McMichael—were members of the Communist Party. Congressman Scherer, exalting the inherently incredible and internally inconsistent statements of two paid informers to the level of unchallengeable truth, asked Bishop Oxnam:

> On the basis of the testimony we had in New York, sworn testimony of any number of witnesses, and on that basis how could any reasonable person come to any other conclusion than that Dr. Ward and Reverend McMichael are dangerous Communists?

Both of these ministers thus learned of these charges for the first time from newspaper headlines. Each at once informed the press that the charges were completely false. The Reverend Jack R. McMichael was thereafter subpoenaed from his church in California. He denied the charges under oath, and, indeed, challenged the Committee to give him a lie-detector test. The Committee then produced Manning Johnson, who, of course, had no more difficulty identifying Reverend McMichael than he had in the case of Dr. Bunche. The witness was denied the opportunity to cross-examine his accuser.

The Committee made no effort to conceal its determination to injure and discredit the witness, or to ornament its exposure purposes with any pretended legislative justification. Before the confrontation, the Committee showed the extraordinary lengths that it was prepared to go to ensnare McMichael:

> Mr. Kunzig (Committee Counsel): Have you ever met Manning Johnson, Reverend McMichael?
> Reverend McMichael: The name is unfamiliar to me. I would appreciate your producing him and let me

look at him. Perhaps I would be able to recognize him by his face. Is he here in the room?

Mr. Velde: Is Mr. Manning Johnson in the audience? Mr. Williams, would you attempt to find Mr. Johnson?

Mr. Williams (Investigator): Yes, sir.

Mr. Clardy: Would you know him if you saw him?

Reverend McMichael: I'll be glad to look at him.

Mr. Clardy: Answer my question. Would you know him if you saw him?

Reverend McMichael: How can I answer that question? I'll let the record show that question—how unfair it is.

Mr. Clardy: If you were a truthful man, you would answer that question, sir.

Here is another example of the crude police-court tactics of the Committee:

Mr. Kunzig: You testified yesterday you were never a member of the Communist Party, and you testified you are not now a member of the Communist Party. I now wish to ask you if you ever at any time attended Communist Party meetings.

Reverend McMichael: Not to my knowledge. I've been very curious and interested in all sorts of things, and I've gone to a lot of meetings of groups I didn't agree with: but never to my knowledge, attended this kind of meeting.

Mr. Kunzig: Will you deny here, under oath, you never attended a Communist Party meeting?

Reverend McMichael: Yes: I will deny, under oath, that I never, to my knowledge.

Mr. Kunzig: I thought that would be the answer, and I think the record should note, you very carefully added, 'to my knowledge'! The question is: Do you deny you ever attended a Communist Party meeting?

Reverend McMichael: The answer is: to my knowledge, I never attended such a meeting.

Mr. Kunzig: In other words, that is an evasive answer.

Reverend McMichael: You keep making charges of evasive answers. What is evasive about that? Isn't it possible for a group to have a meeting and not know the nature of it? . . . Mr. Chairman, will you ask the counsel to be a counsel rather than a prosecuting attorney here?

The conflicting testimony of McMichael and Johnson was referred to the Justice Department for possible perjury prosecution. Understandably enough, the Department has never moved on this issue.

In the wake of these hearings, which signally failed to bolster up the Committee's theories about the clergy, J. Edgar Hoover, in response to a letter, informed Senator Harry F. Byrd that he knew of no minister who had been proved to be a Communist agent. Mr. Hoover had supplied "convincing evidence," said the Senator in a public statement, that the charges against the clergy were "baseless."

The testimony of the July 1953 secret hearing was formally released in September. Its charges of 600 Red-tainted clergymen, the attack on Dr. John Haynes Holmes and two revered dead rabbis, the spectacle of hired informers defaming ministers of the gospel and of the Committee's vicious equation of the social gospel with Communism, brought condemnation from the leaders of every faith. Pressure for curbs on the Committee came from both within and outside of Congress.

By the end of 1953, the Committee was ready to throw in the sponge. In its annual report for that year, it virtually conceded that its "Operation Rescue Matthews" had failed:

A minute number of case-hardened Communists and Communist sympathizers have actually infiltrated themselves into the ranks of the loyal clergy. . . . Only a very small number of clergymen in the United States have been fellow-travelers. . . . The members of the clergy who have associated with Communist causes is a minute percentage of the hundreds of thousands of loyal, patriotic men of the cloth.

The churches may have won the battle, but the war was by no means over. In 1955, the Air Force published a *Security Guide* which stated: "a while back Americans were shocked to find that Communists had infiltrated our churches." The *Guide* charges that the clergy is Communist-infiltrated. "Of course no clergyman admits he is a Communist when he is one (he is required to keep his membership secret), but he still does Communist work." The *Guide* discussion of Communism and religion concludes:

Again to stop Communists, we must be careful not to attack the majority of faithful ministers and church-goers. We must merely search out those who back Moscow right down the line.

We can do this, first, by understanding and supporting the teachings of our religions to the hilt: then by getting rid of those who try to pass off Communist ideas as substitute for what we know are true religious teachings.

The *Guide* was silent about how to tell the difference between Communist ideas and true religious teachings. To the right-wing fundamentalist groups, church-centered efforts in support of the admission of Red China to the United Nations were not "true religious teachings." With the aid of Southern money and support, those race-baiting, anti-Semitic and anti-Catholic groups intensified their smear campaign against the clergy on these issues. And HUAC continued its practice of giving official sanction to material from these groups which could then be re-circulated with greater impact.

In 1957, the Committee experimented with a more open form of support for its right-wing theological allies. It published a propaganda document. *The Ideological Fallacies of Communism,* based on consultations with three religious figures, which rebuked the churches for their lack of zeal in the fight on Communism.

In November 1958, the Fifth World Order Study Conference of the National Council of Churches questioned the United States all-out support of Chiang Kai-shek and our seemingly unalterable opposition to the admission of Red China to the United Nations. The Committee promptly answered by a publication, *Communist Persecution of Churches in Red China and Northern Korea,* which summarized private HUAC hearings. The witnesses for these hearings were supplied by a leading religious Network organization, the American Council of Christian Churches. This document, like earlier Committee material, soon found its way into crackpot fundamentalist pamphlets.

But these hate-mongering groups really came into their own in an *Air Reserve Center Training Manual* of January 1960. This publication charged that "Communists and fellow-travelers and sympathizers have successfully infiltrated into our churches. . . . From a variety of authoritative sources, there appears to be overwhelming evidence of Communist antireligious activity in the United States through the infiltration of fellow travelers into churches and educational institutions." Two proofs that the churches are infiltrated are:

1. The governing body of a prominent Protestant church group have just called for "mutual understanding" with Red China and urged that the Peiping regime be recognized by the United States and admitted to the United Nations.

2. The National Council of Churches of Christ in the U.S.A. officially sponsored the Revised Standard Version of the Bible. Of the 95 persons who served in this project, 30 have been affiliated with pro-Communist fronts, projects, and publications.

These charges, which the *Manual* elaborates, were rewritten from three pamphlets, two of them published by the Christian Crusade, headed by an Oklahoma evangelist, Billie James Hargis, and the third by the Circuit Riders. All of them relied heavily on Committee material.

The *Manual* brought a vigorous protest from the National Council, which demanded its withdrawal and the recall of all copies in circulation. In a letter to the Secretary of Defense, the Council made four points in support of the requested action.

1) Such a document is a patent contravention of the First Amendment to the Constitution.

2) The implication that there is a relationship between the Revised Standard Version of the Holy Bible and Communism is insidious and absurd.

3) To aver by innuendo that the National Council of Churches is associated with or in any way influ-

enced by the Communist Party is an example of ir-responsibility at its worst.

4) The adoption as official Air Force statements of the opinions of prejudiced persons is an incredible reflection upon the judgment and sense of responsibility of all those involved.

A week later, both Defense and Air Secretaries apologized for the *Manual*. Air Secretary Sharp announced its withdrawal and an inquiry into the circumstances of its issuance. Perhaps because the *Manual*, in a discussion of another issue, had termed "foolish" the view that Americans had a right to know what was going on, the press was virtually unanimous in denouncing it. The Washington *Post* pointed out that the author of the *Manual's* attack on religion was merely parroting a line popularized by the House Committee on Un-American Activities. "The Committee had succeeded in persuading a great many who are gullible, that any organization which seeks social justice or racial equality or freedom of expression, a restraint on police authority, has been infiltrated by Communists."

Chairman Walter was not slow to claim his share of the headlines. He accused the Defense Secretary of making a "groveling apology," suggested an investigation, not of the *Manual*, but of its withdrawal, and of the National Council as well. He added: "The leadership of the National Council of Churches which fraudulently claims to speak for 38,000,000 American Protestants, has in the aggregate a record of hundreds of affiliations with Communist fronts and causes." Shortly thereafter, the National Board of the National Council passed a resolution pointing out that the material in the 1955 Air Force *Guide* on religion and Communism was equally objectionable and should be deleted as soon as possible. It asserted that: "An important issue raised by this recent incident is how long the American people are going to allow various agencies of Government to continue the practice of treating false and absurd charges lifted from confidential files as material to be seriously used as a basis for security decisions and for official indoctrination of Government employees."

Fearful of the impact of an adverse public reaction on its future, the Committee called Air Secretary Sharp into executive session. The hearing, subsequently released, was prefaced by Walter's charge that " the Communists have duped large numbers of the clergy as well as lay leaders in the churches into supporting Communist fronts and causes which masquerade behind deceitful façades of humanitarianism." Even before the hearing commenced, Walter anticipated that its conclusions would result in "attacks by Communists, pro-Communists, dupes and misguided liberals who would use the façade of religion to mask Communist activities."

The hearings showed the extraordinary concern of the Committee that the repudiation of the *Manual* might raise doubts about the role of the Committee itself:

> Mr. Arens: Mr. Secretary, when you issued your press release repudiating the publication as representing the Air Force views, and issued your apology to the National Council of Churches of Christ in the U.S.A., did you by that act mean to convey the impression that the Air Force was convinced that the National Council of Churches was not infiltrated by fellow travelers?
>
> Secretary Sharp: No. I did not intend any concurrence with this statement, or objection to the statement as to its validity. I felt simply that this kind of statement should not be made in an Air Force publication. . . .
>
> Mr. Arens: Did you, in your statement of repudiation, intend a repudiation of the integrity, validity or accuracy of the testimony before the Committee on Un-American Activities which is quoted in this manual?
>
> Secretary Sharp: No sir. . . .
>
> Mr. Arens: Chairman issued a statement to the effect that the leadership of the National Council of Churches had hundreds or at least over 100 affiliations with Communist fronts and causes. Since then we have made careful but yet incomplete checks, and it is a complete understatement.
>
> Thus far of the leadership of the National Council of churches we have found over 100 persons in leadership capacity with either Communist front records or records of service to Communist causes. The aggregate affiliations of the leadership, instead of being in the hundreds as the Chairman first indicated, is now,

according to our latest count, into the thousands, and we have yet to complete our check.

Mr. Jackson: The effect of the action taken by the Air Force, Mr. Secretary, was to tell 180 million people in this country by the retraction of this, that the Air Force did not believe it.

Secretary Sharp: Mr. Jackson, I think it is very unfortunate if that is the impression we gave. . . .

Mr. Doyle: My mail is such that it indicates that the work of this Committee in the minds of the people out West that have read the newspaper reports—that the work of this Committee is discredited as a result of the unfortunate apology and letter by the Secretary.

The Chairman: You may call it unfortunate. I call it stupid. . . .

Secretary Sharp: We certainly did not intend any aspersions on this Committee. . . .

The Chairman: This does not charge the National Council of Churches as being a proscribed organization at all. It merely states that the 95 persons who served on the project (for a revised version of the Bible) which they sponsored have been affiliated with pro-Communist fronts. I think that is a great example to show a youngster. . . .

Mr. Moulder: Is it your plan to revise the manuals? . . . In the process of doing that, will you confer with the Committee on Un-American Activities and the Internal Security Committee and the Attorney General's office and the FBI for any information which you may wish to use in the manual?

Secretary Sharp: Yes, sir. I would hope we could, to be sure it is authentic. . . .

The Chairman: I am looking now at an article that appeared in the paper this morning concerning a resolution purportedly adopted by the General Board of the National Council of Churches in Oklahoma City. The resolution stated that the Air Force had violated the guarantee of "the free exercise of religion" contained in the First Amendment.

This is the sort of thing this "fine" organization is capable of. There is nothing in this manual, is there, that indicates an interference with the free exercise of religion?

Mr. Scherer: They don't want freedom of religion.

They want freedom of criticism. . . .

Mr. Jackson: Is any mention at all going to be made in the new manual with respect to the efforts of the Communist Party to infiltrate into church institutions?

Secretary Sharp: I would hope so, yes, sir. . . .

Mr. Doyle: I would suggest that the new manual would direct the attention of the Air Force personnel further than to churches and schools.

Mr. Jackson: I did not mean to limit it.

Mr. Doyle: Directed to all and any organization, such as labor unions, or others. Do not limit it to churches and schools. That is my suggestion. . . .

Mr. Jackson: Is any action contemplated, disciplinary or in reprisal, against Mr. Hyde who was responsible, as I understand, for writing this material?

Secretary Sharp: This matter has not been finally decided yet. I think that people who do not follow their instructions—and it might appear that Mr. Hyde had not—should be certainly reprimanded, if that is the case. . . .

The Chairman: Let me tell you something. If you so much as say "Naughty Boy," to this group of people who are far more expert than you are, it will blow that up out of all proportion. They will have him shot at sunrise, figuratively speaking, for telling the truth.

Mr. Jackson: Furthermore, some sort of hell will break loose on the floor of the House of Representatives. . . .

Chairman Walter went out of his way to show his gratitude to the author of the Air Force Manual, Homer H. Hyde. He asked Billie James Hargis of the Christian Crusade to give him a job on his staff at the same salary if the Air Force fired him. The extent of Walter's links to Hargis are not fully known, but it is certain that his ties with Hargis antedate the Air Force *Manual* episode. Thus, he has inserted in the record publications from the Christian Crusade on the subject of the Red menace. Hargis is a type of cryptofascist radio evangelist who flourishes in the West and South. He is a fervent supporter of hate merchant Joseph P. Kamp, who has charged that "notorious un-American elements support General Eisenhower."

In response to the protests which poured into the Committee as a result of its attack on the National Council of Churches in its support of the *Manual,* HUAC called up its big guns. Fulton Lewis, Jr., with materials from the Committee files maintained a barrage of denunciation of liberal Christianity. The fundamentalist groups initiated a campaign to follow up the Committee's assault. Leading the fundamentalist attack was Carl McIntire, a vendor of hate and president of the International Council of Christian Churches and the American Council of Christian Churches. McIntire is a deposed Presbyterian minister who is not only anti-Protestant, but virulently anti-Catholic and is closely allied with hate sects throughout the country. His organizations oppose racial integration, the United Nations, the Revised Standard Version of the Bible and modernism in religion. Among the familiar Network personalities who have been attracted to his movement have been Gerald K. Smith, Gerald Winrod, Merwin K. Hart and Billie James Hargis.

Also joining in the campaign to discredit the National Council were the Circuit Riders. In 1960, it was disclosed that their leader, M. G. Lowman, had received secret subsidies from the Georgia Legislature for segregationist activities.

The Committee member who assumed responsibility for leading the attack on the National Council of Churches was Californian Donald Jackson, who had specialized in clergy-baiting for the Committee. Jackson had worked closely with the McIntire and Lowman groups in the course of the 1953 attack on the clergy. The fundamentalist and hate groups had briefed Jackson for the 1953 Oxnam hearing. The Bishop's friends had to wait in long lines for admission to the hearing room, but Jackson's guests were assigned special seats. A Committee counsel suggested that as a courtesy to the Bishop and his wife, they be admitted to the hearing by a private entrance, but they were turned back because Jackson was holding court for his hate claque. As Bishop Oxnam himself put it, "They were apparently in for the kill."

It was Jackson who, in a speech in 1953, made what was considered to be the most violent attack on a clergyman ever made on the floor of the House. He charged: "Bishop Bromley [sic] has been to the Communist front what Man o' War was to thoroughbred horse racing, and no one except the good bishop pays much attention to his fulminations these days. Having served God on Sunday and the Communist front for the balance of the week, over such a long period of time, it is no great wonder that the bishop sees an investigating committee in every vestry." Jackson added:

If reprinting Bishop Oxnam's record of aid and comfort to the Communist front would serve any useful purpose, I would ask permission to insert it here, but suffice it to say that the record is available to any member who cares to request it from the Committee [on Un-American Activities].

In 1954, Jackson headed a House subcommittee which subpoenaed Professor John A. Hutchinson, a professor of religion at Williams College and a minister of the Presbyterian Church. Jackson had informed the minister that Mr. Hutchinson and another clergyman had "reported at Communist Party headquarters" before going on to their pastorates in Baltimore during the thirties. Dr. Hutchinson categorically denied the accusation that he had reported to the Communist Party at any time. The Congressman shifted his ground and charged that, as a young pastor in Baltimore, Hutchinson had joined organizations that had since been branded as Communist fronts. It developed that Dr. Hutchinson had joined the American League Against War and Fascism in 1935, and had dropped his membership in 1939. Jackson saw nothing strange in hauling a respected minister and professor of religion before HUAC to answer 19-year-old charges which were in part completely false, and in part false by implication.

On March 3, 1960, Jackson made his farewell attack on the clergy—he left Congress in that year. In his speech entitled "Uncertain Trumpets," Jackson pulled all the stops of antisubversive demagoguery. The speech charged that one of the ministers in the 1953 hearings had been identified as a Communist by "three witnesses," but suppressed both the fact that these were paid informers and perjurers, and that the minister had denied the charges under oath.

Jackson also tried to smear a church-supported desegregation meeting which had been held in Washington in January 1960. The meeting was a mock hearing conducted by a volunteer civil-rights commission of private individuals to dramatize the disenfranchisement of Negroes in the South. The general chairman of the hearing was Bishop Edgar A. Love, Baltimore Area Methodist Church, a vice-president of the Southern Conference Educational Fund. In addition to Bishop Love, there were three other bishops on the platform, including Bishop Oxnam. The sponsors of the meeting were 16 Negro and white religious and civic organizations, including the Mississippi Regional Council of Negro Leadership, the United Christian Movement of Louisiana, the Alabama Christian Movement of Human Rights, the Baptist Ministers Conference of Washington and vicinity, and the Methodist Ministers Union of Washington and vicinity.

Jackson's rebuke of the clergy for participating in the meeting rested on the charge that the Southern Conference Educational Fund, one of the participating organizations, had been "cited" by Senator Eastland's Internal Security Subcommittee. He did not claim that anything that was said at the meeting was un-American or subversive.

The Fund was cited as a result of a hearing held by Senator Eastland as a one-man subcommittee in New Orleans in the spring of 1954. The hearing was about the most sordid ever conducted by a legislative investigating committee. It starred two perjurious informers; all of the subpoenaed officials of the Fund denied Communist Party membership. At its conclusion, Arens, then Staff Director of the Internal Security Committee, asked newspaper reporters if the subcommittee had not proved its case. They bluntly told him no.

As a result of the hearing, Senator Eastland cited the Southern Conference Educational Fund as a subversive organization. The theory of the citation was that the Fund was a "successor" to the Southern Conference for Human Welfare, which had been cited by the House Committee in 1947. But that citation was equally fraudulent. Professor Walter Gellhorn, of the Columbia Law School, in a painstaking analysis of the Committee's citation, which, incidentally, was issued after repeated requests by the Southern Conference to grant it a hearing had been ignored, concluded:

. . . From semi-truths the Committee has drawn

conclusions which would be strained even if the factual assertions of the report were beyond challenge. The report demonstrates, not that the Southern Conference is a corrupt organization, but that the Committee has been either intolerably incompetent or designedly intent upon publicizing misinformation.

Jackson further abused the clergy because Carl Braden, the field secretary of the Fund, spoke at the meeting. The Committee's vindictiveness against Braden has already been discussed. Jackson charged him with being a Communist agent. He failed to tell Congress that Braden, a defendant in the famed Louisville sedition case, had denied under oath that he was a Communist in the course of the Louisville trial. The prosecution did not, in presenting its case against Braden, produce evidence that he was a Communist. When Braden denied membership in the Communist Party under oath, the prosecution, in rebuttal, introduced the testimony of an FBI agent, one Alberta Ahearn, that Braden had attended a meeting of a Communist cell with her. Braden again took the stand to deny the charge. His denials should have impressed even Congressman Jackson, in view of the fact that Braden's accuser had a criminal record.

In the course of his smear attack, he charged that the National Council of Churches had circulated obscene books written by Communist sympathizers. When Representative Edith Green of Oregon demanded that Jackson name one book on any list of books circulated by the National Council that had been found obscene, Jackson was unable to do so.

The irresponsibility of Jackson's attack on respected church leaders for participating in this meeting is well described by an observation of Professor Zechariah Chafee, Jr., about another legislative body which at a period of political tension "repudiated government by representation and substituted government by misrepresentation." The reasons for Jackson's extraordinary performance became clearer a short time after he made a speech in Congress. He was one of 24 Republicans who voted in the House of Representatives with the Dixiecrats against the Civil Rights Bill.

The assault on the National Council by Jackson and other Committee members gave Americans a full measure of HUAC's slop-bucket tactics. In its ruthless eagerness to make a case against the National Council and to provide ammunition for its extremist following, the Committee outraged fair-minded Americans. Some of the farfetched inferences upon which the clergy's subversion was constructed were aptly characterized by the Washington *Post* as "guilt by extrapolation."

The use of this technique to befoul the Revised Standard Version of the Bible was well described by the Washington *Post* as follows:

Dr. Henry J. Cadbury, professor of divinity at Harvard University, was one of the 95 clergymen who joined in the preparation of the Revised Standard Version. Like many another Quaker pacifist, Dr. Cadbury belonged to the Fellowship of Reconciliation. But among the members of the Fellowship of Reconciliation were some individuals who at one time or another were denounced as Communists or fellow travelers before the House Committee on Un-American Activities by one or another of that stable of former Communist professional witnesses whom the Committee kept constantly on hand to assassinate the reputations of their betters.

From this set of facts, the authors and defenders of the Air Force manual have no trouble at all in deducing that Dr. Cadbury himself has been affiliated with a "pro-Communist front" and that, therefore, anything else with which Dr. Cadbury may have become associated—as, for example, the Revised Standard Version, must be Communist-tainted.

HUAC's 1960 attack on the National Council and its defense of the Air Force *Manual* has precipitated a bitter struggle in American religious life. The Committee's leadership has given religious hate groups an enormous impetus. Fortified by subsidies from Southern businessmen, they have formed new alliances in the South with the White Citizens Councils movement, and in the mid-West and West with the John Birch Society, for a showdown battle with the National Council.

The undercover anti-Catholic campaign against President Kennedy was spearheaded by this reinvigorated religious hate movement. It has also instigated vicious letter-writing campaigns attacking the National Council. It now has a new cause—the showing of the film "Operation Abolition." Its followers have tried to force the showing of the film in the churches whose denominations are members of the National Council. But the National Council has stood firm and has resisted pressure to become a propaganda instrument for HUAC, whose values and objectives are basically at war with those of liberal Christianity.

14 BIG BROTHER IS WATCHING YOU

Everybody knows about HUAC's hearings. But hearings are only part of HUAC's far-flung operations. In addition to its propaganda activities, HUAC conducts a vast indexing, surveillance, dossier-building and reporting service which feeds and supplements its exposure hearings, but it also functionally quite independent of it.

When a hearing is completed, *all* the names mentioned in the hearings—the witnesses as well as those indentified or casually mentioned—are placed on index cards. When enough names are accumulated, the Committee prints them all in a "cumulative index." HUAC has already published *Cumulative Index of the Committee on Un-American Activities 1938-1945*, and a *Supplement to Cumulatixe Index to Publications of the Committee on Un-American Activities, 1955-1956*. These telephone-book size compilations are not subject-matter breakdowns, as their titles deceptively indicate. They are lists of names of about 45,000 individuals and several thousand organizations "mentioned" in Committee hearings or reports. They are the reference works used by personnel directors, Hollywood producers, landlords, clearance agencies, Network organizations, boards of education, radio and newspaper columnists.

These blacklister's desk books are supplemented by the famous Appendix IX, of which only one thousand copies were printed in 1944, and withdrawn by the Committee. (It was attached to the Dies Committee's last report on the National Citizens Political Action Committee.) Its seven volumes contain a cross-section of HUAC's files and were published (at a cost of $20,000) to make the files public when it was thought the Dies Committee would be ended. When the Committee was made permanent, publication was suppressed. But there are many sets in existence. In 1954, a private organization reproduced it to meet the demands of Network organizations. Appendix IX is said to list the names of more than 250,000 individuals who are alleged to have joined "front" organizations as far back as the thirties. Several thousand organizations are also listed. One of the Committee's current projects is to bring this priceless piece of incunabula up to date. A prior Committee chairman has promised that, "This document when completed will be a bible of subversive activities in the United States."

Appendix IX is a product of what the Committee calls the "file and reference service." This is a euphemism for a vast collection of dossiers elaborately indexed and cross-referenced. These dossiers—in 1949, the Committee had compiled one million of them—are no different from the files on "subjects" maintained by police agencies; they contain politically "derogatory information" about suspects gleaned from sources such as HUAC's investigative files, the publications of other anti-subversive committees, Federal and state, the records of the Federal Bureau of Investigation, press reports and letterheads of organizations.

The Committee understates when it says that its files "should not be thought of as files in the ordinary sense."* They are a "constantly growing" accumulation of information, a vast political rogues' gallery of individuals and organizations. In 1948 there were 300,000 card references to activities and affiliations of individuals. There were separate files maintained on the activities of 3,040 persons, "top leaders" and "prominent fellow travelers" of the Communist Party. The files list signers of Communist Party nominating petitions in 20 states for various years—

_____

* All of the quotations are from the HUAC's annual reports.

363,110 names. "Since subversive forces try to infiltrate other organizations . . . the Committee has acquired a vast store of information concerning thousands of organizations in the United States." So huge is the number that the Committee tells us only that there are 380 organizations filed under the letter "A."

In 1949, we learn that there were a total of 1,000,000 individual card entries. That year the Committee's dossiers and cards required 300 file cabinets. A major project of that year was indexing and printing its vast collection of Communist Party nominating petitions. New material was added to the collection of information about subversive organizations as a result of "constant research by staff members to ascertain the aims and purposes of new organizations and a constant check of old organizations which appear in new guises."

In 1951, HUAC added 60,000 index-card references to its sources, and consolidated its master index preparatory to publishing a cumulative index. In 1952, the Committee added thousands of new items to "an already voluminous collection," and noted that "the number of clippings cannot even be estimated." No file is ever obsolete or out of date. HUAC does not believe that a "subject" can outgrow his dossier: "Such material does not become obsolete and available for discard or storage but tends to become more valuable as it increases in age and volume." By 1955, the Committee's collection had grown so extensive that it was forced to reproduce part of it on microfilm.

In recent years, the Committee, aware of the frightening implications of this forest of dossiers, has become rather reserved about the scope of its files, except to assure us that they continue to expand.

The dossiers are not assembled and filed as a collector's hobby or because HUAC has a passion for order. This dossier-building function is a highly important aspect of the Committee's work. It gives the Committee an operational continuity, enables it to maintain an unbroken relationship with its supporters and, by servicing other security agencies, to entrench itself as a permanent part of our security bureaucracy.

The files and dossiers feed into what HUAC calls a

"reference service," which makes the material available when it will do the most good. They are used by Government security and intelligence agencies—primarily to check on the background and loyalty of individuals. This is a familiar kind of sharing of confidential data by police agencies.

But HUAC's "reference service" uses another channel to make these files public. A special "reference" activity consists of furnishing reports on individuals and organizations to Congressmen. HUAC thus brilliantly exploits the imperatives of practical politics; it gives Congressmen a free service—"inside dope" on the politics of Americans—as the bribe for Congressional acquiescence in a wholly illegal activity. We can best understand the Committee's relationship to Congress if we see this aspect of HUAC as a captive Congressional FBI, a glorified, self-appointed House detective. A legislative body has no power to act as security police—a "public eye," one might call it. But HUAC is untroubled by the illegality of its role as a Congressional "Red squad." It understands a cardinal rule of American public life: never fire the policeman.

While this reporting service is normally rendered on request, the Committee does not always wait until it is asked for information. If it learns that a delegation of constituents is planning to visit a Congressman, the Committee will supply him in advance with dossiers on its members. Congressmen have reason to be grateful. The material is not turned over to them as a raw, unedited reproduction of file sources. It is far superior to a conventional detective's report. As HUAC explains it, "This reference source goes far beyond the ordinary type which simply points out the best sources of information to the person making inquiry. Whenever references to the subject under consideration are found in public source material, a written report of that information is furnished, setting forth, point by point, what appears and where it appears, together with any pertinent citations by this Committee or the Attorney General on every organization involved."

The demand for these reports is heavy. From 1949 to 1959 reports were submitted on more than 60,000 individuals and 13,000 organizations. In 1960 alone, HUAC received 2,200 requests from Congressmen to check 4,566 individuals and 1,900 organizations and periodicals. Referances were supplied to materials on 1,389 individuals. A total number of 1,945 reports were compiled. To increase its efficiency, HUAC mimeographs reports on "recurring subjects." In other cases the available material is so great that "more than a day is often required to prepare a single report." A report is sometimes "as long as 12 or 15 pages on a single subject."

HUAC members use the reports to attack HUAC's critics. A speech by Congressman Scherer, in defense of HUAC, is usually a solid mass of such reports. Chairman Walter relies on them heavily in his feuds. Other Congressmen make intensive use of them as well. In 1956, and again in 1958, a large number of these reports were turned over to Southern Congressmen, who used them to charge that the NAACP was Communist-dominated and that the school integration movement was a Red plot.

Most important, the reports are used by private individuals who obtain them either by writing to their Congressman* or directly from HUAC. These enable HUAC to condemn the politics of vast numbers of Americans whom it would be inexpedient to subpoena for hearings or to attack more directly.† The reporting service is simply a "do-it-yourself" exposure system which dispenses with the formality of a hearing by furnishing Network members, "Americanism" buffs, blacklisters, security specialists, and clearance fixers, with material to pillory and discredit their fellow Americans. Its uses for blackmail and slander are particularly easy because the reports are submitted on the letterhead of the Committee. Individuals can obtain such a report and then announce, "Our Government in Washington knows all about you and has kept track of you in a special subversive file." The fact that the report is obtained by a Congressman gives it added official prestige. It is a sort of political "wanted" circular lacking only a photograph. One report of the Committee about Bishop Oxnam began, "G. Bromley Oxnam. This

*One Congressman, in commenting on the volume of the requests for reports from constituents and HUAC's efficiency in meeting them, commented. "This beats free seeds all hollow."

† HUAC denies that reports can be obtained directly. But the evidence is to the contrary; it has stated that it supplies reports to "private individuals" who have a "sincere and genuine need for the information of the type which is available here."

267

individual is a Methodist minister and is sometimes referred to as a Collectivist Bishop."

Armed with these dossiers, the Network conducts an unceasing ideological warfare against every local liberal movement, from support of UNESCO to interdenominational brotherhood. Thus, when Dr. Rufus E. Clement, president of Atlanta University and a respected Negro educator, was invited to speak in a white Houston church on race relations, he was attacked by the Network's Minute Women with a HUAC dossier charging affiliation with seven "Communist-front" organizations. He had never heard of four of them.

The Minute Women of Houston also charged the physicist Dr. Arthur H. Compton with subversion on the basis of a HUAC file of alleged subversive affiliations. The American Friends Service Committee received the same treatment when they held an institute on international relations in Houston. The Minute Women also used HUAC files to force the cancellation of speaking appearances of two New York educators—the late Dr. Eduard C. Lindeman, of the Columbia University School of Social Work, and Dr. Ethel Apenfels of New York University.

Here is an example, drawn from a court record, of the use of a HUAC report by a personnel manager of a large plant who needed a weapon to defeat a union's election campaign:

Q. Do you know the defendant John T. Gojack?
A. Yes.
Q. Have you ever participated in negotiations with him?
A. Yes.
Q. He is an official, an officer of the District 9 of the United Electrical Workers, isn't that right?
A. That is right.
Q. Did you ever have occasion to circulate in the plant material obtained from the files of the House Un-American Activities Committee, deal-with Mr. Gojack?
A. Such information was circulated to department heads and factory supervision.

. . . .

Q. I show you a document that has been marked by defendant's Exhibit No. 5-A and ask you what that is.

A. This is a copy of a circular sent from my office to all of the department heads and foremen.

Q. What is the circular to which it is attached?

A. The circular to which it is attached is a report, a copy of a report from the files of the Committee on Un-American Activities.

Q. Mr. McClaren, how did you obtain that copy?

A. Through the Congressman from our district.

Q. What is his name?

A. Ross Adair.

Q. Did you ask Congressman Adair to get this for you?

A. My assistant, on my instructions, asked Congressman Adair to get it.

Q. And you had the information which you received duplicated; is that correct?

A. That is correct.

Q. Verbatim?

A. That is right.

What warrants developing a dossier on a "subject"? How does the Committee decide that a particular piece of information should be filed about him? The most articulate Committee thinker on this point is Congressman Jackson. He has said, "The Committee, in its work, accumulates all pertinent information relative to any given individual whose name is listed in the files, that is the only way by which one can determine the philosophical bent of any given individual." The Congressman gives us an unusually revealing explanation of the political criteria which guide the Committee's investigators in opening and building a file:

A file is based upon the frequent and common occurrence of an individual's name in Communist fronts, his listing as a sponsor, director, editor, or contributor to Communist front or Communist publications, or the editorial comments of the activities of any given individual; consistent and favorable mention in Communist Party or Communist front publications; his personal actions which are intended to be divisive of the American people; the personal advocacy of the socialist state is certainly contributory to any file; a consistent advocacy of any part or all of the Soviet system; his opposition to any form of investigation of the Communist conspiracy or those who comprise it; his opposition to deportation of Communist Party members or alien Communist front members; his opposition to legislation designed to curb Communism; his opposition to the affirmation of loyalty (loyalty oaths); and his opposition to any form of military training. All of these factors are considered by the Committee. In addition, the use of such phrases as 'red baiting' and 'witch hunt' to describe the activities of the duly constituted committees of the United States Congress is indicative of the Communist Party line. One who consistently deplores the suggestion of guilt by association, but who attempts to prove his own innocence by association is in a manner suspect.

As is readily apparent, this is a net so broad as to envelop millions of patriotic and devoted people because of their association with loyal, praiseworthy organizations and causes.

The files reflect in sharp outline the premise—which the hearings sometimes blur—that liberalism is subversion. Every possible form of distortion is employed to make the subject of a dossier as subversive as possible.

The file material uses guilt by association, not occasionally, but systematically, and as a guiding principle. In fact, as Congressman Jackson pointed out, an individual "who attempts to prove his own innocence by association is in a manner suspect."

Another method which the files employ to blacken the reputation of the subject is the slanted selection of sources. If the subject has written a book or made a speech affirmatively establishing his patriotism—even by the Committee's standards—such documents do not appear in the file, for this is a file confined only to evidence of subversion. Similarly, if the subject made a speech reported in two different newspapers, one of which quotes the speaker's remarks out of context and hence makes him sound more radical, while the other, reporting more fully, is unobjectionable, the investigator will invariably clip and file the more damaging. And if one of the newspapers is the *Daily Worker,* or any other Communist newspaper, then that clipping is used no matter how garbled the text.

The files lean heavily on the doctrine of original political sin and retroactively condemn membership in organizations long prior to the time they were cited or officially denounced as subversive. The Committee has recently been empowered to tap a fresh source for material for its secret dossiers: here is what the Washington *Post* for April 30, 1961, has to say under a head "Snooping Unlimited":

> Were you under the impression that the income tax return you filed a few days ago was confidential and to be scrutinized only by the Internal Revenue Service? If so, you were mistaken. Executive Order 10935, reported in the *Federal Register* for April 25, provides that "any income, excess-profits, estate, or gift tax return for the years 1945 to 1961, inclusive, shall during the eigthy-seventh Congress, be open to inspection by the Committee on Un-American Activities, House of Representatives, or any duly authorized subcommittee thereof. . . ."
>
> . . . we wonder what the Un-American Activities Committee wants with such information. Three congressional committees—Senate Finance, House Ways and Means and the Joint Congressional Committee on Internal Revenue Taxation—are entitled to inspect tax returns under the law, as one can readily understand; they are concerned with general problems of taxation.
>
> But the HUAC has quite different interests. Perhaps it wants to know whether someone . . . has been receiving Moscow gold. . . . Perhaps the Committee wants to know whether someone made a contribution to the Institute of Pacific Relations or some other organization of which Committee members may disapprove. It is easy enough to think of mischievous purposes which the HUAC could pursue by riffling through tax returns but not so easy to think of useful purposes. . . .

Not only are HUAC's standards of classification dishonest, but its over-all motivation toward the subject is suspicious and hostile. The file makes a "case" against the subject, and its impressiveness is measured by its size.

If the subject belongs to an organization which has been cited more than once— for example, by two different committees—both citations are listed. This makes the individual super-subversive.

Every charge, no matter how irresponsible, is listed. Moreover, once a subversive entry appears in a subject's file, there is nothing one can do to alter or cancel it. When Bishop Oxnam requested at a HUAC hearing that his file reflect his denials, a motion to that effect was defeated on the ground that those interested in the matter could refer to his testimony.

If Congress attempted to pass a *law* authorizing the Committee to develop secret dossiers on subjects deemed to be subversive merely for internal use of Government agencies in checking on the loyalty of Government employees or defense workers covered by an Executive Order, it could hardly be doubted that such a measure would be invalid. Congress has no law-enforcement powers. Yet the Committee's file and reference service attempts to dossier *all* our people. And these dossiers are intended to be made available to the malicious and the spiteful, to the blacklister and patrioteer, to purge, slander and destroy.

Error is built into the method of constructing a dossier. When the Washington *Post* secured a copy of HUAC's file on Bishop Oxnam, they asked for his comments. There were 305 typewritten lines in the HUAC report. Bishop Oxnam analyzed them as follows:

Two are introductions;

Sixteen are a summary of the organizations mentioned in the report;

One hundred twenty-eight concern organizations never listed as subversive, or quotations from journals that are not related to subversive organizations or activities;

Seventy-two are from an obscure newspaper in Princeton, Ill., the utter falsity of which might have been disclosed in half an hour's conversation had a committee investigator bothered to walk the 300 yards from the capitol to my office;

Sixty-four are devoted to organizations to which I never belonged;

Twenty-three refer to organizations listed as Communist fronts to which I once belonged but from which I had resigned prior to the publication of the Attorney General's list of subversive organizations and concerning which I have made full explanation above [in the same issue of the Washington *Post*].

When Mrs. Agnes Meyer, educator and wife of the owner of the Washington *Post* dared criticize anti-education witch hunts by Congressional committees in 1953, Velde, acting on his own but in the name of his Committee, formally accused Mrs. Meyer of writing a pro-Russian article for a Russian paper. Investigation showed the article had been written by a Mrs. G. S. Mayer of British Columbia. But it took threats of a libel suit to bring a retraction from Velde, and he said: "It's a lot better to wrongly accuse one person of being a Communist than to allow so many to get away with such Communist acts as those that have brought us to the brink of World War III."

To the charge that these home exposure kits are honeycombed with errors, the Committee answers by pointing to the fact that each report recites, on the Committee's official letterhead, this disclaimer: "This report should not be construed as representing the results of an investigation by, or findings of, this Committee. It should be noted that the individual and/or organization referred to above are not necessarily Communist, Communist sympathizers, or fellow travelers, unless otherwise indicated."

In other words, this legislative fact-finding Committee deliberately circulates at public expense material attacking private citizens which it knows may be inaccurate and may give rise to false and slanderous inferences. Moreover, when Network organizations use these HUAC reports to circularize a community, they frequently omit even this disclaimer.

It must be emphasized that the files of which we have been speaking are the raw material of an auxiliary exposure system which is almost entirely privately operated. The Committee's investigative files which are used in its own exposure hearings are the product of other forms of investigation and surveillance.

In order to develop an exposure hearing the Committee

needs names as prime raw material. To obtain these names it must find a friendly witness. Such witnesses sometimes voluntarily make themselves available to the Committee; others are brought to the Committee as part of a clearance arrangement. But the most important single source of friendly witnesses and of possible unfriendly witnesses is the FBI. The FBI plays an enormously significant role in HUAC's operations.

From the chairmanship of Martin Dies to the present, common interests have brought the FBI and the Committee together. The FBI has always had liaison representatives posted in the Committee's offices and using its files. Of the eight investigators now on the Committee's staff, at least four are ex-FBI agents.

The closeness of the relationship between the two agencies has burgeoned with the years. The Committee under Dies played a distinctly minor role in the "security" area. It concentrated on demolishing the organizational structure erected during the united front period of the early thirties. Its attacks on the Communist Party were primarily focused on the functionaries of the Party, a field in which its investigative needs were minimal and were amply served by city police Red squads.

In the late forties, the relationship flowered when the Committtee began its spy-hunting, with which it was preoccupied until the early fifties. The FBI, frustrated by the failure of the Elizabeth Bentley disclosures to yield indictments for espionage, turned to the Committee for vindication and publicity. In 1948, Chairman Thomas, in the course of testimony by Miss Bentley, fresh from unproductive grand jury proceedings, said, ". . . The closest relationship exists between this committee and the FBI. . . . I think there is a very good understanding between us. It is something, however, that we cannot talk too much about."

As the Committee began to see itself as a security agency, it independently undertook to build cases against suspects, sometimes in competition with grand juries then sitting, and examined evidence gathered by the FBI. An outstanding example is the Remington case which, the Committee claims, was "broken" as a result of its investigative efforts. Often the Committee was called by the FBI to punish suspects whom the grand juries refused to indict.

In 1953, Senator Mundt, a graduate of the Committee,

said of Committee espionage probes, according to a press account, that they are "a valuable supplement to the investigative work of the FBI. The Committee may compile such evidence on Communist infiltration, but not enough to justify indictments. Often in such case," said the Senator, "the FBI will tip off a Congressional committee as to a situation where it is convinced American security is endangered.

"The Committee's inquiry then makes it possible to bring the case into the open and, with the suspected Communist spy usually taking refuge in the Fifth Amendment's protection against incriminating himself, it is possible to eliminate that particular threat."

By 1953, the prospect for a smooth relationship seemed especially promising, for when the Republican Congress took over in that year, Harold Velde, a former FBI agent, became Chairman. He announced that he expected "a new era of good feeling between the Un-American Activities Committee and the FBI. . . . There are lots of files that we could make good use of, and I am satisfied the Eisenhower Administration will let us make use of them."

Velde's hopes were richly realized. The trickle of undercover agents who had previously found their way to the Committee as friendly witnesses swelled considerably.

In 1955, Walter became Chairman, and in May 1956, Arens, who has intimate connections with the FBI, was designated Staff Director. A statement by the Chairman made clear that the appointment would inaugurate an even closer collaboration between the Committee and the FBI. Arens, he said, would "coordinate more effectively the legislative and investigative work of the Committee."

This "coordination" was necessary to remove a serious threat to the Committee's exposure operation. By 1957 there were few friendly witnesses—either former FBI agents or bona fide ex-Communists—remaining. The Committee had exhausted the supply of agents who had appeared as witnesses in Smith Act trials and proceedings before the Subversive Activities Control Board. The mine of defectors was pretty well worked out too.

The FBI was in a perfect position to come to the Committee's rescue, for it had a surplus of the very commodity so badly needed by the Committee. By 1957, both the Smith Act prosecutions and the SACB proceedings under the Internal Security Act of 1950 were reaching an end.

Rulings of the Supreme Court limiting the applicability of the Smith Act and requiring the submission to defendants of informers' prior FBI reports made criminal prosecutions hardly worth the candle.

As a result, a large number of undercover informers, who had been held in reserve for antisubversive litigation, had become surplus. These informers, some of them fresh from the shrunken councils of the Party, with increasing frequency make their testimonial debuts as Committee witnesses.

Many Americans have hoped that the corps of planted, paid informers who swarm over our land would be retired with the tapering off of sedition prosecutions. They are doomed to disappointment: even if there is no one to prosecute under the law, the Committee needs them to keep us under surveillance and to find exposure victims.

But the relationship between the Committee and the FBI involves more than an undertaking by one party to supply witnesses in exchange for a promise by the other to glorify them. These agencies have become open collaborators in an integrated security system.

It is an old story that liberty is endangered by legislation creating political offenses, not only because such offenses are direct limitations on free expression, but also because the process of investigation gives enormously suppressive powers to the investigator. As Federal political offenses multiply, the justifications for interrogating individuals about their politics also increase. More importantly, the target of the investigation shifts from the seditious utterance to the nonconformist opinion, from incitement to force and violence to all forms of liberal opinion and expression.

But a police agency in a democracy is an inefficient weapon for attacking liberal or radical opinions and affiliations which violate no law. It is true that the mere interrogation by an agent of a "suspect" interferes with free expression and creates an atmosphere of fear. But as sedition prosecutions come to an end, the jurisdictional pretext of the FBI for use of such tactics against private citizens—Government employees are another story—is rendered increasingly implausible. The role of the investigative agency as a repressive thought police becomes more naked, challenges to its authority more pervasive, and its ability to obtain "cooperation" from ordinary citizens more fragile. It must be remembered that the FBI under our system lacks the power, common in totalitarian countries, to coerce the cooperation of those who withhold it because of a conviction that it is acting beyond the scope of its authority.

The FBI can intimidate by interviewing a subject in his place of employment, making known to his employer his refusal to cooperate, and sometimes bringing about the permanent blacklisting of an individual. It can threaten to have the subject called before a grand jury. But grand juries sit only to investigate the commission of crime; and even if a grand jury is sitting the witness is protected against exposure sanctions by the secrecy of its proceedings. The subject also knows that the grand jury cannot make a "presentment"—an attack which does not charge a crime —against him, for this is forbidden in our Federal court system.

These controls are imperative if the watchmen of our ramparts are not to be transformed into the guardians of our thoughts and opinions. When the FBI was organized, Attorney General (later Chief Justice) Stone was acutely aware of the dangers of such a body encroaching on our basic liberties and sharply limited the FBI to the investigation of crime—or prohibited acts—and barred it from the realm of mere expression. This was wholesome— a necessary limitation. It permits proper scope to true law enforcement without impairing our democratic freedoms.

The weapon which the FBI is tempted to use against the uncooperative subject is to turn him over to the Committee. Fear of exposure may make him cooperate, and exposure will punish him if he refuses. Thus a recurrent pattern in this area is the FBI interview with an uncooperative witness, followed in its wake by a Committee subpoena. HUAC not only subpoenas those who refuse to cooperate with the FBI, but it "clears" those who do cooperate. When a friendly witness designates an individual as a Communist who has cooperated with the FBI, Arens announces (New England, 1959) that "it is our information from authentic sources that he has disassociated from the Communist Party and has cooperated with the appropriate Government agencies."

It is primarily, then, the restoration of a national equilibrium of freedom and tolerance which is cementing the FBI and the Committee into a new security bureaucracy. Our democratic traditions have been too strong to sanction an avowedly antisubversive domestic governmental agency with all the familiar trappings; secret political thought police with power of coercion, dossiers, surveillance of dissenters, and a propaganda apparatus to manipulate public opinion, etc. Many of these functions, however, were performed by the FBI and the Congressional antisubversive committees in indirect and illegal ways. And this usurpation of power engineered a reluctant acquiescence by posing as its alternative the overthrow of the Republic. Illegal and unconstitutional government grew fat on a rich diet of "security." Like an army which dreads the impact of peace on its size, budget and prestige, so this monolithic security agency fears the revival of our democratic values. To prevent it, the propaganda mechanisms which pump fear into the political bloodstream must be rebuilt. Repression of liberal and radical thought must continue without the aid of political prosecutions and antisubversive administrative proceedings.

Thus, the Committee makes common cause with the FBI. It has made criticism of the FBI and of repressive security legislation a hallmark of subversion. By identifying itself with the FBI, it has used the FBI's prestige to ward off attacks, and in turn has obtained the enthusiastic endorsement of the FBI. Indeed, many are convinced that the extraordinary ability of the Committee to silence Congressional criticism springs from the fear that the Committee may use the FBI in reprisal. As one Washington editor has put it, "The FBI will never permit Congress to curb the Committee."

The Committee has become increasingly bold in developing in its hearings tips and leads from the files of the FBI. On occasion it abandons all pretense and uses its hearing sessions to air material which the FBI wants publicized. An example of this aspect of the Committee's collaboration with the FBI is the six-day hearing (300 printed pages worth) which was held in Los Angeles in 1958 and 1959 on "The Southern California District of the Communist Party—Structure—Objectives—Leadership."

The purpose of this hearing was to put on the record material which had come to the Committee from intelligence sources (presumably the FBI) about the Party and its activities in Southern California. Chairman Walter announced: "Information has come to this Committee of renewed Communist Party activities in this, a highly sensitive and important area of the country. The degree and extent of this renewed activity is deemed by the Committee to be of such importance to the national welfare and the defense of the country as to justify this investigation in order that remedial legislation may be recommended in this field designed to meet new threats of public subversion."

The hearings—the term is hardly appropriate to describe what went on—consisted of the interrogation of some 65 individuals, alleged to be present or former Communist Party members or officials. Every one of these witnesses used the protections of the Constitution to resist questioning by the Committee. This hardly seemed to trouble Chairman Walter and his colleagues, for the Committee had not come to Los Angeles to ascertain any information. It came rather to play a game of "cops and robbers" with the local Communists, to brag, either on behalf of itself or the FBI about how much they know about internal affairs of the local Red organization. "It must occur to you," Chairman Walter told the head of the Southern California Party organization, Dorothy Healey, "that someone knows all about your activities to give us this information."

The questions at the hearings dealt almost exclusively with internal Party matters, such as "hard" and "soft" positions taken at the National Communist Party convention in 1957; the views of Dorothy Healey, leader of the Southern California Communists; the disillusionment of a group of members with the Party and ultimate resignation of some of them; the organization of the Party into two districts; the local Party's program on various problems, such as labor, youth, Negro discrimination, and the Party's relationship to non-Communist organizations. Threading the entire six-day proceedings were a series of statements in the form of questions showing how much the Committee knew about who said what in the presence of whom. The "questions" were asked not to gather information, but to demonstrate how much had been gathered, to prove that there was nothing that the local Reds were doing which was not already known.

The Committee subsequently issued a 100-page report to Congress; it was based not on the hearings but on the intelligence information—the names, documents, surveillance reports, and dossiers—which had been turned over to it. The hearings were referred to only to footnote the fact that particular individuals had pleaded the privilege against self-incrimination at the hearings. This report contains about 30 pages of political dossiers, obviously from the files of an intelligence agency, with full descriptions of nine of the ten members of the executive board of the California organization and of 75 individuals billed as "other party personalities."

The report takes us by the hand and guides us to the inmost mysteries: it reproduces a letter signed by 22 individuals protesting against Party policies. The letter, addressed to the National Committee of the Communist Party, is signed only with first names. But the Committee sees all, knows all. "The Committee has supplied the full names in parentheses, with four exceptions." One must not be too impatient to learn the names of the four; the Committee has "reliable information" about their identities and backgrounds, but "it is not reporting its information at this time."

The report also reproduces in 63 closely printed pages a series of 16 documents which were distributed to the delegates to a Communist convention in 1957. The relevance of these dull resolutions and speeches to any subject of Congressional concern is obscure. The body of the report—the voice of the Committee speaking directly to Congress—is little more than 20 pages long. The report warns Congress that the Party in California, "has remarshaled its forces for a new offensive in the Golden State." This and other overheated conclusions of the report are a valiant attempt to conceal what the hearings showed, that the Party in California is isolated, weak and faction-ridden; that it is without influence among the groups which it would like to influence, workers, youth and Negroes, and that dissension and resignations have completely enfeebled it. Although the report is written in the Committee's most frenzied it-is-later-than-you-think-manner and milks the most sinister inferences from the hackneyed materials it reviews, it does not even suggest that its intelligence sources have led it to evils which require the attention of Congress. And it makes no legislative recommendations at all.

It can hardly be doubted that HUAC has, to a large extent, functionally allied itself with the FBI. A striking recent example of the collaboration is the issuance of an FBI report on the San Francisco student demonstration in

1960 to bolster HUAC's Red-plot charge and to clothe its film "Operation Abolition" with authenticity. According to a statement to a reporter for the Washington *Star* in 1957 by a former FBI agent who became a staff investigator for a Congressional anti-subversive Committee, "We wouldn't be able to stay in business overnight if it weren't for the Bureau. . . . We have eight or nine investigators. How could we possibly build up all the cases we have had without outside assistance? It just could not be done. We would have to keep lots of people under surveillance, but how could we do it with our small staff? The FBI has between 5,000 and 6,000 special agents." It is, of course, a violation of a presidential directive to make available to a Congressional agency material from FBI files. The FBI has always insisted that it rigidly adheres to the directive, and the Committee disclaims that it has access to the files. The acceptance of such a disclaimer requires the disregard of too much evidence to the contrary.

Thus, freedom of dissent still faces enormous hazards in our country. Instead of the telescreen of Orwell's "Big Brother," we may well have the combined HUAC-FBI policing every home for evidence of subversion.

15   THE LEGISLATIVE HOAX

As has been pointed out, HUAC has no authority to engage in exposure for its own sake; its investigations must have a legislative purpose. When the *Watkins* case came to the Supreme Court in 1957, Watkins' lawyers argued that he was a victim of exposure and called the Court's attention to HUAC's systematic disregard of legislative ends in all of its hearings. The Court expressly warned HUAC that it lacked the power to expose. Experts thought that this warning was HUAC's death knell as an exposure agency. When the Court spoke, even HUAC would have to listen. HUAC itself was thrown into momentary panic—but it quickly recovered.

It abandoned its former practice of shouting its exposure purpose from the housetops. Descriptions of its functions which used the word "exposure" were denounced as "Communist semantics." Attempts by witnesses to protect themselves against exposure by reliance on the *Watkins* decision were met by a beautifully simple deception which has now become a ritual. At the hearing, HUAC announces a series of "legislative" reasons for holding the session. HUAC has, with practice, learned to apply this legislative cosmetic to its exposure operation with great skill. But immediately after the *Watkins* case, when HUAC was still a novice at applying its new makeup, the blemishes showed through— as we have seen from the 1957 San Francisco hearing. An executive session for two Newark school teachers which occurred a month after the *Watkins* decision was undoubtedly HUAC's most inept use of its then newly acquired legislative makeup.

This affair begins in 1955, when HUAC held hearings in Newark over which Chairman Walter presided, resulting in a move to oust three teachers who had pleaded the Fifth Amendment. In the discharge proceedings, the board of education struck certain testimony on the ground that it had been illegally admitted into evidence at HUAC's hearings. A final decision by the board was scheduled for June 23, 1955.

Now, whenever Chairman Walter presides over a hearing, he is particularly zealous about the "follow up." He wants to make sure that the unfriendly witnesses who have appeared before him suffer the full exposure penalty. Walter was outraged that the board of education had agreed to strike the illegally admitted testimony, and fearful that the final decision might be favorable to the teachers. He took to the floor of the House of Representatives on June 22, the eve of the board decision, and blasted the board for relying on an alleged technicality to avoid doing an unpleasant job. He bitterly complained of the board's "lack of cooperation in a fight to preserve our way of life."

Walter's pressure, on the eve of the board's vote, had its intended effect: the three suspended teachers lost their posts by a 5-4 vote. In an interview which he gave on June 26 to the Newark *Star-Ledger,* HUAC's New Jersey mouthpiece, Walter said that he was "upset" by the slim margin and rebuked the board minority. He suggested that they were subversive, and warned Newark's chief executive responsible for "appointing members of the board of education [that he] should examine his conscience closely as to future and present appointees."

The minority which Walter had abused and threatened in this way had simply taken the view that it was improper for a public body to discharge an employee solely for exercising a right guaranteed by the Constitution—a view which was adopted by a United States Supreme Court decision shortly thereafter. On the basis of this decision, the New Jersey Supreme Court reversed the discharges and adopted the same "subversive" views as the board's minority.

The New Jersey court ordered the matter remanded to the superintendent of schools, with instructions to the superintendent to inquire as to whether or not in fact the three teachers were subversive or unfit. The teachers, the court ruled, could not be ousted merely because they had relied on the Constitution.

After a hearing before Newark Superintendent of Schools Kennelly in the spring of 1957, it became widely known that two of the three teachers would be reinstated. But the likelihood of even two reinstatements stirred the Newark Network to action. Too much was at stake. If the ouster of the teachers could be made to stick, the majority of the board of education was preparing a wide-scale purge of the Newark school system, based on a list of names supplied by an informer.

The Network sent HUAC an S.O.S., and HUAC responded nobly. It summoned the two teachers who appeared to be slated for reinstatement, and who had appeared before it in 1955, to an executive session to be held in Washington on July 24, 1957. The summons was no bolt from the blue. The Newark *Star-Ledger* had carried a statement from Walter that the teachers would be subpoenaed "because they had told the School Superintendent things they had refused to tell the House Committee." The newspaper had also imparted to its readers the ominous intelligence that the reinstatements would depend not only on the testimony before the superintendent, but on the HUAC hearings and on "any future hearings that might be held."

When the witnesses appeared in executive session before a subcommittee consisting of Representatives Doyle and Scherer, Arens interrogated them with a copy of the superintendent's secret, confidential report on his desk. How he obtained it may only be surmised. The first witness protested that "forces in the community working against my reinstatement have exerted pressure to effect my appearance." She pointed out that her call to an executive session had been publicized despite a promise that it would not be, and that in view of the fact that the testimony before the superintendent of schools had been supplied to the Committee, although it was supposed to be private and confidential, there was no assurance that the executive hearing itself would be kept confidential as the Committee had promised it would be.

Neither Arens nor the subcommittee members responded to the witness' serious charges. Instead, they pretended innocence of the whole reinstatement issue. Thus Arens asked the witness, "You refer to some private inquiry before Dr. Kennelly, what was that?" And Congressman Scherer played his role in the game of pretending ignorance of the background of the controversy in this fashion: "You said that this Dr. Kennelly was holding a hearing at the direction of the New Jersey Supreme Court? . . . I am entirely unfamiliar with the litigation involved. Will you tell us about the directive and how it arose? . . . What was the nature of this directive that was issued to Dr. Kennelly? . . . This is the first time I have heard of it . . . tell us what you understand about it. I might want to ask some questions and I might be better able to ask those questions if I know the nature of the hearing and how it came about."

Notwithstanding these protestations of ignorance of the reinstatement issue, the entire hearing was taken up with an attempt to trap the witnesses into discussing their testimony before the Superintendent. ("Is there something you said or failed to say in your appearances . . . which was untruthful?" When the witnesses pleaded the Fifth Amendment to this line of questioning, these pleas in turn were stigmatized as an attempt to shield perjuries before the superintendent. "Did you perjure yourself before the Kennelly inquiry?") In short, HUAC was forging a weapon which could be used by Newark Network organizations either to force the superintendent to change his proposed recommendations or the board to reverse them.

When the first witness protested on the basis of the month-old *Watkins* decision that the real purpose of the session was to forestall her reinstatement, Arens read the following HUAC statement of legislative purpose:

It is the information of this Committee that there was, and perhaps is, in the Newark, New Jersey area, a union consisting of school teachers. That that union, consisting of school teachers was heavily penetrated by members of the Communist Party.

This Committee is considering legislation, with the view toward precluding certain certification of unions which may be Communist controlled or penetrated. It is for that reason, among others, that we have invited you to appear here today to give us information which might be germane to the consideration of such proposed legislation.

This justification is as spurious as the claim of ignorance of the reinstatement issue. Not a single question was asked either witness about a teachers' union or their membership in it. The entire interrogation was confined to the superintendent's hearing, the subject which Walter had assigned to the Newark *Star-Ledger* as the reason for the hearing. When the witnesses refused to discuss their testimony before the superintendent, they were excused from further questioning.

Arens' choice of a legislative pretext was an unhappy one. Under Federal laws protecting collective bargaining rights of workers, labor unions receive "certifications" to establish that they are representatives of the majority of the employees for purposes of collective bargaining. But these certification provisions do not apply to those employed by the government—Federal, state or municipal. Even private-school teachers are not subject to these laws, because their activities do not affect interstate commerce. In addition, at the time of the interrogation, there was a law on the books, the Communist Control Act of 1954, which barred from certification as a collective bargaining agency a labor organization which, in Arens' language, "may be Communist controlled or penetrated." If a possible law was to be selected to justify the hearing, Arens could at least have chosen one which had not been passed three years earlier. And this lapse was particularly strange, for Arens has claimed to be the draftsman of the 1954 law.

What completely demolishes this "legislative" justification is that only the two teachers were called whose reinstatement was threatened. The third teacher who was not called had been the president of the Teachers' Union.

Thus crude pressure to influence the outcome of a judicially ordered hearing was concealed by a wholly fraudulent legislative justification. If the teachers had refused, on grounds not legally protected, to answer HUAC's questions and had been cited for contempt, HUAC would have repeated to the court its fake legislative purpose and disclaimed any attempt to use the executive session to expose them. And HUAC undoubtedly would have been believed—as in the Braden and Wilkinson cases.

In the case of the Newark school teachers, HUAC's labors were not wholly in vain. Three weeks after the hearing, the superintendent filed his report and only one of the two teachers on whom HUAC had worked was recommended for reinstatement. The reinstatement of the other teacher has just been ordered after six years of litigation. Will HUAC once again invent a "legislative" pretext to frustrate the court's decision?

In its annual report to Congress, HUAC makes legislative recommendations. It uses these recommendations as another means of establishing its legislative purpose. These legislative recommendations invite the assumption—by Congress and the courts—that they are the legislative answer to the problems which have been investigated in the course of HUAC's hearings and that the hearings were held to throw light on the desirability of the recommendations. This, too, is a deception to conceal the exposure purpose of the hearings.

Before exploring the relationship of these recommendations to the hearings, we should take a look at some of them. Here are a few examples:

> The mandatory deportation of aliens who advocate any basic change in the form of our government. [1940]
> The statutory period during which citizenship papers can be revoked be extended to at least ten years. [1940]
> That legislation should be enacted that would restrict Federal employment to citizens of the United States and that only citizens of the United States be permitted to hold office in any labor union subject to Federal laws. [1947]

Thought should be given to ways and means of stimulating defections from the Communist movement and of encouraging qualified informants. [1950]

In recent years HUAC has made a specialty of recommendations which are designed to neutralize the effect of Supreme Court decisions upholding civil liberties. When the Supreme Court construed the Smith Act to conform to the requirements of the free-speech guarantees of the First Amendment, the Committee recommended that the Act be enlarged in scope. When the Court struck down restrictive passport practices, unfair security-screening regulations, the denial of hearings to Federal employees accused of disloyalty, and state sedition laws in conflict with Federal laws, the Committee rushed into the breach with recommendations to overturn the decisions. Most of the recommendations rebuke the Court for misinterpreting the law and charge that the decisions endanger the national security.

At the outset, one is struck by the sharp difference between HUAC's recommendations and the carefully drafted legislative recommendations which normal investigations produce. Almost all of the Committee's recommendations have a broad, shotgun quality, ignoring the legal and constitutional problems which they raise.

In its most recent annual report to Congress, the Committee conceded that its rough-hewn warnings are unpromising even as raw material for Congressional action: "The necessity for remedial legislation on these subjects is apparent, but the final form which such legislation should take has been, in some instances, a matter for continuing refinement and development. . . . But due deliberation is a legislative virtue." Still, Congress must not flag in its "due deliberation," for "history must not record that this generation has negligently left its patrimony of liberty to be taken from it by those who pass in the shadows."

What is most remarkable about the recommendations is not their technical crudity and political flavor, but the fact that they are quite unrelated to the hearings from which they are supposed to flow. For example, HUAC's 1953 annual report makes eight recommendations for legislation which, it claimed, were "based upon investigations and hearings" in that year. They range from proposals for wire-tapping legislation to barring second-class mailing privileges to "subversive publications." Most of

287

the recommendations, if adopted, would invade our basic freedoms and raise serious Constitutional questions—all of which are blithely ignored.

Still, the question of "how" these recommendations can be legally adopted is not nearly as puzzling as why they should be. There is no reference to the evil or threat established in the hearings to which the recommendations are a response. And when we look at the hearings—either as they are summarized in the report or in full—we understand why: They do not deal with the subject matter of the recommendations. They could not possibly enlighten Congress as to why these extraordinary proposals were advanced.

The hearings in 1953, as summarized in HUAC's annual report, include six "area" hearings, two subject-matter hearings (education and government-labor), hearings on a Methodist Bishop and minister, and three hearings on foreign affairs involving testimony from iron-curtain defectors.

No rational links to the recommendations are supplied by the area hearings, because they deal not with problems, but with people. The summary of the Los Angeles hearing is prefaced by an honor roll of the names of 42 friendly witnesses, who among them identified a multitude of alleged Communists. The names are all submitted to Congress in 26 closely printed pages of the report. The high point of the Los Angeles investigation was the fact that, "As a result of tireless investigation on the part of the Committee and the cooperation of numerous witnesses . . . more individuals were named as members of the Communist Party in Los Angeles than in any other locality in which the Committee has held hearings." In addition to the news of this record-shattering event, the report shares with Congress the intelligence—of inscrutable legislative relevance—that one Los Angeles witness who had refused to disclose whether he had been a Communist had, however, "indignantly denied" that he had used any other name. The Committee triumphantly produced another witness who testified that he *had* known this man under another name.

The New York City area hearings of that year produced an honor roll of 11 friendly witnesses who named 225 victims. But there is still no link to the recommendations. The Columbus, Ohio, section of the report gives Congress the names of 5 cooperative witnesses and of 12 individuals whom they dubbed Communists. It informs Congress that "the first enemy of the Communist is a belief that you are created by a Divine Creator," but leaves Congress in the dark about the need for eight recommendations—so does the Albany, N.Y. section of the report, in which a corporal's guard of 4 friendly witnesses gets high praise for identifying 90 individuals, all of whom are named. The summary of the Committee's Philadelphia hearings consists of a list of 19 unfriendly teachers who, the Committee ambiguously informs Congress, "are a very small fraction of the loyal American teachers in Philadelphia, Pa." The testimony identifying the teachers was not made public; so no honor list is published—a curious fact, but hardly enlightening as to the need for the recommendations.

The report's summary of the Committee's San Francisco hearings includes a remarkable two-and-a-half page close-printed extract from the testimony of a friendly witness, an ex-Communist, of how he came to join and why he left the Party. One also learns from the report that, in still another area of endeavor, Los Angeles has outstripped its sister city. All that the ten helpful San Francisco witnesses could produce was about 300 names, 13 pages worth—just about half of the Los Angeles record-breaking total.

In the same way, the report of HUAC"s summary of the education hearings is crowned with an honor list of 12 friendly witnesses, followed by a longer list of the 54 individuals whom they named as Communists. The rest of this portion of the report is taken up with such cosmic questions as whether the universities are more effective than the Committee at ferreting out Communist teachers. The government-labor report concentrates on the case of a resigned Government worker who had concealed the fact that he had been a Communist from 1938 to 1940, and concludes with a list of five individuals in the labor movement named as Communists.

Still in the dark as to "why" the recommendations, we study the report of the hearings of the defectors and the Methodist churchmen, but they are equally useless in helping us find our way back to the recommendations.

There is no way back. The recommendations are *not the result* of the hearings, but are *entirely independent* of them. They are not based on evidence and do not reflect the testimony of the witnesses. They are not rooted in a fact-finding process at all, but are simply an expression of the subjective views of the Committee, its members and staff. They resemble resolutions by an American Legion post, and are recommendations in the same dubious sense that the frustrated cry, "There ought to be a law" is a recommendation. They give Congress no more help in the process of law-making than a letter by a private citizen to his Congressman. And since the problems with which they deal are not, even remotely, what the hearings are about, the claim that the hearings have a legislative purpose must be marked down as another deception.

A third response to the *Watkins* decision is HUAC's compilation of a "box-score" of its recommendations, which, it asserts, became law. Like the prehearing statement of legislative purpose, HUAC's box-score is recited at the hearing to brighten its legislative image. It is offered as a record of solid legislative achievement to refute the claim of a pattern of exposure.

But the box-score is characteristically overstated. Just as the recommendations find no support in the hearings, so the laws to which HUAC points are largely unrelated to the recommendations. The box-score, which was published in 1958 (expanded edition 1960) claims that HUAC made 79 recommendations of which 29 assertedly became law. In point of fact, all but one of the 29 laws were processed by other committees. HUAC argues that simply because it made a recommendation and another committee processed a bill on the same subject which became law, HUAC is somehow entitled to credit.

As a matter of fact, in some instances, the reporting of the bill anteceded the Committee's recommendation. For example, the Committee made recommendations in January 1956 for broadening the sedition and espionage acts. It claims that its recommendations were enacted in the summer of 1956. But the legislation was proposed a year before the Committee made its recommendations, and was reported favorably (by the Judiciary Committee) eight months before HUAC's recommendations were made.

The Committee demands not only retroactive but also clairvoyant credit. Thus, it insists that three recommendations which it made in 1941 on the subject of aliens resulted in the enactment, 11 years later, of certain provisions of the Walter-McCarran Act. Proposals made in 1941 for enlarging the statute of limitations in certain kinds of cases are seriously pressed as the source of a statute passed in 1951 and processed by another committee.

One final instance will convey the enormously strained flavor of the Committee's claims. In 1941, the Dies Committee made a blanket recommendation that financial support be withheld from schools which permitted members of the faculty to advocate Communism, Fascism or Nazism. The Committee contends that this recommendation entitles it to assume credit for a law passed 11 years later, Section 228 of the Veterans' Readjustment Act, prohibiting payment of an educational allowance to any eligible veteran who enrolls for a course in a school on the Attorney General's list of subversive organizations! The legislation in question was processed by the Veterans' Affairs Committee of the House, which nowhere indicated that the "recommendation" by a sister committee 11 years earlier had in any way been responsible for the law.

Equally absurd are the Committee's contentions that many of its recommendations, while not in fact enacted into law, are the subject of bills now pending. Here, too, the Committee assigns itself credit for work actually done by other committees. For example, the Committee demands credit for a group of wire-tapping bills which, it says, were inspired by its recommendations. But bills of this sort were pending before the House Judiciary Committee long before any recommendation was made by HUAC. Indeed, the House Judiciary Committee has, from time to time between 1940 and 1950, held extensive hearings on a series of fourteen wire-tapping bills, none of which owes its origin to the recommendation of the Committee. HUAC's relationship to Congress is basically that of an impassioned special pleader. Its recommendations have an agitational warning-from-the-ramparts quality: "Hurry-up and do something," HUAC's recommendations in effect plead, "it is light years later than you think." HUAC seeks to spur other committees to take action which they are unwilling to take—either because of constitutional doubts or for reasons of policy. But our legislative system does not authorize a Congressional committee that lacks jurisdiction, to supervise, bully or coach other committees that have it.

Still another legislative cover for HUAC's exposure system is the Omnibus Security Bill. Beginning in 1957, *and every year thereafter* Chairman Walter, with many flourishes and fanfares, has introduced an Omnibus Bill containing a heterogeneous accumulation of the Committee's legislative recommendations through the years: Smith Act enlargement, passport restrictions, industrial security-screening measures, etc.

This Omnibus Bill is designed to serve as an umbrella of legislative purpose over the Committee's investigations. Its widely assorted provisions could justify any conceivable anti-subversive inquiry. It is frequently summarized at the commencement of the hearing to anticipate and block protests by witnesses that the hearing has no legislative purpose.

This is a short version of this post-*Watkins* gambit recited at the beginning of the Committee's 1958 New Orleans hearings.

> To strengthen our security laws, a number of legislative proposals are pending before the Committee. The most recent and comprehensive proposal is in the form of an omnibus security bill, H. R. 9937, which Chairman Walter introduced and which represents the most comprehensive effort ever made to deal with the many legislative problems in the field of internal security. It is the hope of the Committee that factual information obtained at this hearing will be of assistance in the consideration and appraisal of the numerous provisions of this bill.

But the Committee is playing games. This annually introduced bill has never been reported out to the floor of Congress. Here is a measure which is a bouquet of the Committee's fairest recommendations, the subject of many hearings to develop "factual information," the passage of which the Committee insists is imperative to rescue the Nation from betrayal and ruin. Why has the bill never been reported out? Because as long as it is pending, the Committee can use it as a pretext for more exposure hearings.

Another curious and revealing explanation was recently offered by Chairman Walter. In testifying in the course of a trial last year (1960), Chairman Walter explained the mystery of the bill: "Frankly, we haven't acted on it because parts of it have been acted on in other committees, and parts of it are pending in other committees. You will find it in many different pieces of legislation over which other committees have jurisdiction." This legislative monstrosity has been re-introduced by the Chairman this year (H.R.6,1961). It has no future as legislation, but it can be used for years as a reason for developing "factual information" of the "are-you-now-and-have-you-ever-been" variety—a marvelous violin case in which to carry the machine-gun of exposure.

All of the four methods which HUAC has devised to give its investigations a legislative facade are even more implausible than the preceding pages indicate. The Committee must pretend not only that it is investigating for a legitimate legislative purpose, but that the legislative problem which it claims to be pursuing falls within its jurisdiction. It consistently uses as a cover for its exposure hearings problems and issues which it has no jurisdiction to investigate at all. Its jurisdiction is defined as "propaganda" and "propaganda activities," but it systematically raids the jurisdiction of other House committees—such as Judiciary, Armed Services and Foreign Affairs—for subjects to mask its exposure operations.

For example, in 1960 the Committee grilled the delegates to a youth festival in an exposure hearing complete with informers and surprise witnesses. The justifying ploy was a claim that the Committee was considering the advisability of legislation providing for official, Government-sponsored, politically reliable, delegations to such festivals. But this is a bare-faced usurpation of the jurisdiction of the Foreign Affairs Committee. In the same way, virtually all of the recommendations of which it is so proud involve problems and responsibilities which belong to other committees. And those recommendations which it claims became law, achieved that status, with one exception, only because of the activity of some other House committee with appropriate jurisdiction.

The Committee sheds no tears because there is no jurisdictional pillow on which to rest its weary head. Indeed, its jurisdictional shortcomings are an asset, freeing it from legislative responsibilities so that it can roam wherever it likes and expose at will. The very obscurity of the Committee's mandate has permitted it to set up shop as an exposure bureau for the whole Congress without regard to jurisdictional limitations.

HUAC's restricted and obscure jurisdiction is primarily responsible for its extraordinary record of sterility as a standing Committee. During the entire 16 years of its functioning as a standing Committee, HUAC has processed only one law, the Internal Security Act of 1950. The constitutionality of this highly controversial piece of legislation, passed over President Truman's veto, has not yet been determined by the United States Supreme Court. The Committee also claims credit for another dubious product of the fifties, the Communist Control Act of 1954, termed by some the most repressive and by others the most foolish law ever passed. Whatever the merits of the law, the Committee had little or nothing to do with it. Representative Velde, while a member of the Committee, introduced a bill dealing with the subject of the legislation; but it was the Senate bill which ultimately became the law. The Committee never held hearings on its bill. When the Committee reported favorably on the bill, something unusual happened: a minority led by Representative Walter of the Committee attacked it on the ground, among others, that the bill was "reported by the Committee on un-American Activities without one word of testimony pro or con introduced, or a report from the Department of Justice submitted." Nor is this the whole story. From March 18, 1954 to June 30, 1954, the House Committee on the Judiciary conducted intensive hearings on a group of 20 bills and resolutions, the counterparts of the Senate-sponsored measures which became the Communist Control Act. But the Judiciary Committee refused to report the bill out. Thus the Act was sponsored on the House side by HUAC (which had not held a day of hearings on it) and was rejected by the Judiciary Committee which had extensively convassed its merits.

It can be readily surmised from its puny output that HUAC is no tower of strength as a legislative standing Committee. Those who operate the Congressional lawmaking machinery turn to other legislative agencies to process the bulk of the antisubversive measures which are offered. During the first six years of the Committee's existence, no bill was referred to it, since it was only a special committee. During this period of time, the Committee published some 16,000 pages of hearings and reports, but made no direct legislative contributions. It was indirectly responsible for one piece of legislation, the appropriation rider withholding pay checks from certain Federal employees on the grounds of subversion. This was invalidated as a bill of attainder by the United States Supreme Court in the *Lovett* case.

From January 1951 to the present, scores of bills on various aspects of security and subversion have been thrown into the legislative hopper. These bills are indexed under headings such as "Communism or Communists," "Subversive Activity," "Foreign Agents," "Subversive Aliens," "Subversive Propaganda," and related subjects which the Committee claims as its jurisdiction and which serve as subjects of its investigative hearings. But only a fraction of these are ever referred to the Committee; and most of even that fraction are the brain children of the Committee Chairman or members, which find their way to the Committee in courtesy to their sponsors. Bills covering the same subject, but under different sponsorship, are regularly assigned to other committees. The following table summarizes the Committee's role as a standing Committee from 1951 (82nd Congress, 1st Session) to 1960 (86th Congress, 2nd Session).

Congressional Session	All Committees	Bills Referred to: House Un-American Committee	Anti-Subversive Bills Referred to All Committees
82nd (1951-52)	5,324	2	21
83rd (1953-54)	6,478	4	57
84th (1955-56)	8,796	1	30
85th (1957-58)	10,331	5	31
86th (1959-60)	10,847	19	42
TOTAL	41,776	31 *	181

* 17 of this total introduced by HUAC members.

Thus, in the past decade, HUAC, one of the House's most lavishly financed and staffed operations, has handled seven hundredths of one percent of its legislative business, and a little more than one-sixth of its antisubversive bills.

It is not merely that the Committee is called on to handle so few bills: it rarely holds hearings even on those bills which are referred to it. It held no legislative hearings on any of the 12 bills referred to it between 1951 and 1958. In its entire history, the Committee has held three purely legislative hearings on some six bills. This is, of course, a minute fraction of the hearings which the Committee has conducted as an investigative committee.

You may wonder why the Committee, which is prolific in investigation hearings and frequently holds more of them during the course of a Congressional session than all of its sister committees, is so coy about holding hearings on the bills which are referred to it.

There is no mystery about this. Purely legislative hearings are dull. There may be a headline in some minatory observations of J. Edgar Hoover about the "Menace," but, by and large, they create scarcely a ripple in the news. Besides, a legislative hearing requires a measure of preparation and some familiarity not only with the subject of the bill under consideration, but with the legal problems which it presents. How different from the investigative-exposure hearing, where all that the Committee panel does is to proceed according to a familiar prepared script.

Then, too, many of the bills in the antisubversive area raise serious questions of constitutional law, because they restrain freedom of thought and expression. The legislative hearing forces the Committee to recognize the existence of the Constitution as a limitation on Congressional power. The Attorney General's office might—as it has, on occasion—tell the Committee that the proposed bill violates one or more of the basic freedoms.

The House itself recognizes that the Committee puts no great strain on the legislative talents of its members. It is one of the few committees in the House which is exempt from the rule limiting Congressmen to service on only one standing committee. A member of the Committee may, in addition, have another standing committee assignment. The theory of the legislative hearing is that both expert and representative lay opinions should be freely heard, not as friendly or unfriendly witnesses, but pro or con. The legislative committee needs to know about the legal and constitutional bugs in the measure, but it also wants a sampling of informed popular opinion. It is particularly desirable to get the viewpoint of those adversely affected by proposed legislation. If you plan to raise a man's taxes, limit farm income, or curtail the right to strike, the taxpayer, farmer, and trade unionist ought to be heard. People are more ready to accept and live with legislative decisions adverse to their interests when they have had an opportunity to shape and influence them. And this is never more true than when you propose to take away from their freedoms.

Even HUAC must hear the opposition when it holds a legislative hearing. While HUAC's few legislative hearings are heavily loaded with ultrarightists and security watchdogs, liberal, labor and civil-liberties groups manage to put their objections and constitutional doubts on the record. The Committee enjoys this as little as a poacher would relish an afternoon's sport with the gamekeeper at his side. To HUAC it would be senseless to afford a forum for the "subversives" it ceaselessly harries from which to attack the official version of the "Menace"; it is simpler to expose them. Besides, who needs a statute? The systematic exposure of the dissenter has the effect of a statute, but makes its formal passage superfluous. At the same time, it bypasses the Constitution.

These considerations undoubtedly explain why the Committee majority reported out a version of the oppressive Communist Control Act of 1954, not only without asking the opinion of the Attorney General, but without holding hearings at all.

HUAC may have found a way of combining legislation and exposure in a single hearing. This two-for-the-price-of-one approach—a "legislative" curtain-raiser followed by an exposure hearing—was launched in 1959 when HUAC conducted "legislative" hearings in Pittsburgh on an industrial security bill, introduced by Congressman Scherer, with a full array of Government security officials as witnesses. After their testimony, the Committee switched to an old-style exposure hearing. Scherer's bill, however, had not even been referred to HUAC, but was under consideration by the Judiciary Committee. HUAC invaded the jurisdiction of another committee to conduct hearings on a bill which it had no power to report out. It then yoked this "legislative" hearing to its regular exposure operations. Committee member Scherer wasn't too sure why the Committee was playing in the

Judiciary backyard, except that he personally liked the idea:

> . . . I think it should be noted that H.R.3693, the bill we are discusing, has not been referred to this committee for consideration but is before another committee of the House. Some people may wonder why this committee does not report out this bill. Of course, personally, I feel that this bill should be before this committee, but that is beyond my control.

The Staff Director, Arens, came to the rescue with this smooth explanation of how to saw a bill in half:

> . . . The reason we are making the inquiry and the reason the Committee on Un-American Activities is developing the facts on this is that the bill itself, though technically pending before another Committee, deals with a subject, namely Communism, which is within the jurisdiction of the Committee on Un-American Activities.

If the reader doesn't understand the difference between "technical jurisdiction" (the kind the Judiciary Committee had) and the Committee's jurisdiction, he shouldn't be too troubled. No one else does either.

In 1960, HUAC used this new legislation-exposure approach in two sets of hearings held on bills introduced by Chairman Walter and referred to the Committee. These two bills would deny licenses to seamen and radio operators who declined to answer questions put by Federal agencies (including Congressional committees) about subversive activities. In each of the hearings, HUAC first called Government officials and private individuals who were all enthusiastic supporters of the measure under consideration. It then proceeded to interrogate groups of seamen and radio operators.

Instead of asking these witnesses their views about the bill supposedly under consideration, the Committee launched its familiar exposure-style hearing. An uninformed reader might find these hearings rough going if he forgot to shift gears between the testimony elicited from the supporters of the bills and that coerced from the seamen and radio operators who were the bills' targets. He might ask why was the one group invited to expound at length on the reasons for passing the bills, while the very individuals directly affected by them were denied an opportunity to give their views and instead subjected to the exposure treatment.

It was a foregone conclusion that these subpoenaed witnesses would be unfriendly: at the very time they were subpoenaed they were involved in litigation contesting the power under the Constitution of Government agencies to impose loyalty tests as a condition of employment. In the guise of conducting a legislative hearing, the Committee merely sought to create new reasons why they should be deprived of a livelihood. And it was not one whit abashed by the circumstance that it was intervening in pending litigation. As a matter of fact, it had before it the files of some of the witnesses obtained from the Federal Communications Commission, and asked them the same political questions which were then being challenged in court on constitutional grounds.

HUAC may thus have found still another way to mask its exposure operation—by using the rare hearings which it does conduct on legislation as a form of camouflage for exposure.

As a standing Committee, HUAC plays the same non-legislative game that it plays as an investigating Committee. The legislative process is important to HUAC—but only as a cloak for its exposure system.

The Committee's case in support of its legislative contributions gives fresh proof of its extraordinary affinity for the arts of deception. The punishment of the witness and the invasion of his rights cannot be written off as the price we must pay for getting on with the business of government, for the business the Committee is engaged in is not the business of government. The Committee's business is really exposure for its own sake. We must face the fact that a revolutionary organ of governmental power has come into being in our time which performs functions irreconcilably in conflict with the way in which we have agreed to govern ourselves.

CONCLUSION

A fresh wind is rising in America. We are bestirring ourselves from an era of complacency, fear and conformity and are beginning to count the heavy price we have paid for the stifling of individuality and dissent.

During the fifties, we were warned by our intellectual leaders—educators, statesmen, writers—that repression would bring us to political, social, and cultural disaster. We were squeezing America into a mold of sterility, mediocrity and intolerance which would fatally handicap our ability to solve the problems which confront us. But these warnings were met, for the most part, with apathy, or were outweighed by a fear of using our freedoms.

Today, this apathy and fear have been replaced by a growing concern. There is spreading among our people a deepening mood of self-consciousness and self-searching. There is an uneasy feeling that as a people and as a Nation we have somehow lost our way. Americans are worried about our lack of initiative, educational inadequacies, cultural shortcomings—about our insensitivity to the oppression of minorities, the mediocrity of our mass media, the unimaginativeness of our foreign policies. We make best-sellers of the books that give a name to our plight, that tell us how unenthusiastically we are regarded abroad, or why we are so conformist at home.

Many are asking, how did this happen? How can we change this? We are looking for answers. Do we have a national purpose? What are our goals? Are equality and democracy mere slogans or basic articles of our political faith? What about Little Rock and its sequels? How much freedom are we prepared to stand up and fight for in our daily lives?

It has become desperately important for us to see ourselves clearly, to face courageously and honestly the causes of our failures and frustrations at home and abroad. The old cries about the need for security cannot offset a dying sense of individuality. Sloganized hate for the Reds cannot explain away every error, cannot hide our bewilderment over the mess we have made of the values by which we are supposed to live as a people. We cannot avoid a reckoning with the governmental, security, corporate and military controls that breed submissiveness and tie us into the straitjackets of orthodoxy and safe nonthinking.

This self-questioning brings us face to face with our key dilemma—the erosion of our basic democratic freedoms. We are the leaders of the free world. Our greatest asset as a Nation is the strength of the democratic way. The integrity of our entire system of government depends on the defense and protection of freedom of political expression, association and dissent. Our security and progress as a Nation require the most vigilant safeguarding of freedom of thought, of criticism, investigation, expression and controversy. We must not just believe in freedom, we must practice it— buoyantly and passionately.

We can defend our freedoms against totalitarian threats only by steadfastly upholding those freedoms, not by fostering our own brand of totalitarianism. We can rescue ourselves from the tranquillizing influences which sap our independence only by reasserting and implementing our dedication to the free mind and the free spirit.

Americans in growing numbers are coming to this realization. The era of fear and anxiety is being challenged by a new mood of faith in freedom.

The movement for HUAC's abolition of which I spoke in the opening pages of this book is a clear indication of this new determination to regain our freedoms. The swelling cry that HUAC must go is something new in America. McCarthy and his "ism" met with protest, but it was discouraged and isolated. The anti-HUAC movement is a large-scale assertion of a demand for an end to repression and the techniques and institutions which engender conformity.

Among those who have called for the ending of the Committee are Mrs. Eleanor Roosevelt, Governor Gaylord Nelson of Wisconsin, Dr. Reinhold Niebuhr, Norman Thomas, Stanley Isaacs, Dr. Lewis Mumford, Algernon Black, Carey McWilliams, Bishop James A. Pike, Bishop G. Bromley Oxnam, Helen Gahagan Douglas, Professor Henry Steele Commager, Professor George S. Counts, Professor C. Wright Mills, Lloyd K. Garrison, Dr. Frank P. Graham, Dr. Millicent McIntosh, A. Philip Randolph,

Professor Arthur Schlesinger, Jr., Dean John C. Bennett of the Union Theological Seminary, Dean Douglas Horton of the Howard Divinity School, and Dean Liston Pope of the Yale University School of Divinity—to name only some.

Outstanding leaders of the American religious denominations have attacked the Committee, as have many professional, civic and labor organizations, including the American Civil Liberties Union, Young Democratic Clubs of America, Americans for Democratic Action, American Jewish Congress, Commission on Social Action of Reform Judaism, the American Association of University Professors, Amalgamated Clothing Workers of America, United Packinghouse Workers of America, American Federation of Teachers, and the United Electrical, Radio and Machine Workers of America. Some 250 Southern Negro leaders have protested HUAC's attempts to frustrate the Supreme Court's decision against racial segregation.

Over a thousand members of the faculties of such American universities as Harvard, Yale, Princeton, Northwestern, Columbia, Stanford, University of California, Wisconsin, Michigan and Brown have joined in demands for HUAC's abolition.

Congressman James Roosevelt, a California Democrat, has emerged as HUAC's leading Congressional opponent. His April 25, 1960, speech on the House floor, "The Dragon Slayers," called for the Committee's abolition on eight counts:

First—the Committee had spent "large amounts of time, money and energy ponderously exploring the absurd and self-evident."

Second—the Committee was blindly fanatic in evaluating the political orthodoxy of its victims; its "world is one of black and white moral judgments on matters of immense intricacy and great shadings."

Third—the Committee systematically encroached on the jurisdiction of other Congressional committees.

Fourth—the Committee makes no contribution to the defense of the Nation's security and, in fact, was not created for that purpose.

Fifth—the Committee has transformed itself into a "roving police force and prosecuting agency to haul persons and groups before it, accuse them and force them either to answer under oath or claim their constitutional protection.

Yet it acts with the aid of immunities and powers we would not dream of granting our police and public prosecutors."

Sixth—the Committee had similarly usurped the functions of the courts; here again, it has ignored the standards "of fairness and impartiality which we impose upon our judiciary."

Seventh—the Committee's mandate is "inherently contrary to our democratic traditions. How did we come to establish a committee to decide what was 'Un-American,' forsooth, and still worse, how did we persuade ourselves that propaganda, speech, was a fit subject for regulation by inquisitional techniques such as the Committee employed. To me the very nature of that commission is at war with our profoundest principles. We have, in effect, created and empowered an agency to supervise the exercise of First Amendment rights, an organ for censorship and suppression."

Eighth—the "most serious criticism of the Committee," Congressman Roosevelt charged, was the fact that it had become an agency for the destruction of human dignity and constitutional rights. "We have become accustomed to think of those whom it subpoenas or labels as victims rather than witnesses. Endlessly they are dragooned before the Committee and accused. Secret sources, arrogance, rudeness, that maximize defamation and the threat of prosecution either for perjury or contempt if they do not seek the refuge of silence are the constant ingredients of this degrading spectacle. Beyond this the Committee is sanctimoniously cruel. Those who would answer the charges against themselves are forced to accuse others and become the agents of further havoc."

The press has raised its voice for HUAC's abolition. Shortly after Congressman Roosevelt's speech, the New York *Times* editorialized as follows in support of the Congressman's charges:

Fortified by ample appropriations almost automatically renewed each year by the House, the Committee pursues its heresy hunt, endangering constitutional guarantees in the process, weakening at home and abroad America's reputation as the land of the free —and all to what avail?

If the security of this nation were dependent on the kind of exposure for exposure's sake the Committee has repeatedly indulged in, whether investigating actors in New York or school teachers in Washington, then our country would really be in a dangerous condition.

At the same time, the influential Washington *Post* wrote that the "House of Representatives ought soberly to ask itself if it wants to go on indiscriminately punishing Americans for resisting a Committee which has long since ceased to serve any useful purpose and which has probed relentlessly into the area of private conscience and belief."

In 1957, the Louisville *Courier Journal* wrote that the Committee "had dragged the Communist fish pond dry without revealing any plots, truths or conspiracies that weren't already known;" that it had conducted its activities "with an eye to the notoriety that might be gleaned but without any real legislative purpose in mind or any objective other than the embarrassment and humiliation of witnesses and the gathering of headlines."

The San Francisco *Chronicle* has repeatedly denounced the Committee, most recently charging it with "vicious defamation of character, inane irrelevancies and crashing boredom."

The Newark *Evening News* of February 9, 1960, dismissed the Committee's 1959 annual report: "Time and events have not been kind to the Committee. Its early days were sad, and its methods never quite earned full public confidence, so perhaps it is time to receive and file the 1959 report, discharge the Committee with thanks and leave the fight against Communism in all dimensions to the FBI and other agencies more adequately equipped."

The San Francisco student demonstrations have made it plain that youth does not intend to surrender its freedom to the compulsions of the Establishment. Youth everywhere in our country is in ferment and in revolt against complacency, conformity and Madison Avenue orthodoxy. They know that for them protest and dissent are fraught with special dangers. There is the problem of preserving a record of discretion and noninvolvement so as to qualify for a Government job. Our large corporations do not choose junior-executive material from the ranks of the "controversial." Our defense connected institutions stand ready to bar a scientific career to such "security risks" who speak up against nuclear testing, go on peace walks or support the sit-ins in the South. Fellowships do not reward the rebel, nor do our large foundations succor him, gifted though he may be.

Nor, as was true a generation ago, are there ready-made organizations through which youth may voice its protests. The youth of our day have come to their causes and commitments by stirrings of individual conscience, by the pull of questioning curiosity and the hatred of sham and injustice. Risking much, they have proceeded from choice to painful choice—shattering the shell of repression, mediocrity and intolerance with which a decade of controls has cramped our society.

Youth wants to recapture the humane, truth-seeking tradition which has vitalized our democracy from the beginning. It knows that only in this tradition can it fulfil itself, find its significance and define its purposes. And fulfilment to be meaningful must come from engagement and involvement in the social, political and economic problems of our times, not in beatnik self-exile.

The freedom that our youth wants is not an abstract exercise in political theory, a form of self-advertisement to prove how much better "we" are than "they," but a tool for living and growing. Youth demands freedom now because freedom is a precondition to finding the answer to all the other momentous problems which involve our future and their fate. They reject the dogmas of Communism as sharply as they reject the dogmas of anti-Communism.

The opposition of America's young men and women to HUAC was inevitable—because the Committee is the enemy of freedom. The March 1960 *British Journal of Sociology* has published the results of a survey on civil-liberties attitudes on the University of California campus at Berkeley. The survey was based on 894 completed questionnaires, considered to be a reasonably reliable sample of campus opinion. Four of the questions in the questionnaire dealing with anti-subversive investigations drew the following responses:

1. It is reasonable to suspect the loyalty of a lawyer who represents accused Communists before a Congressional committee. Disagree, 79%; agree, 14%; don't know, 8%.

2. A high school teacher who pleads the Fifth Amendment while being questioned by a Con-

gressional committee should be fired at once. Disagree, 75%; agree, 13%; don't know, 11%.
3. Legislative committees should not investigate the political beliefs of university faculty members. Agree, 61%; disagree, 29%; don't know, 9%.
4. A former member of the Communist Party who refuses to reveal the names of Party members he had known should not be allowed to teach in a private university. Disagree, 60%; agree, 27%; don't know, 13%.

In 1960, the United States National Student Association, America's largest, and most respectable, student organization, strongly condemned HUAC and launched an intensive informational campaign about its activities. On virtually every large American campus, students have challenged HUAC and attacked its film. Student leaders, molders of opinion, have been in the vanguard of the anti-HUAC drive. This prickly, uncompromising opposition is the new "treason of the intellectuals."

HUAC may have good reason to fear that American youth may be its nemesis. This is why staff member Fulton Lewis, III, has so zealously attempted to peddle "Operation Abolition" on American college campuses. But the Red plot, the old reliable shield against attack, may fail HUAC. What can be done with a generation of 18 to 23 year olds with no political past to serve as an exposure target who are insistently and increasingly demanding their full heritage of freedom?

HUAC's strategy to turn back this new abolition movement is the same strategy of terror which has served it so well through the years. No Communist is as unhappy about the numerical decline of the Communist Party in this country as HUAC. No Communist tries so hard to conceal the lack of power of the Party in America and its rejection by the overwhelming mass of our people. HUAC warns us against the fearsome non-Reds, the questioners and challengers who are even more dangerous than the Reds because they want to abolish HUAC and are harder to expose and attack. But fewer and fewer people can be persuaded that the hosts of HUAC's opponents are merely dupes.

Ever more frequently and loudly, HUAC yelps, Wolf, Wolf: the Reds are at our throats; the conspiracy grows stronger by the hour; visual "proof" is created of Red-inspired violence within our borders; our defenses are powerless to cope with it. In this security racket, nothing succeeds like excess. The wilder and more dishonest the charge, the better. The cornerstone of this manipulative technique is a falsehood—that our country is under a permanent internal threat of subversion with which the courts, the FBI and our mountainous pile of antisubversive statutes are powerless to deal.

It is this security blackmail that has kept many ordinary Americans from a definite commitment to the abolition movement. What would happen to our security, they ask, if HUAC were abolished?

The answer, of course, is that we would be far more secure than ever before. If recent history has taught us anything, it has confirmed the truth of Benjamin Franklin's reminder that "They that would give up essential liberty to obtain a little temporary safety, deserve neither liberty nor safety."

But HUAC offers no "safety" of any kind—temporary or permanent. HUAC is not a security agency and has no mandate to safeguard our security. The investigation of violations of our security laws is a function of the FBI, not of HUAC. If there is evidence of subversive acts, the suspects under our system are entitled to formal charges and fair trials—not exposure by HUAC. And if all that is involved is speech—divorced from action—then our Constitution decrees that no law can punish it or restrain it.

If our present laws are inadequate to check threats to our security, then those Congressional committees which have been authorized to process security legislation—primarily the Judiciary Committee—are available to do so and to conduct investigations.

If HUAC were abolished, Americans could exercise their freedom to dissent and to criticize without fear; organizations could take stands on controversial issues without the risk of a HUAC "citation"; the never-ending stream of political propaganda pouring from HUAC's hate mills would dry up; there would be no more indexes for use by blacklisters, no more heavy annual appropriations. The image of America, at home and abroad, would no longer be shamed by an agency of Government which exploits fear, promotes hate and uses falsehood as weapons of ideological warfare.

The Network groups, deprived of access to HUAC's forest of dossiers with which to slander and pillory their opponents, would have to fend for themselves in the open arena of free expression, without a protector, a voice, and a friend at court—as extremists of any kind have to do. This is as it should be. An active, functioning democracy assumes that its citizens are capable of exercising their freedom of choice without governmental intervention. The price of democratic freedom comes high. It demands awareness, it demands education, it demands knowledge of the whole spectrum of political, cultural and humanitarian thinking, it demands that we run the risk of listening to all voices. This is our pride, our strength and our most solemn commitment. Only in freedom can the rich promise of democratic government become a reality.

SOURCES AND ACKNOWLEDGMENTS

The argument of this book, that the Committee is not a legislative investigating committee but an illegal law-enforcement body with a dominant purpose of punishment and exposure, was first developed in a brief which I prepared for the United States Supreme Court in 1955. The elaboration of the argument here is based primarily upon the official records of the Committee: its printed hearings, reports, indexes and miscellaneous publications. I have also made use of *Congressional Investigations of Communism and Subversive Activities,* Summary-Index, 1918-1956, compiled by the Senate Committee on Government Operations (1956), and the *Internal Security Manual,* Senate Judiciary Committee (1960 ed.)

In addition, I have drawn extensively upon newspaper reports about HUAC in particular areas where hearings have been held. Accounts of HUAC's activities which have appeared over the past decade in the New York *Times,* the Washington *Post,* the San Francisco *Chronicle* and the New York *Post* have been especially helpful. The Easton *Express,* a newspaper published in Congressman Walter's home district, is an invaluable source of information about HUAC's Chairman.

The *Congressional Record* supplied a great deal of revealing material both about the Committee and its members. I have also made extensive use of court records, briefs and decisions in cases involving the powers of the Committee.

Many of the witnesses before the Committee have generously granted me interviews. For obvious reasons, their names are withheld—as are the names of other unfriendly witnesses who have requested me to do so. I have also profited from interviews with lawyers who have appeared professionally before the Committee and, in some cases, have been permitted to consult legal files dealing with activities of the Committee.

An invaluable source of information and leads have been the files of the *Nation* and *Reporter* magazines. Scores of pamphlets have been written about HUAC. Many of these have been very useful—especially those dealing with the Committee's early years. I have also drawn on the files of various civil organizations and groups.

The authoritative study of the Committee from 1945 to 1950 is by Robert K. Carr, *The House Committee on Un-American Activities* (Cornell University Press, 1952). The pre-1945 period is the subject of an admirable work, *The Dies Committee* (Catholic University Press, 1945) by Father August R. Ogden. I have drawn on these two books, although the major stress in this one is the recent period of HUAC's functioning.

In addition to the general sources to which I have referred and the specific ones cited in the text, I have relied on the following material and documents:

The summary account of the San Francisco demonstration in Chapter 1 is based on an article "Black Friday" in the July 1960 issue of *The Californian*, and on a newspaper series by Hadley Roff and Wes Willoughby which appeared in the San Francisco *News-Call Bulletin*, January 23-31, 1961. The statistical material dealing with the Committee's appropriations is from the *Congressional Record*, and from statements by Representatives William Fitts Ryan (D. N.Y.) and James Roosevelt (D. Cal.) made on February 21, 1961 to the House Administration Committee. Supplementary material about such matters as HUAC's expenditures and contempt citations appears in a Committee publication, *This Is* Your *House Committee on Un-American Activities* (1954) and in HUAC's Annual Report for 1960.

The source material for Chapter 2 is the *Congressional Record*. The account in Chapter 3 of the attacks on Wilkinson and his organization is based on interviews. The Berkeley *Daily Gazette* for January 19, 1961, carries a story of the Farmer affair. The discussion of HUAC's rightist ties relies heavily on David Wesley's *Hate Groups and the Un-American Activities Committee,* a recently published pamphlet. Other sources are Carlson, *Under Cover* (New York, 1943), and Gellerman, *Martin Dies* (New York, 1944). A fascinating survey of the Network appears in the *American Right Wing,* by R. E. Ellsworth and S. M. Harris (Urbana, 1960). The discussion of the Committee members relies largely on the *Congressional Record*. The Washington *Post* has devoted much space to Chairman Walter. I have also heavily relied on the files of Charles R. Allen, Jr., who interviewed Walter in 1956 and published two articles about him. The account of Arens' background is based on press stories in *The Compass,* September 2, 1952, Washington *Post & Times Herald,* January 12, 1955, June 19 and July 13, 1956, and the New York *Times,* May 2, and July 13 and 30, 1956.

Two excellent books on the abuse of the investigative power (Chapter 4) are Telford Taylor's *Grand Inquest* (New York, 1955) and Alan Barth's *Government by Investigation* (New York, 1955).

The foundations of Chapter 5 on How Exposure Works are a series of interviews with witnesses, lawyers, psychiatrists and psychotherapists. The statement of William T. Gossett in Chapter 6 is from an article, "Are We Neglecting Constitutional Liberty?, A Call to Leadership" in Volume 28, p. 817 of the American Bar Association *Journal,* and the Elmer Davis quotation is from a lecture at the University of Minnesota given on November 3, 1951. The California Bar censure of staff counsel Arens is reproduced in the *Frontier* magazine for May 1957. The discussion in Chapter 7 about informers' credibility is based on my article, "The Informer," which appeared in the *Nation* for April 10, 1954. Cvetic's current activities are described in an article in the same periodical (March 11, 1961) by Hans Engh on the John Birch Society.

Chapter 7 on the press is based on a newspaper survey made in 1960 by a research group in leading American cities; on articles by Alan Barth, "A Moral Challenge to the Press," *Colorado Quarterly,* Autumn 1952; Dozier C. Cade, "Witch-Hunting 1952: The Role of the Press," *Journalism Quarterly,* December 1952; and Irving Dilliard, "Congressional Investigations, The Role of the Press," *University of Chicago Law Review,* Spring 1951; and on an address on June 19, 1953, by Gordon A. Sabine, "Journalism, Journalists and Joe McCarthy," to the Oregon Newspaper Publishers Association. The story of the Cincinnati *Enquirer* and Cecil Scott was first aired in an article, "Cincinnati's Phantom Reds," by James A. Maxwell, in the *Reporter* for September 26, 1950. The account of the Miami *Daily News* and its exposure operation is based on my article, "The Miami Formula," which appeared in the *Nation,* January 22, 1955.

The background of the Baltimore hearings described in Chapter 9 (The Road Shows) is based on local research and interviews. In addition to the press accounts, which gave unusually full coverage to the San Francisco hearings (Chapter 10), I obtained factual material about the hearings and their background from local lawyers and Mrs. Barbara Sherwood, the widow of William K. Sherwood.

The 1959 teacher subpoenas are discussed in detail in Congressman Roosevelt's April 25, 1960, House speech. Further revealing data came to light as a result of a series of questionnaires submitted to the teachers. The student demonstration and the film have been extensively discussed and analyzed in print. By far the most reliable version of the 1960 hearings and student demonstration are the tapes recorded by Berkeley radio station KPFA. A study of the film itself yields rewarding insights into HUAC's techniques. The Bay Area Student Committee has issued an analysis of the film, "In Search of Truth," and the National Council of the Churches of Christ has published "Operation Abolition," a survey of opinion and comment about the film. A closely detailed analysis (unpublished) has been made of the film's accuracy by Russel Joyner, a 36-year-old senior at the University of California who has specialized in content analysis of propaganda. A challenge to the accuracy of the Hoover report appears in *The Californian* for March 1961.

The discussion of HUAC's harassment of the ECLC (Chapter 12) is based both on the record and on material in the organization's files. A full account of HUAC's quarrel with The Fund for the Republic appears in its Bulletin for September 1956.

The classic study of the religious hate groups (Chapter 13) and what makes them tick is Ralph Lord Ray's *Apostles of Discord* (Boston, 1953). Much of the material in this chapter is based on publications of the National Council of Churches and The Religious Freedom Committee. The National Council has published a comprehensive compilation of documents on the Air Force *Manual* controversy. The most useful study of HUAC's files (Chapter 14) appears in Bishop Oxnam's admirable *I Protest* (New York, 1954). Valuable supplementary material may be found in Ralph S. O'Leary's "Minute Women, Daughters of Vigilantism," *The Nation,* January 9, 1954. The relationships between HUAC and the FBI are acutely explored in *I. F. Stone's Weekly* for November 2 and 9, 1959. A highly illuminating article on "FBI Data and Congress," by L. Edgar Prina, appeared in the Washington *Sunday Star* for April 28, 1957. In the *Syracuse Law Review,* Fall 1956, J. Edgar Hoover discusses "The Confidential Nature of FBI Reports."

The Fund for the Republic's carefully researched two-volume *Report on Blacklisting* by John Cogley (1956) is basic to an understanding of the blacklist phenomenon (Chapter 12). Vivid supplementary material appears in the records of several lawsuits brought to challenge the legality of blacklisting. The Hollywood blacklist is the subject of a useful article by Elizabeth Poe, "The Hollywood Story," in the May 1954 *Frontier*.

The story of the Newark school teachers (Chapter 15) is based on HUAC's records, stories in the Newark *Star-Ledger* and personal interviews. Helpful in evaluating HUAC's legislative claims are the calendars of bills published by the House legislative standing committees (but not by HUAC) and the *Index of General Public Bills,* compiled by the Legislative Reference Service.

The conclusions about the extent and meaning of the anti-HUAC movement among youth are based on a survey of representative campuses, interviews and a study of college newspapers.

Among those who have been most helpful in furnishing information and suggesting leads are Charles R. Allen, Jr., Max Dean, Joseph Forer, Ruth France, Victor Rabinowitz, Millie White, and Burton White. I am under heavy obligation to Bertram Edises who not only read and commented on two chapters of the text, but made available valuable material from his files. I am grateful to my law partners, Marshall Perlin and Eleanor Jackson Piel, who were generous, patient and cooperative.

Grand Inquest

The Story of Congressional Investigations

by TELFORD TAYLOR
Chief Prosecutor of War Criminals at Nuremberg

The Bill of Rights was written into the Constitution to protect the basic freedoms of citizens from governmental encroachment. At the same time the Constitution gives Congress the power to investigate in order to pass sensible legislation and revise out-of-date statutes. In certain crucial periods this power to investigate has been in conflict with basic human rights. Since the end of World War II, a host of congressional committees have literally thrown the Bill of Rights to the wind, transforming legitimate investigation into an inquisition attacking Americans because of their beliefs, their ideas, the books they read, and even on the grounds of their associations and their friends.

> "GRAND INQUEST is in the greatest tradition of American political writing. It deserves the widest possible audience for it speaks eloquently, sanely and informatively on one of the greatest problems of statecraft now facing our nation."
>
> Robert K. Carr, New York Times

DEPT. 510, BALLANTINE BOOKS, INC.
101 Fifth Avenue, New York 3, N.Y.